Dario Fo

Tom Behan

Dario Fo
Revolutionary Theatre

Pluto Press
LONDON • STERLING, VIRGINIA

First published 2000 by Pluto Press
345 Archway Road, London N6 5AA
and 22883 Quicksilver Drive,
Sterling, VA 20166–2012, USA

British Library Cataloguing in Publication Data
A catalogue record for this book is available from
the British Library

ISBN 0 7453 1362 0 hbk

Library of Congress Cataloging in Publication Data
is available from the Library of Congress

Designed and produced for Pluto Press by
Chase Production Services, Chadlington, OX7 3LN
Typeset from disk by Stanford DTP Services, Northampton
Printed in the European Union by T.J. International, Padstow

Contents

Acknowledgements

It is strange to thank people in a language that is not theirs: many of the people named on this page will need to get all that follows translated.

Ditto chisto, thanks in general to all those who agreed to be interviewed: Dario Fo, Emilio Orsino, Arturo Peregalli, Nanni Ricordi, Piero Sciotto and a member of *The Commune* who wishes to remain anonymous. Specific thanks to Lanfranco Binni and Chiara Valentini for their enthusiastic agreement to release copyright for the two passages reproduced as appendices.

Having seen some live Fo performances over the years and others on video has been a great help in the writing of this book. Dario Fo and Franca Rame's massive personal archives have also been invaluable in terms of collating documentation. So thanks to Franca for her help in this area, and thanks also to some of the staff: Chiara Bonfatti, Marina De Juli, Marco Scordo and Valentina Tescari.

In financial terms I wish to acknowledge the receipt of a grant from the British Academy.

Last but not least my thanks go to the people who read the book in draft: Ed Emery, Colin Fancy, Diane Fieldes, John Foot and Barbara Rampoldi.

Naturally, the final paradoxical result is entirely down to me. The paradox is that this is a political biography of a man (and a woman) who has never had 'political ambitions' in the conventional sense of the word. But then again, much of Fo's theatre is built on paradox.

Brief Chronology

1926   Fo is born in San Giano, near the Swiss border.
1943–45   Deserts from fascist militia. Helps partisans to smuggle people
            into Switzerland.
1945–52   Moves to Milan and begins to study architecture. Starts to
            gravitate towards the theatre and performs in amateur shows.
1953   Co-writes and performs in his first major theatrical production:
            A Poke in the Eye.
1962   Seven controversial appearances on the television variety
            show *Canzonissima*.
1968   A year dominated by student protests. Fo leaves the commercial
            theatre, founds *New Scene*, and performs at branches of ARCI,
            the communist cultural association.
1969   Performs *Mistero Buffo* for the first time. The year concludes
            with a 'Hot Autumn' of working-class struggles and the
            anarchist Giuseppe Pinelli dying in police custody.
1970   Founds a new theatre company: *The Commune*. *Accidental
            Death of an Anarchist* premières exactly a year after Pinelli's
            death.
1973   Writes *People's War in Chile* immediately after Pinochet's
            coup. Fo is briefly arrested.
1974   Première of *Can't Pay? Won't Pay!*
1977   Première of *Tale of a Tiger*.
1980   Crushing defeat for FIAT car workers, traditionally Italy's
            most militant workers. Revival of *Can't Pay? Won't Pay!*
1981   Première of *Trumpets and Raspberries*.
1997   Wins the Nobel Prize for Literature.
1998   Première of latest play: *Free Marino! Marino is Innocent!*

Introduction

Political theatre has become a kind of byword for boring theatre, conceited theatre, pedantic theatre, mechanical theatre, a non-enjoyable theatre.
Dario Fo, 1973

If you're reading these lines in a bookshop and wondering whether to buy this book, and you see a video of a Dario Fo performance on another shelf, buy the video. That way you're sure to come back and buy the book.

The most difficult task one faces when either writing or reading a book about Dario Fo is that you can't see him. There are, in fact, no videos of Fo available in the UK or North America. There can be no other actor in living memory who is capable of holding a crowd of thousands for hours in a variety of locations, with no props, costumes or supporting actors whatsoever. Fo can do this, and it is these acting abilities which have played a large part in his popularity in Italy, and possibly with his winning of the Nobel Prize for Literature in 1997.

After 50 years on the stage he still commands tremendous support from the Italian public. For example the TV audience for some new tales he had written on St Francis of Assisi, broadcast from half past midnight to 1 a.m. on New Year's Day 1998, was 3.5 million. Less than three months later his latest play, *Free Marino! Marino is Innocent!* was broadcast on national television. The show started at nearly 11 p.m. on an ordinary weekday, yet live audience figures grew to nearly 2 million from midnight to 1 a.m., when the two-hour show finished.[1] It has been estimated that 3 million Italians have made the even bigger effort to go and see him on stage in his performance masterpiece, *Mistero Buffo*.

Outside Italy his popularity has also been immense for decades. He became the world's most performed living playwright for the first time in 1964 and has held this distinction for many years since.

One explanation for his popularity is that for much of this period he has been a Marxist, a revolutionary. Indeed it must be one of the fundamental reasons for his success, given that most of his plays contain one scene after another attacking the rich and powerful, while other plays contain workers and shop stewards as their central figures. Fo's art demolishes the stereotype of humourless left-wingers as well as illustrating the enduring relevance of far-left ideas.

The rich, powerful and the right wing have consequently attacked him and his wife, Franca Rame, both physically and personally, as well as criticising his work theoretically and making it difficult for him to work.

For example, Fo has been arrested for obstructing a police officer, been challenged to duels by right-wing journalists, been the object of over 40 court cases with accusations ranging from blasphemy, obscenity, slander, to subversion – and for many years his performances ran the risk of bomb attacks from neo-fascists. Both his house and theatre have been firebombed. In 1973 Rame suffered even more: she was kidnapped, tortured and raped by neo-fascists. For years Fo has had to endure the presence of police agents in the audience, who were there to make sure that he did not go beyond the scripts handed in to the authorities who had vetted them for blasphemy and obscenity. He has been accused of sympathy with left-wing terrorists and of materially helping them. The Vatican once defined *Mistero Buffo* as 'the most blasphemous show ever transmitted on television'. And in 1980, at the height of his success, he was denied a visa to enter the United States, an action which led to a demonstration by artists and intellectuals including Norman Mailer, Arthur Miller and Martin Scorsese.

In Italy the attitude of many sections of the political and cultural establishment has not changed significantly over the years. Less than six months after Fo won the Nobel Prize for Literature, the new play by the most popular actor and playwright for most of the last 40 years, *Free Marino! Marino is Innocent!*, was essentially boycotted by politicians and cultural figures alike. The best-known member of the audience at its première was Licia Pinelli, the widow of the anarchist who died 'accidentally' nearly 30 years earlier.

So with enemies like these, who have his friends been? Given the fact that many of his early plays dealt with the difficult and precarious existence of the working class, from the beginning his audience was often made up of left-wing and working-class people. As well as being a source of inspiration, Fo's commitment to the working class has also been repaid by their support. As far back as 1962 he was banned from television for dealing with a whole series of taboo subjects: the Mafia, building speculation and working conditions in factories. When he refused to accept the censor's cuts he stormed out of the building, provoking spontaneous demonstrations outside the television studios as the news was broadcast. The problem for the television channel was that he had built up an audience of 15 million in just seven weeks!

The reason Fo developed such popularity so rapidly was that he didn't engage in sermonising against the rich and powerful – he simply laughed at them. Through the use of satire he ridiculed the sanctimonious hypocrisy of church leaders and the ridiculous explanations given by politicians and police officers in the hope of escaping from accusations of corruption, torture and murder.

Fo's consistent and passionate support for the working-class struggle has been at the base of both his popularity and his inspiration. Those who view these struggles with various degrees of cynicism, incomprehension or hostility often face great difficulties in assessing accurately Fo's place on the political map.

When the news of his Nobel Prize award was announced in October 1997 the British *Guardian* claimed that 'in Italy Fo is known primarily as a former member of the Communist Party'. Fo never joined the Italian Communist Party (PCI), he always denounced its Stalinism, bureaucratism and reformism. He is famous for being to the left of the PCI, someone who believes that a better society will be created out of mass struggle and not by laws coming out of parliamentary chambers.

Another article in the same newspaper also mistakenly explained that Fo left mainstream theatre in 1968 because he was 'too anarchic to submit to the disciplines of the orthodox left'.[2] Yet the reason for Fo's break with commercial theatre in 1968 had nothing to do with any belief in anarchism or refusal of any sense of discipline. A mass movement had exploded on the streets, and for the next ten years Fo performed in his 'own' squatted theatre, in big public squares or in occupied factories. And it is not by chance that these were the years in which he wrote and first performed some of his best plays, such as *Accidental Death of an Anarchist*, *Can't Pay? Won't Pay!* and *Mistero Buffo*.

By the late 1970s this mass movement had declined and, therefore, Fo had less inspiring material to draw on. As a review of one of his shows put it in 1980: 'The crowd was huge, yes, but different ... it was almost a normal audience, left-wing but not militant, mixed in with theatregoers ... Ideas like socialism and revolution and the working class have become much more complex, and seeking an impetus for action has now become somewhat difficult.'[3]

After often writing and performing two or three full-length plays a year, Fo wrote very few between 1976 and 1981 as he tried to find a new direction, given the downturn in the working-class struggle. He became more and more interested in women's issues as well as in producing plays by other authors such as Bertolt Brecht, and was also increasingly forced to return to the commercial theatrical circuit.

Another outlet for him was to perform overseas, where he often demonstrated the radical spirit which had already guided him for nearly three decades. For example, there was a degree of heckling and some walkouts when he performed in London in 1983, as some people thought they had bought a ticket to see a 'revivalist of classic Italian medieval theatre'. At one point he launched into an unscripted satirical explanation of the real cause of the recent Falklands War – given that they were such barren islands Fo's explanation for the war was that Margaret Thatcher wanted to keep a good supply of *guano* for the back garden of 10 Downing Street! If this wasn't the reason, he claimed, then it was simply an occasion for Prince Andrew to parade in his new military uniform.

As well as attacking the Thatcher government, Fo also engaged with arguments on the left. While applauding their commitment, Fo criticised some of the ideas of women protesting against Cruise missiles at Greenham Common: 'How can you believe in "non-violent direct action" when the state constantly engages in "non-direct violent action" against you? It isn't Margaret Thatcher or Michael Heseltine who beat you up and arrest you, they send their police to do that. And it isn't Ronald Reagan who flies the B52s and the nuclear submarines.' In 1985 the profits from his Roman shows were donated to Britain's National Union of Mineworkers, led by Arthur Scargill, which was engaged in a no-holds-barred strike against the Thatcher government, no easy task in that period as the union's funds had been seized by the courts.

In subsequent years the cutting edge of his plays was blunted by the continuing downturn in mass struggles, yet his response to receiving the Nobel Prize shows that he is far from being out of touch. His explanation for the award was that 'the system today no longer has any ideas. It is a recognition that awards all those who have fought and struggled'. He continued: 'The phone calls which have moved me the most have been from Turkey, Afghanistan and Argentina, all from people who have ended up inside for having put on some of my plays. This Nobel Prize is theirs as well.' He concluded: 'Loads of friends, or people I don't know, or others I've met during my shows in occupied factories – or the people I met in the street coming here to the theatre today – they all said, "We've all won a bit of this prize".'

Fo's success is due to one stark fact: his commitment to giving the working class a voice, a voice which is infinitely louder and richer than that of the establishment. What follows is a political biography of Dario Fo. But to tell the full story you also have to tell the story of the Italian working class: both its struggles and its organisations.

This book can be read conventionally, that is from cover to cover. However while Chapters 1, 2 and 6 generally take the form of a political biography and have a chronological structure, Chapters 3, 4 and 5 concentrate on three of Fo's most famous plays.

The Bourgeois Period

Looking back at the age of 70 to his birth in 1926, Dario Fo reveals both his paradoxical sense of humour and his understanding that much of human life history is dictated by work patterns: 'I must thank my mother who chose to give birth at San Giano on Lake Maggiore. To be honest my mother didn't make the choice, State Railways had decided to send my father to work at that station.'[1]

San Giano is a small town in Lombardy, near the Swiss border, where his father worked as a stationmaster and his mother was a peasant. His father, Felice, had previously worked as a builder in France and Germany, although he had also occasionally played roles in amateur drama productions. His mother, Pina Rota, was from a long line of peasants and came from a tradition of oral storytellers. But perhaps the biggest early influence on Fo's future career was his maternal grandfather Giuseppe – nicknamed *Bristin* – a kind of travelling greengrocer who used to entertain his customers with outrageous and scandalous stories. Fo remembers that as a young boy he travelled with his grandfather:

> We left when it was still dark, wrapped in blankets during the winter ... We travelled to farms which seemed like small towns – in the Aosta valley there were 30 families living on one big courtyard. When they saw us a party started. He began shouting and telling stories in dialect ... cases of adultery in a farmhouse nearby. People laughed because *Bristin* adorned the scene by holding up big marrows and leeks to explain the dimensions ... In order to take part you had to buy some potatoes.[2]

Furthermore, Fo grew up in an area which still had a strong tradition of *fabulatori*, oral storytellers who recounted grotesque and paradoxical stories in public squares. He also listened to the stories of the local fishermen, who told tales of towns at the bottom of the lake, where traditional roles were reversed, such as women getting drunk in bars, priests confessing their sins and landowners who would get beaten up by peasants. Another influence was the fact that a nearby town specialised in glass-blowing: 'The basic disease was silicosis, but with an intermediate stage which provoked some real lunacy. I can often remember the council van full: it was used to take the lunatics to Varese.' All in all, 'The mixture of different people created a fantastic cultural environment: people told tales.'[3] These influences were to stay with him throughout his life, indeed about a quarter of his acceptance speech when he received the Nobel Prize was a story he heard from a *fabulatore* when he was a child. What Fo absorbed at a very impressionable age was the art of storytelling, without the use of a theatrical cast and props.

As regards politics, his adolescent years were dominated by the Second World War, which broke out when Fo was 14. He was called up for military service in May 1944 but deserted and worked briefly with his father in the anti-fascist Resistance movement, helping Allied prisoners and Jewish refugees escape to Switzerland. His father had been secretary of a small branch of the Socialist Party before fascism, and had become military commander of the Resistance movement for his local area, while his mother gave medical assistance to wounded partisans.

Although Fo had absorbed the left-wing ideas of his father far more than the fascism of the regime, he never joined the Resistance in any real sense. Indeed, even after obeying the call-up in 1944 and deserting, he presented himself again for military service with a parachute regiment in 1945, but deserted once more. This time he made attempts to find a local partisan brigade but, as it transpired, it had just been annihilated. His father was on the wanted list, as was Fo for slightly different reasons, so as he couldn't go home he lived rough for a few months, witnessing fascist and Nazi atrocities.

At the end of the war Fo went to the Brera Academy in Milan to study architecture, but didn't finish his degree course. Instead, he discovered politics and a cosmopolitan atmosphere: 'We were coming out of total ignorance. We knew nothing so we started to read frenetically anything that fell under our noses ... And then we talked, each of us transmitting to the others an effervescence, an angst, a desire to know and to do everything. I almost didn't sleep at night.'[4] Or to put it another way, 'We talked until dawn, Paris seemed round the corner.'[5]

A painter friend of his, Alik Cavaliere, has recalled that 'Fo had a larger than life personality, but politically he was not very advanced. He matured more slowly than the rest of us; he committed himself to political activity through purely personal channels'.[6] Nearly all his friends at this time were Communist Party (PCI) members, but Fo never joined the party.

One of these friends was Elio Vittorini, an established author, PCI activist and editor of a cultural magazine named *The Polytechnic*, closely linked to the Communist Party. Fo's friendship with Vittorini is significant because a party dispute over *The Polytechnic* dominated left-wing cultural circles in the immediate postwar years. What began to upset PCI leaders was that the magazine would not only take up positions on culture which clashed with the rigid Stalinist dogma of the time, but it would directly comment on political issues without consulting the party leadership. The fact that the Vatican was attacked for its collusion with fascism, or that subjects such as divorce were discussed, made PCI leaders very nervous as they wanted to avoid such issues so as not to upset the Catholic hierarchy.[7] A public party discussion on what policy *The Polytechnic* should follow ensued, but the issue was settled when the leadership withdrew its support from the magazine, thus leading to its closure.[8]

A very influential intellectual at that time was the Marxist Antonio Gramsci, who had died in prison in 1937 and whose *Prison Notebooks* were published by the PCI in 1947. Although the first edition often censored any mention of Marxists such as Amadeo Bordiga, Rosa Luxemburg and Leon Trotsky (portrayed by the PCI as 'fascists' at the time), one of the central arguments developed by Gramsci was the importance of intellectuals in creating a counter-current of thought which would eventually overcome the ideological dominance of the ruling class. Even though Gramsci was clear that this counter-current was only a part of a more general war against the ruling class, the PCI emphasised the importance of ideology rather than class war and so managed to entice many intellectuals into its orbit.

Although these issues were keenly discussed in left-wing intellectual circles, it would be mistaken to bestow sophisticated and unified political understanding on a young man barely out of his teens, experiencing democracy and a big city for the first time. Looking back, almost 40 years later, Fo recalled:

> Mine has been a revolt, a rebellion, against a hypocritical and deceitful order, which dates back to my experience as a student. As Marx says, 'The ruling ideas in society are the ideas of the ruling class', and at that time it was only the ruling class which expressed its culture. Therefore my class, the peasantry, was viewed as being a parasite that lived off that culture and aped some of its products.[9]

Throughout the late 1940s Fo socialised with artists, writers and actors and he slowly drifted towards the theatre, since he often used to amuse his friends by recounting the tales he had heard as a boy. He began to act in review shows a series of sketches performed in small theatres around Lombardy where the conditions were very much 'rough and tumble' far from the staid, comfortable theatres of Milan. It was both an environment and a theatrical style in which improvisation was at a premium. Fo and his friends sardonically called these tours 'punitive expeditions', after the same phrase used by fascists to describe their attacks on prominent left-wingers in towns and villages during the 1920s.

After a while Fo started to take theatre more seriously and came under the influence of three traditions: French farce, neo-realist cinema and the theatre of Eduardo De Filippo. He also had an interest in set design as he was a gifted painter and because it was a field not too distant from the architecture degree he had been studying for.

In 1952 Fo had his first big break when he wrote a series of shows for RAI, the state radio channel. All the shows (they were monologues) had a constant theme, that of turning a common-sense view of the world on its head, of emphasising paradoxes. These shows were collectively known as *Poer nano* (*Poor Lad* in Milanese dialect), and in them Fo made use of some of the tales that he had heard years before from the Lake Maggiore *fabulatori*. He wrote 18 shows until the censor put a stop to them. These shows were important in his theatrical development as they were a training ground in how to write and stick to a script rather than simply perform and improvise.[10]

Fo's first significant theatrical appearance was in a revue of 24 sketches, *A Poke in the Eye*, which was first performed in 1953 and was co-written by Fo. The mime sequences were created by a French mime expert, Jacques Lecoq, who differed from contemporaries such as Marcel Marceau in that he also used dance, song and language. Although they were later to disagree over the usefulness of mime, Fo has never denied that Lecoq taught him many physical movements such as using the whole of the stage, how to express different kinds of laughter, how to use facial expressions which communicate the opposite of what you are saying, as well as different ways of walking, and so on.[11] Another development was the fact that Fo also designed the costumes and the set.

It was an ambitious project, to 'poke in the eye' traditional history, as Fo once explained: 'The key was destroying the myths which fascism had imposed and the Christian Democrats had preserved. The myth of the hero, according to which only great people make history. The myth of the family and a certain kind of morality. Of culture as the product of an elite of intellectuals.'[12] Consequently, there were sketches about the Egyptian workers who had built the pyramids rather than the Pharaohs, the ordinary soldier who told Ulysses to build a fake horse to enter Troy, of Napoleon and Nelson squabbling like two spoilt brats, and so on.

Yet this show was being performed in the midst of the Cold War, which, in Italy, took a very virulent and repressive form due to the strength of the Communist Party. Between 1948 and 1956 57 PCI workers were killed by the authorities during various disturbances and 4,572 were wounded; a total of 58,286 PCI members were convicted of crimes, for which a total of 19,682 years of custodial sentences were handed down, not counting 19 life sentences.[13]

Such was the atmosphere that Rame, who also starred in *A Poke in the Eye*, recalled:

Every night there would be an inspector in the auditorium checking our words one by one against the script and the Ministry for Entertainment would obstruct our touring arrangements, while the most reactionary theatre-owners would refuse us their buildings and the bishops would ask the police to tear our programmes from the walls of the cities.[14]

Even though it opened in the summer, and the actors and writers were essentially unknown, the show was an immediate hit. There were several reasons for this: the impressive scenography, the use of mime, Fo's acting in particular, and the political content of the show. Despite the harassment described above, as Rame explains, the show had clearly struck a chord: 'The workers, the students and the progressive bourgeoisie were supporting us, thereby allowing us to move on and make ourselves known.'[15]

The second review show, or series of sketches, opened the following year (1954) and was called *I sani da legare* (*These Sane People Should Be Locked Up*). On this occasion the political targets were even clearer, more contemporary and familiar. Most of the sketches were set in a big city of the North, with its factories, hospitals, jails, police stations, trams and unemployment. Influential journalists were taken to task, as were the middle-class women who organised charity for poor people to alleviate their own boredom.[16]

The most significant sketch was entitled *Vassilic's Return*. In just three minutes it deals with the horrors of Stalinist Russia, as well as attacking anti-communist censorship. The anti-Stalinist aspect is interesting because although Stalin had died a year earlier it was way ahead of its time – Khruschev's denunciation of Stalin was to occur two years later, in 1956, and would cause huge crises within communist parties throughout the world.

Vassilic's father, a scientist, had found himself on the wrong side of a Kremlin power struggle and had been condemned as a 'deviationist'. Or, as his son put it, he had taken:

42,350 pages to show that when it rains birds hide under leaves ... and he only managed to get people to believe it because Stalin supported him. But as soon as Stalin died 250 pages of his opponents were enough to show that birds don't hide under leaves when it rains, but under branches![17]

Not only does this sketch highlight the scheming bureaucratic nature of the Kremlin leadership, but it also ridicules the false production achievements outlined in the five-year plans. Fo demonstrates a great deal of political perception here, because at that time nearly all communists outside Russia believed that the Soviet Republic was a land of abundance and efficiency. Consequently, when the scientist learns that his wife has given away his bicycle in an attempt to curry favour with a general, he exclaims: 'It was the only bicycle with brakes in the whole Republic!'[18]

In the script the final lines are spoken by 'voices', but in the performance the public understood that it was the director who turned to the audience and said provocatively: 'Now I want to see if the censor has something to say!'[19] This whole sketch clearly condemns the horrific nature of Stalinist Russia – indeed at the end the son shoots his father to prevent him from experiencing the trauma of a show trial which would almost certainly end in death. Yet the very fact that such an attack could be made by left-wingers was a polemical statement against Cold War hysteria – which simply argued that all left-wingers or communists were in favour of censorship and state repression as well as being uncritical supporters of the Soviet Union. Indeed the new US ambassador to Italy, Clare Booth Luce, had recently made her blinkered view clear, stating: 'Shut the communists up.'

Such was the power of censorship during this period that the cast had to give a private performance for the censors, who had travelled up from Rome, as well as the local authorities. Many cuts were made, but the anti-communist paranoia of the period was so strong that, as Rame recalls, 'On the first night the theatre was peppered with police agents who, with a script and a torch handy, ruined their eyesight in checking whether one comment or mimic gesture went outside the cuts that had been established.'[20]

While the Milan performances were successful, the cast experienced severe difficulties when the show went on tour. Some police chiefs cancelled authorisation for the show, and elsewhere priests put up posters outside their churches telling their parishioners not to go to the performance. Questions were even asked in Parliament, and many of the shows were performed in a very tense atmosphere, in front of a suspicious provincial bourgeois audience.

On a personal note, Fo and Rame were married in June 1954, and the following year their only child, Jacopo, was born. They went to live in Rome for almost three years; there, Fo worked in the cinema, mainly writing scripts, although he played the main role in the film *Lo svitato* (*The Screwball*). The film, like most of his period in Rome, was a failure. Fo found it difficult to adjust to the tortuous meetings and the arrogance of certain individuals. In the end the offering of an important theatrical contract to Rame led them to move back to Milan, which in 1958 was in the midst of an enthusiastic discovery of Bertolt Brecht's plays, such as *The Threepenny Opera* and *The Good Person of Szechwan*.

After an absence of four years, Fo's next work was a series of four farces collectively entitled *Thieves, Shop Dummies and Naked Women*. Instead of brief sketches, Fo was now writing quite lengthy pieces and, for the first time, writing alone. The subject matter was also different: these pieces dealt with misunderstandings, adultery and mistaken identity.

Another series of four farces, collectively entitled *Comic Finale*, was produced after just a few months. Not only was Fo spurred on by his long absence from the theatre, but he was also helped by the fact that the texts were inspired by some old scripts from the previous century kept by the Rame family, which they had performed in the squares of many northern towns and cities. Indeed, Rame's family was one of the most famous theatrical acting families of northern Italy, with a performing history that could be traced back almost three centuries.

Fo once said that what struck him when he read these old scripts were notes which stated that the public 'had to' laugh or applaud at certain moments, a small but significant point, as it views the public as an integral part of the show. As Fo explains, the writing of farces helped in a more general sense:

> For me these farces were a very important exercise in understanding how to write a theatrical text. I had learned how to take apart and reassemble the mechanisms of comedy, how to write directly for the stage without any literary diversion. And I also understood how many old and useless things there were in so many theatrical texts, in the theatre of words.[21]

This was also perhaps the first time that Fo had studied some of the traditions of popular theatre. However, he was far from being an archivist. He rewrote texts, enriching and distorting their original intentions. With these elements in mind a comment once made by the co-director of the show, Gianfranco De Bosio, makes perfect sense:

> Dario was in a period of great tension, he had decided to create a profession for himself, to fully become a man of the theatre. At that time political commitment was a secondary issue. His comedies were big machines to make people laugh, even if you could already sense an underlying gut feeling, working-class derision of the rich and powerful.[22]

Fo's next success was his first full-length play, *Archangels Don't Play Pinball*. This was presented at the prestigious *Odeon* theatre in Milan and was to be the first of seven new plays written and performed during each season of the 1959–67 period, which is commonly referred to as his 'bourgeois period'.

As with his earlier plays, the setting is working-class Milan, although more specifically the world of petty criminals. After focusing on humour in his previous farces, Fo now returned to a more overtly political stance: 'The starting points were from the news, from the events that struck me the most, the most paradoxical contradictions of the Christian Democrat State.'[23]

Yet his criticism was still muted: comical attacks on state bureaucracy, references to political corruption and so on. Fo later admitted that during his bourgeois period he had to tailor his arguments to fit a particular shape:

> [these arguments] were conducted in a way that could be picked up by the audience one found in the commercial circuit. Once we had accepted that system and that audience, the truths we were telling about politics and the nature of society at that time had to be put over in the guise of satirical licence.[24]

In any event, this show earned the biggest takings in Italy for the 1959–60 season. His success was now becoming international too. *Archangels Don't Play Pinball* was soon translated and performed in Czechoslovakia, Holland, Poland, Spain, Sweden and Yugoslavia.[25] The local company which put on the show in Yugoslavia chose to stress the anti-bureaucratic themes in the text, perhaps the first case of what was rightly to become a tradition of Fo in translation, that of adapting his plays in order to hit domestic political targets.

Challenges to the System

The political conditions which had favoured anti-communist hysteria and zealous censorship began to be challenged in a serious fashion in 1960. The year had begun positively for the Christian Democrats: in January the *Financial Times* had awarded the *lira* with its 'Oscar' for being the most stable currency of 1959, and in the spring Fernando Tambroni formed a new Christian Democrat government. However, for the first time ever, the government was installed through a vote of confidence which included support from the neo-fascist *Movimento Sociale Italiano* (MSI), a party which openly stood in the tradition of Mussolini's dictatorship. The political situation rapidly became unstable in June, when the MSI announced it would hold its annual congress in Genoa, a city which had been awarded a gold medal for its part in the anti-fascist resistance movement. The MSI also announced that the honorary president of the congress would be the hated fascist Prefect of the city.

Demonstrations turned to riots, barricades were put up and an ad hoc committee declared it was ready 'to take over the government of the city'. The MSI congress was postponed and the city celebrated, but elsewhere Tambroni made it clear that the police could open fire, which they promptly did, killing one demonstrator in Sicily and five others in Reggio Emilia. The main union federation, the CGIL, called a general strike which proved hugely popular. Two weeks later Tambroni was persuaded to resign.[26]

Building workers took significant strike action, as did Genoa dockers, and at the FIAT car factory in Turin the communist-controlled FIOM engineering union won an absolute majority for the first time.[27] The three union federations, which up to then had been rigidly divided according to their ideological differences, began to work together.[28] Following the successful general strike in Milan against the Tambroni government, an editorial in the Lombardy employers' association newsletter complained: 'The most aware and objective opinion-makers had warned in vain of the danger of creating the widespread feeling of the socialists' and communists' new-found dominance of the streets.'[29]

This explosion of working-class activity influenced the writing of Fo's second full-length play, *He Had Two Pistols and Black and White Eyes*. This is the story of mistaken identity between a fascist petty criminal and a Christian Democrat priest. But the normal role-play of a farce is inverted: it is not so much the underdog, the petty criminal, who feels important, but the priest, who is transformed and takes to his role of street thug with enthusiasm, while still maintaining some of his original characteristics.

Many of the comments in the play would seem quite tame by today's standards, but such irreverence, and Fo dressed up in a priest's tunic, were too provocative for the authorities, who severely censored the script. Fo recalls:

We decided to perform the show without taking the cuts into account whatsoever. There was a tense struggle between us and the Milan Prefecture, which threatened us with immediate arrest but in the end, perhaps worried by the scandal which could have ensued, the Ministry withdrew the cuts.[30]

Fo and Rame's next production was a return to more traditional farcical elements of mistaken identity and frustrated love, *He Who Steals a Foot is Lucky in Love*. The setting was also more naturalistic, essentially a bourgeois apartment with stylish furniture and large pictures. Despite this, because of the reputation they had acquired, officialdom would not leave them in peace: 14 major cuts were insisted upon, as well as the substitution of certain words. For example, the adjective 'catholic' had to be replaced by 'religious'. And when the show went on tour local police chiefs felt it was their duty to insist upon their own cuts.[31]

Some biographers have made the point that Fo and Rame's apparently inconsistent attention to strong political themes during this period was partly due to material factors: the success of their shows meant that they were earning a lot of money. They lived in a luxury apartment, were often interviewed in family magazines and photographed in big cars and fancy restaurants. On one occasion they visited the San Remo casino to play roulette, and Rame won £56,000 at 1999 prices![32] To a certain extent, the couple had also become part of the left-wing establishment. Leaders of the PCI such as Palmiro Togliatti, Giancarlo Pajetta and Luigi Longo, as well as Socialist Party leader Pietro Nenni, often went to see their shows in Rome.[33]

On the Wavelength of Lies

Italian television broadcasting began in 1954, at the height of the Cold War. For those parties in political opposition, principally the Italian Communist Party, times were hard. In big workplaces, where the bulk of communist membership was concentrated, many employers had designated *reparti confini* – isolated parts of the factory – where communists would be confined and obliged to engage in repetitive tasks.

The state television company, RAI, was set up by the Christian Democrat government, which at that time was intellectually characterised by strong doses of Catholic moralism. On one notorious occasion during this period, the future President of Italy, Oscar Luigi Scalfaro, publicly slapped a woman because he thought that her dress exposed too much of her breasts. On another occasion RAI management forced the elimination of a contestant from a quiz show because she had a habit of wearing tight sweaters.

Censorship was very prominent, particularly in the cinema, which was by far the most popular source of entertainment throughout the 1950s and most of the 1960s, that is, before most people bought televisions. What emerges from many official reports is that police attitudes towards the left had changed little since the fascist period; indeed many senior officers of the 1960s had begun their careers under fascism. For example, in December 1960 the Prefecture of Cagliari felt the need to write to the Ministry of the Interior in tones which could easily have been used under Mussolini's dictatorship:

> Out of a sense of duty I report the news of ... a public debate on the film *Rocco and His Brothers* and the abuse of censorship ...
>
> About 80 people were present, and the following individuals were identified: the local correspondent of *l'Unità* [the PCI daily paper] Livio Fadda, and Gesuino Murru, the distributor of publications of Marxist doctrine.

The issue being debated, which was becoming an increasingly common one, was that the film had been accused of being immoral.

Michelangelo Antonioni's *L'Avventura* had already been banned temporarily for very similar reasons. As the Prefect of Milan argued in

October, the film 'is intrinsically obscene, and in the construction of various episodes acts are carried out which offend public decency'.

In February of the same year the Prefect of Naples reported to the Ministry that many priests of the city's archdiocese had sent a telegram of protest to his office about the showing of Fellini's *La Dolce Vita*. They had demanded 'effective and irrevocable measures to create realistic barriers against the worrying spread of immorality which threatens ... Christian civilisation itself'.

Hardline Catholics were encouraged by this harassment of what was at the time challenging cinema. Flaminio Piccoli, who was to become a senior Christian Democrat politician and minister throughout the 1970s and 1980s, wrote in a Catholic newspaper published in Trento that these films 'have taken the road of pornography with a cynicism unworthy of a civilised country'. However he went on to say that Catholic parents 'have found in public authorities an immediate and perhaps significant and decisive response'.

Not that such harassment went without any kind of opposition. On 1 November 1960 the police chief of Rome reported to the Ministry of the Interior that a thousand-strong meeting, made up of actors, directors and technicians, had been called to discuss the wave of censorship engulfing the country. The most important outcome of the meeting was a call for a one hour strike of cinema workers on 3 December.[34]

Such battles were to continue throughout the 1960s. In January 1963 the Prefects of Milan and Palermo confiscated copies of Luis Buñuel's *Viridiana* on the grounds that it insulted the Catholic religion.[35] Later in the year it was reported that Francesco Rosi's *Hands over the City* could finally be shown as the police had withdrawn their accusation that it showed 'contempt for the police force'.[36]

Because of the Christian Democrats' control of television, the communists felt that their own positions were either distorted or simply ignored. At one of the PCI's summer festivals the workers from a Milan engineering factory once built a model exhibition of a television set, which at that time was black and white with three manual controls. They described the left-hand button as being the 'false tone' control, the central one the 'volume of deceit' and the right-hand one the 'wavelength of lies'.

Even before Fo and Rame agreed to present a series of television shows in 1962 they had experienced RAI's obsessive censorship. In 1959 RAI had broadcast one of their mini-farces, *Dead Bodies are Sent, Women are Undressed*, but the title of the farce that went on air only included the first four words.[37]

Fo and Rame presented their first *Canzonissima*, a show which mixed songs and variety acts, in October 1962. Fo had agreed to present a series of shows back in the summer for the very high figure of £13,000 per show.[38] He had also insisted that there should be no censorship, although he had given the script in two months before the show.

The opening jokes were unusual to say the least: tramps criticising the rich in Milan, criticisms of German Nazis, sarcastic comments about other television presenters, all this punctuated by established singers performing sugary songs about the moonlight shimmering over the silver sea.[39] What was even more unusual was that Fo was talking about the world of work and production. At one point Fo played a worker being interviewed about his boss:

> He's everything ... Grass, who makes the grass grow? Him, with his chemical fertilisers. Who gives that lovely violet, yellow and brown colour to the river? Him, my boss with the effluent from his dye-works. Who is it (Fo coughs several times) who gives the air that lovely sour taste? Him, with his big chimneys.[40]

In the most controversial scene Fo portrayed a worker in a meat-canning factory who was so enamoured of his boss that he kept a candle lit in front of his portrait and greeted him every morning with the words, 'Here's a kiss for you.' One day the worker's aunt came for a visit, got caught up in the machinery and was processed herself because the production line wasn't allowed to stop. But the worker was allowed to take 150 cans home with him as a 'memento'.[41]

Sarcasm like this struck a raw nerve. One industrialist in the north complained that he had felt obliged to remove a bronze bust of his father from the entrance hall of the factory that he had founded as the workers were now greeting it with the phrase, 'Here's a kiss for you.' The managing director of RAI phoned Fo and told him to drop issues such as accidents at work. Fo replied that if the law didn't take any interest in the matter, then it was necessary for satire to do so. The managing director hung up.[42]

The scripts for future programmes were now looked at again. The following account by Fo could easily have emerged from one of his comedies; alternatively it closely resembles the kind of obsessive censorship which took place in 'communist' countries such as the Soviet Union:

> There were three kinds of crossings-out: red, blue and black. A low-level official started and he cut almost everything, either things he didn't like or something that he thought his superiors would find unpleasant. Then the middle-level official went into action with a blue pencil and endorsed some cuts but cancelled others. Finally it ended up with the man who had the fatal black biro. And nobody could discuss his cuts.[43]

The second show was extremely toned down compared to the first one, a change which was highlighted in the left-wing press. Fo resumed polemics again in the third programme, when he often appeared surrounded by placards which read 'Satire is banned here' and 'It is forbidden to talk about politics'. The attacks became more explicit in the fourth show, with Fo performing sketches about prisons and the Mafia. The show began with Fo being 'arrested' by fake policemen, who were there 'to monitor and check up on the programme'.[44]

There were more questions in Parliament. One senator objected to the sketch on the Mafia with the following reasoning: 'It insults the honour of the Sicilian people by claiming the existence of a criminal organisation called the Mafia'. Other politicians simply demanded that Fo be sacked, while many newspapers accused him of 'corrupting the nation'. One newspaper revealed both condescension and real fear in a single sentence: 'It is infamous to feed such wickedness, worthy of the basest political propaganda, to an audience as uneducated and easily swayed as the great mass of TV viewers.'[45]

A mini-crusade was unleashed; a nun from near Naples publicly called on Fo and Rame to respect 'the sacred duties of Christian dignity' and warned that if they didn't 'I'll give you a good thrashing.' Two priests in Lombardy took Fo to court accusing him of using a swear word in a song, but then admitted under cross-examination that they had made a mistake, thus ending the court case.[46]

The demands of the censors went into overdrive: they now insisted that Fo cut words such as 'orphanage', 'charitable institution', 'bed' and 'liberty' because they were viewed as being ambiguous. Fo's tactic then appears to have changed to creating a guessing game, accepting some cuts but challenging others. The underlying problems for the Christian Democrats had become enormous: to sack Fo would create a huge row about censorship and, furthermore, the row would be magnified simply because of the massive audience he had built up. Public bars with televisions were packed for these broadcasts, and the incredible figure of 15 million Italians watched the last episode of Fo's *Canzonissima*.

Fo claims that at a certain point the pressure really got to the programme manager, who begged him thus: '"Cut that line, at least that one. Do it for me, don't ruin me." Once he even got down on his knees with tears in his eyes.'[47] This trench warfare also took its toll on Fo, and the seventh programme was universally criticised for being mechanical and very rudimentary.

The preparations for the eighth show clearly revealed that the full series of 15 shows could never be completed. Fo had planned to perform three sketches: the first was banned outright, the second was passed, but he was then asked to perform the third and longest scene live in Milan so that censors in Rome could watch and make a decision. It was about a building employer who is shocked by one of his workers falling off some scaffolding and admits to all the safety measures that he hadn't followed, and promises to change everything. But as soon as he learns that the worker is virtually unhurt he reverses his decision.

The authorities insisted that the whole sketch be cut, openly justifying the decision by the fact that building workers were on a national strike.

Indeed one passage in the sketch had the boss saying: 'They're going on strike to have £1.30 a day more ... I'm saying ... £1.30? ... That's the same amount I give as a tip to the bloke who opens my car door when I'm leaving the nightclub.'[48] More arguments ensued, lawyers were called, and the conclusion was that Fo and Rame left the studios and the series a few minutes before the show was due to go on air.

An RAI announcer explained to a bemused public what had happened, pointing out that one sketch dealt with a building worker and his employer, and that in the current dispute both the employers and the union had asked the government to mediate: 'RAI cannot and does not intend to interfere in the course of trade union disputes.'[49] How viewers could even begin to think that a Dario Fo sketch constituted RAI interference in a union struggle was not explained.

The issue became a national sensation. One right-wing newspaper defined the key sketch as being 'uneducative, inappropriate, offensive towards the institutions, too politicised and not funny.'[50]

The moribund actors' union suddenly became a real trade union and strongly supported Fo and Rame, with its president stating in one meeting, 'If we stay united we'll see RAI on their knees time after time.' Two very famous comedians, who were initially tempted to replace Fo, were persuaded not to take his place. A delegation of building workers presented Fo with a bunch of red carnations while he was giving a public lecture.[51] The furore surrounding *Canzonissima* may even have contributed to the building workers winning their dispute, as an agreement that they would now be paid for the hours of work interrupted due to bad weather was soon reached with employers.[52]

Back to the Theatre

In retrospect it is clear that the *Canzonissima* experience was a turning point in Fo's life – 'I had tried to overturn it [television] from within from the very first show',[53] – but he had learnt that he was simply a cog in the wheel of a very large organisation and could be neutralised, muzzled or dispensed with. In essence he was an isolated source of irritation who only represented himself. Professionally, this forced him to concentrate now solely on theatre, but in a political sense Fo had understood where the core of his following was – among left-wing workers. He also drew a broader political conclusion the day after the fiasco, comparing his fate to that of Italy's apparently reforming centre-left government, sworn in earlier that year: '*Canzonissima*, born with the centre left, has more or less suffered the same fate.'[54]

Despite being Italy's two most popular actors, Fo and Rame were deliberately kept off television screens for the next decade and a half – in 1966 Fo complained: 'They don't even mention my name. My wife and

I are beyond the pale. When we arrive at an event they pack the television cameras away.'[55] Yet when they did reappear on television in 1977 their bargaining power had increased massively – they returned as probably the most popular cultural figures of a mass left-wing movement that was turning Italy upside down. Under those conditions the censors didn't even have a walk-on part to play in Fo's performances.

It should also be said that Fo was pushing at an open door in terms of the mood of the working class. The total number of hours 'lost' through strike activity rose from 46 million in 1960 to 79 million in 1961 and 182 million in 1962. Another key event, in June 1962, was a strike of 60,000 FIAT workers in Turin, which also included thousands of white collar workers. This was significant because FIAT had been the most notorious anti-communist and anti-trade union employer during the Cold War.[56] This is also the period in which Fo's theatre began to develop close organisational links with the working class. During this period Nanni Ricordi was Milan secretary for ARCI, a national cultural association closely linked to the PCI, and recalls that: 'As ARCI in Milan, but also in many other places, we brought people to the theatre on discounted tickets: special discounts for factories, for students. This was something that was going on for five or six years before 1968.'[57]

Fo's new plays reflected the experience of *Canzonissima*; he had performed to a television audience of millions of working-class people and fully understood that his stature had increased immensely. To some extent theatre owners and middle-class spectators now had to grin and bear some of the targets that Fo started to attack in his work. Yet for the theatre owners there was also something to celebrate: Fo and Rame's first play after the *Canzonissima* fiasco broke all box office records at a time when theatre audiences were stagnating or declining.[58]

In this play, *Isabella, Three Sailing Ships and a Con Man*, Fo had a specific axe to grind: 'I wanted to attack those Italian intellectuals who, through the centre left and the Socialist Party in government, had discovered power and its advantages and leapt on it like rats on a piece of cheese.'[59] The historical parallel drawn in the play concerns the eventual demise of Columbus at the hands of the Spanish court. One point that Fo illustrates at the end of the play is that the system can often use and discard those who don't fully belong within it. Facing execution, in his last lines Columbus admits:

Here I am reduced to a skeleton. In my last voyage over there I caught all the fashionable diseases ... I've gone and knocked on the king's door loads of times, and even been kicked up the backside by the court midget ... I've always had faith in the kindness of the great and the good, I've always had confidence in their forgiveness. And here I am still waiting for that pardon, cut adrift once more'.[60]

The final action of the play is the beheading of Columbus.

The political context of the time was that the Socialist Party had just joined a centre-left coalition government with the Christian Democrats. The political idea that Fo was developing was that reformist parties such as the Socialists end up being reformed themselves – and for the worse – by the system that they were initially committed to changing. Indeed this was the beginning of a 30-year period in which the Socialists ended up gorging themselves on state funds, only to be thrown into the cesspit of history when some of the scandals emerged in the early 1990s and their electorate deserted them.

Another interesting political development in this play was that Fo's political range finder was moving further leftwards. He felt the need to attack certain characteristics of what he started to view as being a false left. Not that this play has telepathic qualities and accurately foreshadows the Socialists' demise in the early 1990s; more than anything else it represents Fo's full immersion into left-wing politics. In many ways the student explosion of 1968 was intellectually fed by debates within the left wing of the Socialist Party, who criticised their party's gradual but irrevocable absorption into the corrupt system of government dominated by the Christian Democrats, and the party's increasing abandonment of working-class struggle.

One long-term theatrical development which starts to emerge in this play is a serious level of historical research. The play is centred around the figures of Christopher Columbus and Queen Isabella of Spain, and much of the dialogue was generated from Fo's poring over ancient texts. Although it occurred at sporadic intervals, this interest in historical documents was to become a constant theme in much of his future work.

But not everything had changed. As Rame explains:

> We were attacked by fascists at the exit of the *Valle* theatre in Rome, and oddly enough the police had disappeared right at that moment. Another evening the audience was evacuated during the show because a bomb threat had been received. Threatening and insulting letters were arriving by the avalanche, and Dario was even challenged to a duel by a cavalry officer.[61]

Following that attack, members of the PCI and groups of workers would make a point of going to the show, partly to ensure that the performance could take place. The show also received some harsh criticism in Genoa, the home town of Christopher Columbus.[62] In Milan some right-wingers let off a stink bomb inside the theatre, and the police intervened ejecting and charging 17 of them.[63]

Despite all these attacks, Fo's popularity continued to rise both at home and overseas. *Isabella, Three Sailing Ships and a Con Man* was performed in Sweden two years after its debut in Italy, and a few years later in Paris.[64]

Fo also became the most performed living author in Europe for the first time during the 1964–65 season, with his plays being staged in Amsterdam, Bucharest, Budapest, Copenhagen, Hamburg, Malmö, Oslo, Prague, Reykjavik, Stockholm, Vienna, Warsaw, Zagreb and Zurich.[65]

Fo's success was such that he could pick and choose which theatre to perform in and also negotiate a contract with rather unusual conditions. As the Milan secretary for ARCI explains: 'Dario said to them – "You want me to come to the *Odeon* theatre? Instead of 50 discounted tickets, I want 300. Take it or leave it." He then gave them to me, and we dealt with the distribution.' Normally this meant that 'maybe the first two evenings were set aside for PCI branches and factory workers'.[66]

The final play Fo wrote before his break with bourgeois theatre was *The Lady Is to Be Thrown Away*. Written at the height of the Vietnam War, the 'woman' in question was the United States. More a series of sketches than a full-length play with a plot, here Fo ridiculed issues such as the official explanation given for the Kennedy assassination, the trial of Lee Harvey Oswald's killer, Jack Ruby, and other issues such as racial discrimination and the virtual worship of domestic appliances.

There were boos even on the first night. Criticisms had been building up for over ten years, normally along the lines of enthusiastic appreciation of Fo's writing and acting abilities, but increasing exasperation over his desire to make polemical political points. After the last show in Siena Fo was called in by the police chief and threatened with arrest as he had added some jokes 'offensive to a foreign head of state' (in this case Lyndon Johnson of the USA) which had not been in the script handed in to the authorities.[67]

The Break with the Bourgeoisie

Italy, and the whole world, were changing rapidly in the 1960s, yet very few of these changes were being absorbed by the Christian Democrats. Fo still had to be careful about every word he said on stage, in order not to upset both the authorities and a sizeable proportion of his audience. As he explains:

> It was becoming more and more difficult for us to perform in theatres where everything, including seating arrangements, reflected class divisions. Where, despite all our efforts, we were still famous artists who once in a while came down off the pedestal of their social and professional position. Above all staying in bourgeois theatre became more and more contradictory in terms of what was starting to be understood in that period. The most coherent choice for intellectuals was to leave their gilded ghetto and put themselves at the service of the movement.[68]

Rame fully concurred: 'In order to feel at one with our political commitments it was no longer enough to consider ourselves democratic, left-wing artists full of sympathy for the working class.'[69]

Anticipating one of the audience responses they consciously tried to avoid in *Accidental Death of an Anarchist*, what they found particularly annoying was that most of their middle-class audience tolerated their attacks. As Rame continues:

The high bourgeoisie reacted to our 'spankings' almost with pleasure. Masochists? No, without realising it, we were helping their digestion. Our 'whipping' boosted their blood circulation, like some good birching after a refreshing sauna. In other words we had become the minstrels of a fat and intelligent bourgeoisie.[70]

Fo and Rame broke with the bourgeois circuit in the summer of 1968, following many discussions with the actors of their theatre group as well as with workers at the *Sit-Siemens* factory in Milan. Another decisive influence was the close relationship they had developed with the ARCI cultural association and its network of clubs. As Nanni Ricordi explains: 'There were already links as regards bringing people to the theatre on discounted tickets. And in fact, I came to some of these meetings with the entire ARCI National Committee.'[71]

This decision meant an end to a guaranteed income, to easy money and a relatively easy life. They were rejecting unbridled success, as Rame explains: 'From 1964 to 1968 we always enjoyed the largest takings among the major Italian theatre companies, and our ticket prices were among the lowest.'[72] In a celebrated sentence Fo explained his reasons thus: 'We were tired of being the *giullari* of the bourgeoisie, for whom by now our criticisms had the same effect as *Alka-Seltzer*, we therefore decided to become the *giullari* of the proletariat.'[73]

As he later explained in more detail:

The bourgeoisie even accepted violent criticisms through the use of satire and the grotesque, but only on the condition that you criticised them from within their own structures. In the same way as the king's jester can get away with saying harder things against the king within the court, among all the members who laugh, applaud and comment: 'But look how democratic our sovereign is.' For the bourgeoisie it was even a method to prove to itself how understanding and democratic it was. Powerful people, and important kings, who understand certain things very well, have always paid court jesters to engage in irony against them. But every time one of them left this structure to go and talk with peasants, workers or the exploited, in order to tell them certain things, then they're not accepted any more. You can laugh at the system from within its own structures, but they'll never allow you to do it from the outside.[74]

The 'break' with conventional theatre meant a no-holds-barred struggle with the authorities, who viewed Fo's message with hatred and contempt. The decision was largely the product of two factors: the slow but steady radicalisation of both Fo and Rame, and the growth of a mass movement outside of the control of the PCI.

Nor was it an isolated incident internationally. In the UK Peter Brook had produced *Us*, a play openly against the Vietnam War. The most famous French theatre director, Jean-Louis Barrault, was sacked from his management of the *Odéon* in Paris in the summer of 1968 after supporting the students who had occupied it. And in Italy, a few months before Fo's decision, Giorgio Strehler had resigned from the prestigious *Piccolo Teatro* in Milan in a short-lived act of rebellion.

The Revolutionary Period

Franca Rame once described the first performance that she and Fo gave after their break from the commercial circuit. Not only does such an inspiring account deserve to be quoted at length, it also sets the tone for much of what they were to do for several years after 1968:

I remember our first show at the *Sant'Egidio* club in the suburbs of Cesena ... We were assembling the scaffolding for the stage with the help of the lads in the organisation (ARCI [the cultural association closely linked to the PCI]) and a few workers and students. However, the club members went on playing cards at the other end of the hall, looking at us now and again, but with diffidence. Clearly for them we were a group of intellectuals, mildly affected by the populist bug ... What took them by surprise was actually to see us working, working with our own hands, lifting boxes, carrying steel tubes, fixing nuts and bolts, setting up the stage lights. What? Actors, both male and female, slogging away? Incredible!

In the meantime a rather serious problem had arisen: voices reverberated too much in the hall ... We had to first arrange some cables underneath the ceiling and to hang a few acoustic panels. We decided to use egg boxes, the kind made of cardboard ... We started stringing the boxes together with the help of some upholstering needles, but it wasn't at all easy. After swearing for a couple of hours trying to get the needles through the cardboard, we noticed that the comrades from the club had interrupted their games and were looking at us, following our work with interest but in complete silence. After a while an old comrade muttered, as though talking to himself: 'You want a much longer needle for that job.' Then, silence again for a few minutes. Then someone else said: 'I could easily make one with a bicycle spoke.' 'Go!' they all said. In a moment the comrade was back with ten very long needles. Then everybody started to help us to get the string through the boxes and hang them, climbing on stepladders, like jugglers ... A few hours later there were so many people in the hall that we could hardly move. Even the most stubborn billiard players had come to help us and some women too, who had just come to get their husbands back home ...

We had won their sympathy by showing that we too could work and sweat. In the late afternoon, after work, they would come to help us and, when we started rehearsing, they would sit at the opposite end of the hall looking at us very quietly ... Then little by little they loosened up. At the end of our rehearsals we would ask for their views, whether they had any criticism to make. At first they wouldn't unbutton, saying that they knew nothing about theatre, but later they became less shy and began to make critical remarks and give us some advice too, which invariably was as unassuming as it was pertinent and to the point ... Later on, when we moved to other clubs in the vicinity, those comrades followed us and introduced the show to the local comrades. They went out hanging posters and were always the first to speak in the debates. They supported us, we were their team.[1]

Fo and Rame had abandoned financial and critical success to launch themselves into a mass movement. The following decade, recounted in this chapter, was to witness – not uncoincidentally – both the high point of their political commitment and the writing and performing of their most popular and enduring plays.

Following the student rebellion of 1968, organised workers took centre stage in 1969, as strikes multiplied fourfold between 1968 and 1969.[2] At the highest point of the 1969 'Hot Autumn' workers in some northern factories had rendered these almost ungovernable for their bosses. Mass meetings generally decided what form of action to take, and these were often called spontaneously. As one FIAT worker recalled: 'People just jumped on the tables in the cafeteria during lunch break, and that's how mass meetings started.'[3] As part of negotiating a new contract, between mid-September and Christmas 1969 engineers went on strike for an average of nearly two hours a day: some days there were no strikes, other days there were two, four, six hour or whole day strikes.[4] Strikers often remained within the factory and, as the Milan employers' association complained, this led to 'material prevention of work, using all means: from the usual threats to the siege of workers and the cutting off of electric current to stop all machines'.[5] Strikers would often march round the factory banging drums and blowing whistles looking for scabs. As one worker recalled, once they were caught the strikers would 'place them in front of the rally ... It was the right thing to do to catch them, yank them out of the dumpsters where they hid, and put them right in front of the rally, kicking their butts'.[6] In the most militant factories managers also became targets: 'Hunting for the bosses soon became a habit. Sometimes, we caught them and threw them out over the gates; other times we roped them up, stuck a red flag in their hands, and forced them to march along like that in front of the rally.'[7]

Membership of trade unions began to grow rapidly: members of the communist-oriented FIOM engineering union at FIAT's *Mirafiori* plant rose ninefold between 1969 and 1971, from 539 to 4,799.[8] Similarly, the number of teachers in the CGIL union federation rose from 4,000 in 1968 to 90,000 in 1975.[9] The same trend occurred for all main categories of employment, with membership of the three main national union federations rising from 4 million in 1968 to 6.6 million in 1975.[10] New groups of workers began to take action for the first time; by 1969 striking 'became a conventional expression of dissent or a bargaining tool among such groups as civil servants, bank clerks, doctors and lawyers'.[11] Workers were making all sorts of demands, and wage demands were increasingly awarded in equal amounts across the board rather than in the less egalitarian form of percentage increases. A major survey indicated that in 1970 equal wage increases were obtained in 71 per cent of all cases, this figure rising to 74.5 per cent in 1971.[12] Other widespread reforms were also obtained: by 1973 piecework had been abolished in many factories, and the working week generally reduced from 48 to 40 hours, with workers granted 150 hours of paid leave per year for non work-related education classes – often basic literacy classes.[13]

A mass movement of radical students, angry workers and newly-created revolutionary groups had come into being. And Fo and Rame made it clear they were joining this 'movement' rather than a particular party or a precise set of political ideas. A long-term collaborator of Fo's, Piero Sciotto, outlines a common misconception of what 1968 represented in Fo's career:

It is stupid to say he started doing political theatre in 1968 – it's idiotic. It wasn't a break with his own dramaturgy, his own kind of theatre ... The form of his theatre did change though, because you had to adapt to not having conventional stages, or any wings. They were all haphazard situations: stages that were erected and dismantled – in the open air, in factories, in suburban cinemas. So the technique of writing changed, above all in the presentation of a play. You couldn't write complicated plays because we had to load and unload the lorries – you couldn't have three articulated lorries full of stuff, you had to try and simplify. It wasn't as if the intention was different; the search for a different audience definitely was though. This was the essence of his separation from ordinary theatre.[14]

So 1968 represented the first time that Fo began writing for an essentially working-class audience. And perhaps this is why, as one biographer of Fo has described, his first play of this period (*Big Pantomime with Flags and Puppets*) was 'full, perhaps too full, of things left unsaid for many years'.[15]

There are no real characters, just social categories: *Capital*, *The CBI*, the *Archbishop*, the *Puppet-king*, the *High-Finance/queen* and the *Dragon* – representing a militant working class. There is also a ten-foot tall *Big Puppet* representing the State, from whose insides emerge corrupt industrialists, generals and bishops. It isn't easy for the *Dragon* to defeat the *Big Puppet* however, indeed the first leader of the proletariat gets seduced by the 'buxom bourgeoisie'.

The principal theme is undoubtedly the struggle between the *Dragon* and the *Big Puppet*, but there is also the 'demonstration that there is not one fixed arena of exploitation and alienation, because they are made up from all aspects of life'. But apart from a very strong attack against the world of politics, this play also contained a polemic against 'the society of entertainment' and the consumer society – also a target for writers as diverse as Herbert Marcuse and Pierpaolo Pasolini – in which everything is on display in such a way that people are manoeuvred into forgetting about their own problems. For instance, at one point 'the indecisive rebels risk getting hypnotised by a magician whose main tricks are football-weekend-adverts-music'. There are also lines such as 'switch on the television/and you switch off the revolution'.[16]

However, the entire plot changes in the second act: here factory job applicants are undergoing a medical, in preparation for working a production line which requires that they also use their feet.

The final scene is an argument taking place during a student demonstration, in which Fo explicitly attacks the apparent 'communism' of the Soviet Union. One demonstrator asks: 'Is it true that the Soviet Union has lent several billion to the Greek Colonels?' (They had recently seized control in a military coup.) The answer is thrown back: 'Whoever is curious is playing the game of reactionaries and imperialists.' Another demonstrator then states categorically: 'The USSR has lent billions to the military in Jakarta, the people who massacred 600,000 communists', only to receive a classic bureaucratic Stalinist reply: 'Talking about this is low-level propaganda, it's demagoguery, stupid moralism.'[17]

A New Audience

Most of these performances were taking place in *Case del popolo* (literally 'houses of the people') run by the PCI's cultural wing ARCI. These establishments had been created by the socialist movement at the turn of the century and were a more politicised version of Britain's working men's clubs as they remained a meeting place for the mass membership of the PCI and the Socialist Party.

Fo's new theatre company, *New Scene*, were performing in what were new venues for them, to a new audience, and were guests of a new organisation. In 1968 Nanni Ricordi was both a PCI member and secretary of the Milan ARCI branch; he recalls: 'We drew up a map of possible ARCI branches. Those that were feasible both in a structural sense (a physical space, good acoustics), and in the sense of political willingness.' Many *Case del popolo* and ARCI branches had essentially become meeting places deprived of any strong political commitment. Ricordi recounts that for these shows to succeed, 'You needed two or three preliminary meetings beforehand to understand what needed to be organised. You had to work out what was needed technically, to explain the legal aspects of the ticketing arrangements.' In order to win over these branches, which were often politically dormant, Ricordi used his PCI contacts to ensure that *New Scene*'s proposals were taken seriously: 'The groundwork had already been done before we arrived. I didn't go and talk to Bologna if Longo's or Berlinguer's office had not phoned beforehand.'[18] (Longo and Berlinguer were the two main leaders of the PCI in this period.) Both the PCI and ARCI were making a political commitment towards *New Scene* – which eventually became problematic once the political content of their shows became clear.

Initially, Fo had a captive audience of people who regularly attended the *Case*. Yet enthused by Fo's reputation and radicalised by the general political atmosphere of the period, members of local ARCI branches went out to build the biggest possible audience. As one contemporary account explains: 'The young organisers of the branches volunteer to get rid of the tickets; they approach workers coming out of factory gates and scour the rural areas, farmhouse by farmhouse.'[19]

In another account of this period, interestingly enough entitled 'A total experiment', one journalist described how Fo's company

> presents itself in town without posters or programmes. Its stages are improvised, it doesn't have any dressing rooms, it doesn't place adverts in newspapers, during the day it doesn't rehearse but holds debates ... The actors, who are also the technicians of the company, set up the equipment in front of the first arrivals.[20]

The company was often performing in small semi-rural towns, and local people leapt at the idea of going to the theatre. The PCI daily *l'Unità* reported that only two people in the 450 strong audience at San Martino in Fiume had gone to the theatre before. At Sant'Ilario d'Enza 1,700 people packed into an unheated aircraft hangar in mid-January. In the town of Fabbrico, population 5,000, on two rainy winter nights in midweek, the audience totalled between 800 and 900 per night. On the second night about half the audience had attended the previous performance, and as one spectator explained: 'I came back this evening because there was something I wanted to understand better.' After the opening night of the tour in Cesena 200 people had come back the following day to continue discussion with the cast.[21]

Fo's reputation – built up over more than a decade – was preceding him wherever his new company went. The decision to jump head first into a growing mass movement was clearly paying off. Apart from the explicitly political nature of the play, what stood out even more was the insistence upon a 'third act', a discussion between the cast and the audience immediately after the end of the theatrical performance:

> Entire families, the young and the old, are in the 'theatre' up to an hour before the start of the show. Fo calculates that he would have performed in front of half a million people by the close of the season ... At the end there is no discussion about whether one particular scene is good or bad, or whether it was pleasant or not – but of whether that social reality was true or false, whether it was familiar or not.[22]

Indeed the debates sometimes went on for longer than the show itself, finishing in the early hours of the morning. One of the participants in these debates recalled:

> You could feel the pulse of the political situation. There were all sorts; you would see workers speaking. People who didn't know how to make speeches were speaking up anyway because they had something to say. If somebody was illiterate people would say, 'Let him speak, you've got to talk!' Maybe they got their tenses mixed up, but people said, 'Speak, speak, go on, tell your story.'[23]

These debates committed the cast to an exhausting schedule, as one member recollects: 'It was a sports stadium, with one of our big stages. And we left there at 5 a.m. because the debate had ended at 3 a.m.; then we had to dismantle the stage, load it up, and leave for another town and the following evening's show.'[24]

These accounts are also backed up by a *New Scene* report written after their second season of performances:

> In the small towns the audience was often 80 per cent working class (farm labourers, manual workers, home workers etc., depending on the area) and the same percentage found themselves at the theatre for the first time.
>
> The most interesting and positive piece of information is the audience's real participation in the debate, during every debate. Everyone feels the need to discuss what they have seen. Most evenings the discussion goes on for one or two hours after the performance; very often the entire audience remains seated for the first hour.
>
> Those who speak are often old activists or workers who have never spoken in public before; they are encouraged to do so by the unusual atmosphere and the provocatory nature of the topics raised in the show.[25]

Although the debates may have been more political than theatrical, as a writer Fo also listened, interpreted and acted on the arguments that arose: 'The text *is born* from the public. The author has slowly adapted and modified it listening to successive reactions and criticisms. Fo says that from when it premièred to today he has had to modify at least 45 minutes of the show.'[26]

When *New Scene* returned to Milan they would then 'debate the debates' in which most members had taken part during the tours. Nanni Ricordi remembers that people would say: 'This theme has been raised four, five, six or seven times. Maybe if you can get an idea on this, Dario, you should develop it theatrically?' And as regards actual creative production: 'Ninety per cent of it was Dario's show, however, everybody else had contributed, as they had taken part in the discussions on the tour.'[27] Another member of *The Commune*, again after a gap of nearly 30 years, has a different recollection of the collective's influence over Fo's writing: 'They were trifles. If Dario wanted to say "grey" and we said "green", he wrote "greenish".'[28] Minutes were not taken of these meetings, so it is impossible to verify the precision of individuals' memories. The recollections of Piero Sciotto, a long-term collaborator of Fo's, of the debates held within *The Commune* collective, which was founded in 1970, are more negative and revolve around ideological divisions within the collective:

> Dario's proposals for the production of a play were discussed, not really on the basis of whether they were right or wrong, but because the production hadn't been developed collectively. There were misunderstandings that became dogma, rules ... There were irritations due to an atmosphere, a [political] methodology ... There was a tendency to make Dario write things that he had never intended to say, that he didn't think were right ... There was a tendency to pressurise, almost as if Dario was writing for them.[29]

In terms of the actual performances, *New Scene's* 'political' hosts, the PCI, were slow to understand what was really happening. An early review innocently stated that the nature of post-performance discussions 'was the result of misunderstandings – a joke about Czechoslovakia or a line concerning Lenin which wasn't *orthodox*'.[30]

Given the size of Fo's audience and the nature of the debates that were taking place, alarm bells eventually started to ring in the upper echelons of the PCI, as Fo recalls:

> We made a big impact and this is why the intermediate members, the bureaucrats, almost immediately started to view us with mistrust. I remember one leader in our second year, who without a hint of irony said to me: 'No more than ten people ever came to meetings last year, now there are never less than 50 – and each one has got their own axe

to grind.' The fact was that we gave people courage, often the secretary of the *Casa* would end up being criticised.[31]

It was slowly beginning to emerge that the PCI and Fo's *New Scene* theatre group, although they were working together, had two totally different political agendas.

The Politics of *New Scene*

The company was characterised by an extremely egalitarian organisational structure and performance rationale. All members of the company were paid the same wage – the trade union minimum wage – and all actors received equal (alphabetical) billing in all of the company's shows. Fo initially wrote his new plays, such as *Big Pantomime*, in such a way that there could be no leading actor with a much larger part than others – he himself played a minor rebel in it.

The founding statute of the company, published in late 1968, defined its members as follows: 'A collective of militants who put themselves at the service of revolutionary forces. Not to reform the bourgeois state through opportunistic policies, but to encourage the growth of a real revolutionary process which effectively brings the working class to power.'[32]

Yet it may well be the case that *New Scene* had not fully thought through the implications of such a position. Nanni Ricordi remembers that they published a collection of Antonio Gramsci's writings on trade unions which argued that 'Trade unions tried to douse the flames, to put on the brakes. It was definitely the case that at that point these articles by Gramsci were explosive, because Gramsci had been the founder of the PCI'.[33] For PCI members, used to conceiving of union federation leaderships such as the CGIL as a 'transmission belt' for PCI policies, the very idea that the founding father of their party could conceive of union leaders as opponents of the working-class struggle was a very disturbing concept. Tension between union leaderships and rank and file workers was to become widespread after the 1969 'Hot Autumn', and only from then on did the concept of communist yet 'conservative' union leaders become a familiar concept. *New Scene*, along with the rest of the Italian left, were in turmoil in these years, discovering a range of new writings and opinions within a very short space of time.

A tense relationship developed between these ideals and the venues that *New Scene* was intending to use for performances. Essentially *New Scene* depended on ARCI for providing both venues and an audience. Although formally independent, ARCI's activities largely followed the wishes of the PCI leadership. What is essential to grasp is that during 1968–69 Fo, Rame and many other members of *New Scene* had illusions that the PCI could be pushed to the left. One illustration of this was Franca Rame's decision to join the PCI as far back as 1960.

Despite these illusions, the perpetuation of a mass working-class movement in Italy continued to provide further justification for the content of Fo's plays. And it was the strength of this movement which determined the nature of the clash between *New Scene* and the PCI: on the one hand Fo felt obliged to use this structure, and on the other the PCI found it difficult to ban *New Scene* officially, given that so many activists were attacking the Soviet Union for the repressive nature of its society and its invasion of Czechoslovakia.

There were also political divisions within *New Scene* which centred around the kind of relationship that should be maintained with the PCI, but these divisions could not be resolved to everyone's liking. These internal and external tensions continued. For example, in an internal *New Scene* document of September 1970 it was tentatively suggested that attempts should be made to develop 'firm organisational links with local political groups (supporters of the *Il Manifesto* group, members of the Maoist "Marxist-Leninist" Communist Party, activists of the student movement and individual members of the Communist and Socialist Parties) in order to organise initiatives in suburbs and small halls independently'.[34]

With hindsight, as Fo explains, it was clear that as a group *New Scene* profoundly misunderstood the nature of the PCI: 'We had the illusion that we could change the leadership structures by working with the rank and file; that the PCI would have adopted a revolutionary line thanks to the pressure coming from the student movement and from workers.'[35] It was an illusion that was destined to founder on the rocks of protracted political arguments.

The Break with Reformism

By autumn 1969 Fo had written two new plays, both of which drew directly on the experience acquired during the previous year of writing and performing for a working-class audience. He had set himself a new series of tasks: 'It was necessary to overcome the typical pessimistic outlook of intellectuals, according to whom art should only criticise and never propose anything. In those shows, which were created directly from living concrete problems, I also tried to provide some solutions.'[36]

The first play in question, *The Worker Knows 300 Words, The Boss Knows 1,000–That's Why He's The Boss*, continued the theme of dealing with the political issues which dominated the left in this period, essentially whether to take the road of revolution or that of reform proposed by the PCI.

The setting of the play itself was provocative in that it focused on nine workers in a *Casa del popolo*. Indeed these very performances constituted a virtual earthquake for a structure (the *Casa del popolo*) which had become moribund, as Rame explains: 'The original need that workers and peasants had to create their own place for studying and producing culture together had been completely lost. Those *Case del popolo* had mainly been reduced to the dispensing of alcoholic drinks, dance halls and billiard rooms ... There were virtually no debates any more.'[37]

The plot revolves around a group of workers sent to a *Casa del popolo* to dismantle the library and build a billiard room. The removing of the books from the shelves gives rise to a number of scenes in which some of the authors 'come alive' and their lives and ideas are debated.

Much of the play argues that workers have to reclaim the revolutionary tradition represented by figures such as Antonio Gramsci, the main leader of the PCI from 1921 to 1926. While the PCI leadership were happy to see one of their founding fathers praised, what probably provoked their outright hostility was the overt and repeated criticism of Stalinism: various scenes and lines attacked the exploitation of Russian car workers at the FIAT car factory in Togliattigrad, the murky dealings of Stalinists in the Spanish Civil War of the 1930s, the Stalinist show trials in Eastern Europe during the 1950s, and so on.

The question of politically defining the nature of Russia was not one which primarily related to events of several decades earlier; in a very real sense the issue at hand was whether Russia was a valid model of what one thought socialism or communism to be. Fo never believed that Russia played this role since Stalin's rise to power in the early 1920s, but the PCI maintained its support for Russia long after Stalin's death in 1953. One useful example is a front page article from the PCI daily, *l'Unità*, written by the PCI central committee to the corresponding body of the Communist Party of the Soviet Union. The article was published on 7 December 1972, to honour the 55th anniversary of the 1917 revolution: 'A warm and fraternal greeting is sent to you from the PCI's central committee and the members of our party.' The article then went on to express 'the willingness of Italian communists to act so as to extend and consolidate the unity of the international communist and working-class movement ... the Italian communists and the Italian people understand more and more deeply the decisive function of the USSR'. There is no room for any ambiguity here, as the concluding paragraph and sentence of the article shows: 'With the hope of new successes in the building of the USSR's socialist society, and with the commitment of developing even further our friendship and collaboration.'[38]

Such was the PCI's attachment to Russia that it supported traumatic events such as the Russian invasion of Hungary in 1956 and effectively avoided working through the issues surrounding the far more recent invasion of Czechoslovakia in 1968. Indeed from 1968 onwards hundreds of thousands of Italian students, as well as considerable numbers of PCI members, had for the first time begun to question whether the Russian system ought to be reproduced in Italy. Despite all these countervailing tendencies, the PCI leadership still continued essentially to propose the tired old formulas which were becoming less and less convincing for political activists. However, the continuing increases in both its electoral performance and total membership illustrate that in the political context of the times, the PCI was becoming less and less radical.

The ideas represented by Fo put forward an existing alternative to Russia, in the shape of Mao Zedung's China. Along with probably most of the revolutionary left (albeit often on the basis of misinformation), Fo genuinely believed that Chinese society was much more open and democratic than Russian, and that the working class exercised significant power through the Chinese Communist Party. However, Fo also debated critically the failures surrounding the building of socialism in Russia, and furthermore his attitude towards the Eastern Bloc was not a purely theoretical issue. For example, he withdrew permission for his plays to be performed in Czechoslovakia following the Russian invasion of 1968. He also refused permission for performances in virtually all of the Eastern Bloc countries in that period, due to the excessive level of censorship that was demanded.

Indeed the longest scene of *The Worker Knows...* concerns a notorious Stalinist show trial held in Czechoslovakia in 1952. Despite its remoteness in time, Fo must have decided to highlight this case due to the topicality of the Russian invasion of Czechoslovakia, which occurred the year before the play was performed. Rudolf Slansky was general secretary of the Czechoslovak Communist Party in the immediate postwar period. He and his ten co-defendants became the victims of probably the worst show trial in Eastern Europe during this period. Although he had joined the Czech Communist Party in 1921 and been prominent in resistance to the Nazis, he 'confessed' to the court: 'I have never been a real communist.' It has since been revealed that his 'confession' was in fact written by Kremlin officials, and just to make the whole thing more believable the defendants were shouted and sworn at during the hearings. After their conviction and hanging for 'Titoism', Slansky and the others had their ashes spread over an unknown piece of ice over a river. In order to consolidate their power the Stalinists turned Czechoslovakia into a prison camp: 60,000 members of the Communist Party were imprisoned, and a total of 130,000 people were sent to labour camps. [39]

Parts of Slansky's trial are acted out on stage, and towards the end he understands that the basic reason for his impending death is the fact that party leaders are no longer in contact with ordinary people. Slansky realises that the working class has come to play a passive role in Czechoslovak society and within the Communist Party, being invited to 'come to the meetings, listen to the speeches, applaud, agree, make a few criticisms as long as they're lightweight, encourage us, support us, give us your vote'. The worst thing workers could do was to harbour any doubts: 'Doubt is a bourgeois weakness, held by intellectuals ... By people who've got time to waste ... Socialism is in a hurry.'[40] The final scene of the first act is the hanging of Slansky.

Another central political polemic raised in *The Worker Knows...* is the ingenuous amalgamation of the 'patron saint' of the PCI, Antonio Gramsci, with contemporary students who were criticising the PCI and making alliances with workers. In the play, as in real life, Gramsci was a student activist in Turin who often gave speeches in factories during and immediately after the First World War. *A Worker in Overalls* looks at *The Student* and says, 'But he's a student! He belongs to another race! He's nothing to do with us lot!' Yet the references are more to contemporary students than to those in Turin in 1919: 'He's come here to stir things up, him and his group of extremists. They want us to start complaining – right now – just with all the improvements that the boss has made.' It would have escaped very few people in the audience that this was a criticism of the PCI's contemporary moderatism. An argument then ensues between this worker and *The Student* over the impact of new technology, and Fo now allows *The Worker* to address *The Student* with his real name: 'You know what, Gramsci? You, with those ideas, you'll never get the party you've got in your head off the ground! And I'm someone who understands these things.'[41] The irony is quite vicious: Fo puts the words of the contemporary PCI bureaucracy into the mouth of a worker of 1919, who dismisses the ideas and intentions of the man who did perhaps more than anyone else to create the basis for the PCI's growth into a mass party.

At the end of the scene the student, now renamed *Gramsci*, effectively addresses the audience:

> Those who have very little faith in the proletariat and its resources are terrible Marxists ... Workers are lazy by nature they tell us, let's not tire them out with complicated discussions, let's give them what they understand, let's keep things simple ... Be careful, comrades, doing things that way means that our culture remains stuck at the level of village fetes![42]

The problem for the PCI leadership was that tens of thousands of their members were going to see Fo because they admired his talents; however, as well as entertaining them he was also giving them an alternative view of their party. As one writer has argued: 'The company was not isolating itself from the working-class left, but simply articulating a position which had grown more and more widespread, even among party rank-and-file membership, since 1968.'[43] PCI members often agreed with many of the play's observations, as *l'Unità* admitted: 'The other evening virtually nobody expressed any doubt that the agreement between FIAT and the

Soviet government represented a serious error by the leading group of the USSR.'[44]

A very representative speech concerning the internal life of the PCI was given by an industrial worker and party member during a debate following a show in Florence:

at [PCI] branch meetings discussions go on for two hours ... and nothing gets said. At this point workers get fed up and go and play billiards at the *Casa del popolo*. So I say to those left-wing intellectuals that workers understand any issue, they can force their minds to confront any problem as long as the language that is used is concrete. At this point I must say that the language used by these young people is the most concrete that I've heard in my 43 years, and I ask myself why certain obstacles are placed in front of these shows, and for this reason I want to ask ARCI, *l'Unità* journalists and party leaders whether they really want workers to develop their ideas or not. I believe that if you carry on calling people Maoists, splitters, adventurists, or worse, then you're not heading towards workers developing their own ideas.[45]

The PCI's local federation in Genoa, where the show started its tour, was thrown into turmoil from the very beginning. The chair of the federation's cultural committee expressed his 'drastic dissent' over the show, whereas the federation secretary had spoken of a 'backward show when compared to reality'. Frenetic phone calls then ensued to the national leadership in Rome, which intervened to stop a favourable review by a local PCI member and theatre critic. His article was removed from the party daily, *l'Unità*, and an aggressive editorial was inserted accusing Fo of 'crude sentimental amorality, which offends the objectivity of facts by deforming them'.[46] In protest, the author of the original review resigned from his post on the paper.

The controversy started to snowball, with the national organiser for ARCI making sure that he caught the next show. During the debate after the performance he attacked the actors for touring with a show intended to change the PCI rather than a play which denounced how people were being exploited. Rame read between the lines and responded to the whole audience: 'You've all been either participants or spectators in how you torpedo a theatrical enterprise.' Aware of the difficulties which could arise if ARCI pulled the plug on them she burst into tears and caused pandemonium in the audience, which either applauded her or attacked her with cries of 'shame' or 'people are slinging mud at the party here'.[47]

The PCI's major theatre critic resumed the attack a few days later, arguing that 'you cannot put General Franco's police on the same level as that of the Socialist state' (that is, Russia). He also thought that events such as Slansky's trial and execution should not be put on stage: 'They are very painful pages in the history of the working-class movement, which no theatrical sketch can ever resolve – let alone confront adequately.'[48]

To their credit, l'Unità allowed New Scene to reply to the criticisms, in which they argued, 'You can only build a real alternative to the bourgeois state by working together.' Yet part of this common work must be an acceptance of the need to discuss issues: 'We think it is our duty to stimulate discussions about everything, without taboos or prejudices, because we believe our audience to be very mature and "adult" and therefore able to take part in our activities with a critical eye.'[49]

However, the gap between New Scene and the PCI was now unbridgeable. L'Unità made it clear that Fo had gone too far: 'Criticise the Communist Party and mass organisations? Certainly – this can and must be done. But it has to be from the inside, as part of a move forward, and not as encouragement to bring things to a halt.'[50] The PCI now moved to deny Fo and Rame a working-class audience. In practical terms the tour now had great difficulties: on one occasion the Trades Council hall in Milan was denied to them, so they ended up performing in a real circus tent where lions, tigers and elephants were caged up backstage. In central Italy New Scene were often denied the use of ARCI premises under flimsy pretexts.[51] Alternatively bookings were made in out-of-the-way places, and no effort was made by ARCI and PCI members to publicise them or sell tickets; dozens of shows were cancelled. Local PCI leaders would sometimes stand up in the 'third act' and demand that political discussions should not take place.[52] In any case the debates were beginning to change, in that PCI members would read hostile reviews in l'Unità and go to shows with preconceived criticisms. As Nanni Ricordi later recalled: 'It wasn't a question of bad faith, neither on one side or the other. But if somebody comes to my house and starts criticising my son – well, what would you expect me to say?'[53] In any event, towards the end of 1970 Rame handed back her PCI membership card to the party secretary, Enrico Berlinguer.

One of Fo's comments, made with the benefit of hindsight, illustrates that the PCI and New Scene were destined to part company, the differences simply being too deep. It was Fo and New Scene who were moving forward and discovering new ideas, and the consequence of this was to lead to an irrevocable break:

We had a much deeper dissent. We wanted to put our work at the service of the working-class movement. But for us 'at the service of' didn't mean becoming part of a ready-made package, or essentially being 'left-wing artists' who accept orders and compromises and allow the party to work out the line. We had decided to contribute to the movement, to be part of it, to be directly involved in the struggle – basically to be revolutionary militants.[54]

It wasn't only the PCI hierarchy which was concerned about the combination of Fo's popularity and his political message: the state was also worried. Fo and *New Scene* had set themselves up as a private cultural association, and in order to see their shows you first had to become a member of *New Scene* by buying a membership card, and then buy a ticket for a specific show. This made their performances private shows, and in legal terms, beyond the reach of the censor and police interference. The police either disputed the legal basis of *New Scene*'s operation and entered theatres anyway or used the pretext of ensuring that 'no crimes were being committed' to check up on safety regulations. Dozens of shows were cancelled by the company during the early 1970s when policemen were identified in the theatre. Alternatively, plain-clothed policemen would buy membership cards and performance tickets and hope that they would not be identified. This occasionally led to hilarious consequences, as Fo explained to an audience in Florence before a performance: 'It is forbidden for members of the police or armed forces to join an association which has a specific cultural and political programme [*New Scene* was clearly a 'communist' theatrical group]. I pointed this out to the policeman who was in the stalls, who was kind enough to leave.'[55]

The second play in this season – *Tie Me Up and I'll Still Smash Everything* – opened just two days after *The Worker Knows*...[56] and was made up of two single-act plays: *The Loom* and *The Boss's Funeral*. However, both acts deal with the exploitation of workers, and both are set in the Emilia region, a PCI stronghold where the party has traditionally run many large-scale cooperative workplaces.

The Loom begins with a growing series of complaints from workers: 'I'm a CGIL activist at the SNIA factory. More than a thousand workers, all the factory, went on strike for me! ... indefinite strike ... until the bosses reinstated me.' The next worker continues: 'They sacked all of us, they wanted to close things down because they say we're not profitable.' A third worker goes even further: 'We occupied the factory for almost a month ... In the end the boss gave in and gave us loads of things, including the right to hold meetings, but on allowing the union into the factory, no ... he doesn't want them around.'[57]

Other workers list their bad working conditions, even though some of them suffer from bronchitis or rheumatism and others from deafness or convulsions. At one factory an unusual solution was provided for these health problems:

> Every day at 3.30 a girl from the gatehouse who also works as a nurse comes round with a tray with various pills on it: for headaches, for whoever feels a bit tired and wants a pick-me-up, for whoever is nervous and wants something soothing ... it's all free – it's on the house to ensure good work ... The fact is that so many of us have got used to them

... some people are already taking pills on their own account in the morning, they take two or three a day ... otherwise they can't work efficiently and there's always the worry you'll get the sack.[58]

Women workers go on to complain about their monotonous work and the lack of nurseries, while other home workers complain they work illegally for 15 or 16 hours a day.

At the end of all these complaints comes the killer blow which ends the first scene: 'The lovely thing is that in many areas the bosses, and some of the people who go round collecting the finished work, are members or leaders of left-wing parties.'[59]

The piece then proceeds to illustrate the growing exploitation, alienation and, ultimately, frustration of a family of home workers almost literally chained to a loom, working for *The Buyer*, a PCI member. He defends his actions by saying that he got 50 people to join the party over the last year, but he is immediately attacked on the basis that these were people over whom he exercised an exploitative power, to which he replies: 'I don't exploit them, it's the market that does that.' *The Buyer* then voices what was the PCI's line at the time: 'They've always explained to us that our enemy is only big Capital, and that small-and medium-sized Capital should be our allies.' From such a general statement he then moves to the specific: 'If you wanted I could tell you loads of names of small businessmen and small factory owners, big hoteliers and big shop owners, who have been elected as mayors, party branch secretaries and all sorts.'[60]

Dialogue like this acted as a lightning rod among a working-class audience, a high proportion of whom were PCI members. Not only in the historical and ideological themes that he presented in his plays, but probably more so in the themes of everyday life, Fo obliged party members to examine the contradictions of their membership. One example out of many is a speech by a PCI member following a performance of *The Loom*:

The problems raised in the show and which exist within the party are a real can of worms. A while ago I proposed what the loom worker proposed: revoke membership from loads of people. In my case it was the scabs in my factory, or rather there was someone who scabbed, was a union member and had a party card. When everyone else protested about working on holidays he went to work, when people went on strike he did twelve-hour shifts. Apart from wanting to revoke his membership, I thought someone from the party would call him to tell him that they thought what he was doing made him unworthy to be a party member, that he gave such a bad example by being such an individualist and flashing his membership card while he was scabbing. At this point, if we really were to revoke membership from small businessmen and scabs there would be absolute chaos.[61]

The arguments flowed on night after night. One night Fo would take the chair following a performance of *Accidental Death of an Anarchist*, *Big Pantomime* or *The Loom*, while debates raged on about the nature of the state, the crimes of Stalinism, the pro-capitalist policies of the PCI, and so on. However it is important to remember that what was driving these debates was not purely Fo's skill as a writer and performer. Workers were pushing back management's 'frontier of control' in many workplaces, and as a consequence felt far more confident about their own strength, including the strength to take part in debates at the theatre. The following worker from the FIAT *Mirafiori* factory raises several issues which are extremely representative of the debates that took place:

> How did I, someone who had always been in the PCI, leave the party? Because I realised that going to the PCI branch you played cards or bowls, they didn't politicise people. There was no education, no nothing ... Today at FIAT we hold meetings in the factory, on the shop floor. We talk about politics, we really do tell the foremen to fuck off, we've already reduced the line speed to a decent level, all of this is freedom.[62]

The two plays described in this section, *The Worker Knows...* and *Tie Me Up...* were performed during a single tour which stopped at the same venues, with just a few days' interval between them. Given their confrontational political content, by the end of the tour in summer 1970 the political relationship between *New Scene* and the PCI had essentially collapsed, although organisationally ARCI would continue to book *The Commune*'s shows.

The Commune

New Scene split into two political factions in the autumn, with the majority deciding to maintain the name and a close relationship with ARCI, while a minority – principally Fo, Rame and Nanni Ricordi – founded *The Commune*, named after the working-class Paris Commune of exactly a century earlier.

They created a permanent base for themselves in Milan, in the *capannone*, an old factory in via Colletta, and set about converting it into a rudimentary theatre. They bought 800 wooden seats at the knockdown price of £3 each and, as Rame says: 'We got blisters on our hands through working with saws and hammers for a month.'[63] A student who often attended these performances recalls: 'It was full of draughts, and the acoustics were terrible.'[64] Despite the rudimentary nature of the building, Nanni Ricordi remembers: 'It was our own home. There was more freedom there; our freedoms had been restricted.'[65] *The Commune*'s aim was to create a permanent theatrical laboratory, politically based among the revolutionary left.

It quickly became apparent that all these changes had caused an alteration in the political composition of Fo's audience. The fact that their fixed base at the *capannone* was very close to the centre of a major city like Milan meant that their audiences were quite mixed. In mid-1971 an internal *Commune* document noted after the first season's activities that performances

> often tended to become 'the community's cultural event of the year' for certain social strata. The result has been the attendance of a generically democratic audience, prompted more by curiosity than by the political content – an audience which needs to be added on to the 'bourgeoisie in crisis', the activists, the students and workers – who are the real foundations of *The Commune*.[66]

Not that the entire experience of the *capannone* was a comfortable one for middle-class people. A famous writer once described what happened when he went to write a magazine article and arrived at the entrance without a ticket:

> We were stopped by a pale, stocky, coarse man with a big nose and blue eyes, wrapped up in a regulation khaki revolutionary jacket with its hood pulled up into a conical shape which compensated for his small stature ... In vain I tell him that I'm a friend of Fo's and that I have to write an article ... 'This isn't a bourgeois theatre, this is a communist theatre!' I repeated that I was a friend, and that I was coming here to work and not to enjoy myself. Another swearword: 'And what about me? What do you think I'm doing here? I've been working all day, and I've been working for 30 years!'[67]

During the 1968–70 period Fo and Rame had undoubtedly been performing by and large to the working class, whereas over the next few years the political composition of their audience was to be predominantly one of committed revolutionaries. As regards the social composition, in January 1974 Fo stated: 'Our audience is made up of students (50 per cent), workers (20 per cent), with the rest being made up of the petty bourgeoisie and some elements of the bourgeoisie proper.'[68]

The social composition of his audience was an important political issue on the left, as the PCI often argued that Fo's extremism had led to his isolation from the working class. On a statistical level, working-class audiences were far larger in numbers in the 1968–70 period, yet two further comments need to be made: firstly, there were important regional variations, in that most big cities had audiences which were predominantly made up of students and the lower middle class, while in the small towns where *The Commune* played in their long tours audiences were largely working class. Secondly, Fo and *The Commune* had a far larger following among all social classes than any other theatre company.

All of this should not obscure the fact that *The Commune* achieved the remarkable feat of quickly becoming a sizeable organisation with a mass audience. In the first few days of the *capannone* 6,000 people took out membership of *The Commune*, and within a month 18,000 people had become members.[69] By the following spring membership had reached 20,000,[70] rising to 30,000 after a year of activity – five times the number of season ticket-holders at Milan's most prestigious theatre, *Il Piccolo*.[71] By February 1973 Fo claimed: 'We can now rely on an annual audience of 700,000; there are 27,000 *Commune* members in Milan; every evening we sell 200 copies of our plays at cost price, which means 50–60,000 per year.'[72]

In addition, *The Commune* continuously called for the creation of an alternative theatrical circuit on a national level, and at its highest point the organisation could count on 85 cultural centres or branches, with 700,000 members.[73] *Commune* branches largely did their own thing according to the political and cultural persuasions of their active members, although politically all branches could be classified on the revolutionary side of the argument that Fo and others had engaged in since 1968. For example, in Bolzano, a town near the Austrian border, 150 people founded a local branch in January 1972, with a programme of debates, exhibitions and plays which was not aimed at integrating the working class into the current system 'but on the affirmation and development of their autonomy against the capitalist system'.[74] In November the Roman branch organised a series of films on the 1943–45 anti-fascist movement, followed by debates hosted by Resistance heroes.[75] Nine months after its founding in October 1973, the branch in the northern town of Brescia had 15 activists, 1,000 members, and had organised two shows by Fo, a concert by the singer Enzo Jannacci, political debates, photographic exhibitions, film shows, as well as printing 1,000 copies of a book which recounted a recent revolt in the town's jail.[76]

The essential purpose of *Commune* branches was that of organising cultural activities which contained explicit arguments for revolution and, for any branch, the biggest activity was organising a show starring or written by Fo. The overall political purpose of the organisation was spelt out in the group's first preparatory document: 'For us theatre only has a use if it is connected on the one hand to the masses and their just demands, and on the other to the organised vanguard; in order to become one of the thousand vehicles, one of the thousand weapons, in the process of socialist revolution.'[77]

A key difficulty which would dog Fo over the coming years was that *The Commune* was operating in a political environment in which there were several small competing revolutionary organisations of a similar size. In this context, the group made a key decision, as Fo explains: 'We understood very well from the start that our role would have become one of disunity if we had become the theatre group of Lotta Continua or Il Manifesto.'[78] Although the key figures of Fo and Rame never joined any of these organisations, many Commune members did, and these competing political agendas would periodically rock the group, frequently leading to expulsions and splits. However, it is beyond doubt that the dominant strand of Marxism within The Commune was Maoist: for example, for two years they printed and distributed a collection of writings by the Chinese Communist Party from the early 1960s, which attacked the PCI and its leader Palmiro Togliatti.[79]

Collectively the revolutionary left was sizeable: at its height it could count on tens of thousands of activists, three daily papers, six MPs and several local radio stations. This collective strength was weakened by the fact that it was divided into several competing ideological strands. Consequently, it was far from being dominant on the left as a whole, although there were enough revolutionaries around essentially to dominate the atmosphere at Fo's shows, as the following hostile description of a show at the capannone illustrates:

> It's enough to look at the majority of the audience (which is largely made up of young people, who are visibly people who belong to Lotta Continua, Potere Operaio, etc.) and follow their reactions, or rather the applause that breaks out upon extremist statements, to public appeals, to the most obvious statements made in a 'revolutionary' sense.[80]

These small revolutionary parties and groups provided the organisational backdrop to Fo's activities from 1969 to 1976, and for that reason the major forces will be presented in turn, in descending order of size and influence.[81]

Lotta Continua (Continuous Struggle) was founded as an organised movement and weekly newspaper in November 1969. Of all the revolutionary groups, it was the one most influenced by a spontaneous form of organisation. Indeed it was only in December 1973 that a conference sanctioned the creation of a party, which officially came into existence at the first party congress in January 1975, with a constitution modelled on the Chinese CP. In its early years it was essentially a loose federation of revolutionary activists, opposed to participation in elections, although it dropped its abstentionist electoralism in the spring of 1974 when it called for a vote for the PCI in regional elections. Along with many other groups, it had a dangerously ambiguous attitude towards armed actions, together with another common feature of a cliquish leadership group largely unaccountable to the membership. However, for several years it enjoyed considerable support among young radicalised workers in the north, who had often migrated from the southern countryside a few years earlier. The death knell of *Lotta Continua* sounded in late 1975, when it was decreed that its male stewards would forcibly join a women-only demonstration. This debacle, followed by the growth of the idea of an 'autonomous movement' which could fight capitalism, led to the dissolving of the party into 'the movement' at its second congress in 1976, even though the newspaper of the same name continued until the early 1980s.

Avanguardia Operaia (Workers' Vanguard) was a more orthodox Leninist party, better organised and with a more in-depth understanding of Marxism than *Lotta Continua*, and it was more critical of Russia and less sympathetic towards Mao's China. While *Lotta Continua* had greater influence among students and the unemployed, in its early years *Avanguardia Operaia* had a significant following in many northern factories. As the likelihood of imminent revolution receded, *Avanguardia Operaia* also became an increasingly top-heavy party; for example, its congress in autumn 1974 opened with a three-hour speech by leader Aurelio Campi. As a body of ideas, it provided probably the most dominant current within the organisation which was to emerge from the collapse of these groupings in the mid-1970s, *Proletarian Democracy*.

Il Manifesto was originally the name of a group of intellectuals expelled from the PCI in 1969, who quickly founded a monthly journal which became a daily newspaper in April 1971 and is still published today. Attempts were made to build a political party named *PDUP* for most of the 1970s, yet ultimately this attempt foundered because most of the membership were keen to maintain a close relationship with the PCI rather than build a revolutionary party.

Other smaller groups included *Potere Operaio* (Workers' Power), another Leninist-inclined but rather sectarian organisation. A significant number of theoreticians later became leaders of the 'autonomist' movement of the 1970s, and a few even joined the Red Brigades. Another sizeable organisation was the virulently Maoist Communist Party of Italy (Marxist-Leninist), which was viewed as being rather crude and sectarian by the other groups. In the early years the semi-Stalinist *Movimento Studentesco* (Student Movement) had a significant following in Milan and a charismatic leader named Mario Capanna.

Fo's creative work was now taking place in a situation in which these conflicting organisations would do battle not only within *The Commune* in Milan, but in every branch in the country. As long as the movement was growing overall this tension did not matter too much – Fo appears to have been willing for his writing to be subject to the critical approval of *The Commune*. However, when a distinct political downturn was experienced by the left a few years later, Fo was then to move to maintain a distance between his creative production and any collective political monitoring of its content.

In this most frenetic of periods *United We Stand! All Together Now! Hang On, Isn't That the Boss?* was the next play which emerged from Fo's almost boundless imagination. The subtitle of the play specified the period: *Workers' Struggles 1911–1922*. It concerns a period when the Italian working class was close to launching a revolution and it argues that the struggle was sold out by Socialist Party and trade union leaders – the play then moves on to the fascists' seizure of power in 1922. It deals extensively with the factory occupations of September 1920, but it develops a contemporary comparison between the Socialist Party's reformism of 50 years earlier and the PCI's contemporary reformism.

The play was born out of a seminar that Fo and others gave in August 1970, in which they made speeches and brought along archive material. This initial research soon went further: 'We then started to look for other documents, transcripts of trials held against workers and trade union leaders, the indictments, statements for the defence, the diaries of female activists of the working-class parties. Then we went on to conducting interviews in Turin, Emilia-Romagna, with people who had taken part in the birth of the Communist party.'[82]

In yet another example of the political symmetry which characterised much of Fo's work in these years, 'It premièred at Varese while there were two factories in occupation. The workers came from those factories with their banners which attacked the bosses and their bullying actions.'[83]

Although it is perhaps the most wordy of his plays, it does have some plot. A lumpen proletariat tailoress from Turin, *Antonia Berazzi*, falls in love with a revolutionary activist of the Socialist Party. She becomes politicised, and when he is murdered by fascists she takes revenge for his death by killing a fascist in the prefecture, and then dies herself on the way to *confino*, or internal exile. Most of the play is told by *Antonia* in flashbacks.

In 1911 *Antonia* was arrested for unwittingly having taken part in a subversive meeting. We then move forward four years to Italy's preparation to enter the First World War, a decision which revolutionaries in the Socialist Party opposed. By now she shows clear identification with the views of revolutionaries: 'Proletarians of all lands, unite against all war! Patriotic wars do not exist in the world of Capital, only imperialist wars, that is those waged against us. Proletarians, oppose your governments through any means: wars are really legalised massacres which the bourgeoisie and Capital use to increase their profits.'[84]

At the end of the play she kills the fascist who had murdered her husband. But she immediately realises:

I've shot the dog, rather than the masters ... all of you have got to be destroyed ... all thousand, two thousand ten thousand or however many you are ... bosses, bandits, exploiters! All the ten thousand who live off the backs of millions of poor wretches by keeping them on a lead ... and there's so much talk about thieves ... they make me laugh! At any moment of any day you lot commit a robbery without even saying 'hands up' ... every minute and every hour you're armed ... you murder every hour![85]

Antonia is clearly referring to the contemporary issue of trying to get the neo-fascist MSI party declared illegal, but she is moving much further and arguing that capitalism, which periodically supports fascism, should also be eradicated.

A journalist in Genoa described the show in very disparaging but, at times, accurate tones:

> The audience 'participated' in the play with exactly the same enthusiasm as children – an enthusiasm which reached its highest point when Franca Rame ... killed with a pistol volley a fascist responsible for the murder of her husband, a communist activist.
>
> The young people with red armbands, members of extra-parliamentary pro-Chinese groups suddenly leapt to their feet, and with their clenched fists raised towards the ceiling, chanted for a good five minutes: 'One, Two, Three a Thousand Venturinis! Viva Marx, Lenin and Mao Zedung!'[86]

Another journalist from the same paper made similar comments, but in some sense he describes an audience which appears to be participating in a political rally rather than a theatrical show:

> [the audience] greeted dozens of lines with applause and shouts of approval, above all during the parts when the Communist Party was being praised and during the violent accusatory speech of the finale. Here Franca Rame seemed to be strongly conscious of and enthusiastic in her role – in which she states her specific desire to kill without mercy all fascists and bosses, and without sparing those who might still dare to preach patience and moderation.[87]

This last point is a fairly unsubtle reference to how some revolutionaries viewed the contemporary policy of the PCI. Surprisingly enough, in Trieste the play was put on at the federation of the PCI. The musician of the show, Paolo Ciarchi, recalls that the show went well:

> But during the debate insults started to flow between us and some PCI comrades, and we practically ended up hitting each other with chairs. I had jumped on to a table and had started to improvise a provocatory gag by shouting with a fire extinguisher in my hand: viva Marx, viva Lenin, viva Mao Zedung. At this point some furious dockers tried to throw me down the stairs.[88]

The improvised gag with the use of a fire extinguisher was particularly provocative because it was a metaphor often used on the left to describe somebody who wants to stop struggles either breaking out or continuing, in short someone who wants to extinguish the flames of revolt. In what was now a typical response, *l'Unità* headlined its review: 'Farce and sermon, without dialectics.'[89]

Yet when *Accidental Death of an Anarchist* was performed the following night (the two shows alternated on tour) there was no tension. During the debates everyone agreed that there should be a common response to the 'strategy of tension' – acts of terrorism carried out by neo-fascist groups with the help of the secret services, aimed at criminalising the left and ultimately creating an authoritarian government (for further details see Chapter 3). A similar response occurred in Genoa, where 'hundreds and hundreds of spectators – students, workers, dockers – packed the hall', and Fo in particular 'earned ovations and shouts of approval, underlined by forests of clenched fists, with his monologues halfway between a speech for the prosecution and a speech at a public rally'.[90]

Apart from the occasional example of quick tempers, this apparently contradictory behaviour towards the two plays is not surprising: what united these two different responses was a common sense of purpose, the clear understanding among this predominantly working-class audience that they had important issues to thrash out. Should the fascists be resisted violently or not? Should all struggles within workplaces remain within the boundaries of the law? And ultimately, was the correct political strategy to aim for fundamental change from within the parliamentary system or to argue for an eventual revolutionary overthrow of the existing structures? On some issues, such as the need to oppose fascists as outlined in *Accidental Death...*, people were united. But there was rarely unity on the right strategy needed to create socialism. What is fascinating about Fo's shows at that time is that they *also* constituted one of the most appropriate forums for workers to debate these issues.

During the debate held in Genoa an industrial worker who had also taken part in the wartime Resistance movement drew parallels between the play he had just seen and his own personal history:

> After 25 years of political activity with the PCI I've had to draw some conclusions. In 1944, when I was just 16, I was one of the Ligurian partisans, and you can check this out if you go through the Appenines. The partisans gave me some important responsibilities as they thought I was already a communist, since my father had been killed by fascists. It is difficult to leave a party like the Communist Party, after 25 years of struggle, sacrifices, learning within the PCI. They didn't push me away. It is very difficult, it's hard, you end up crying, you change your mind: I've been dragging this problem around with me for five years. But what has communism taught me? What has the PCI taught me?

What has Gramsci taught me? Leave a party if you think it is no longer suitable for the working class! ... For example you heard it said that those people are mad, when they talk about power coming out of the barrel of a gun. But power does come out of the barrel of a gun, and it is defended by the barrel of a gun, in every country in the world ... Italy was born out of the barrel of a gun! Even out of the barrel of my gun, of my rifle! And a proletarian Italy, a red communist Italy, will again be defended out of the barrel of a gun. And this is independently of the fact that this group is called *Potere Operaio* or *Lotta Continua*, we're comrades, you're comrades who have taught us, after 25 years, to leave.[91]

Fo often faced two kinds of criticisms. The first one was that he was simplistic – yet given the fact he wasn't writing books of history his unadorned structures were perfectly understandable. The second one regarded 'sectarianism', the notion that his attacks on parliamentary socialism led him to inhabit a political ghetto, akin to belonging to some obscure religious sect. The reality of the situation, however, was that Fo's plays were part of a widespread and passionate political battle which was raging among workers as to whether reform, often called revisionism – as opposed to revolution – was the correct road to follow. Fo once gave an interesting response to these attacks when discussing the political purpose of *United We Stand!...* in 1971: 'Underlying this play is a denunciation of reformism and revisionism as the primary cause of the movement's defeats, and the collapse of every struggle. Lenin wrote more pages against revisionism than against the Tsars.'[92]

The Gathering Storm

By 1972 the authorities seemed to have moved beyond a policy of harassment of Fo's work to one of deliberate repression. Some of Fo's shows were subjected to incredible intimidation; for example, in April 500 police assembled outside the main theatre in Reggio Emilia and the show was called off in protest.[93] In July *The Commune* were suddenly evicted from the *capannone* due to police headquarters' pressure on the owners – and they no longer had their own base for two years until they occupied the *Palazzina Liberty*. In the autumn Judge Mario Sossi started proceedings against them for 'subversive activities'.[94] The precise accusation, eventually discovered to be a total invention, was that they were encouraging jail uprisings.[95] Fo and Rame were also evicted from their rented flat in Milan, as the Jewish owner didn't like their pro-Palestinian play, *Fedayn*.[96]

Perhaps the activity which irritated the authorities the most was the creation within *The Commune* of *Soccorso Rosso* (*Red Help*), specifically focused on helping left-wing political prisoners. This was mainly the work of Rame, who quickly managed to organise 3,000 people to send detainees little parcels, books, or letters every month. As Fo explained, the arrival of these letters and parcels had a huge impact among the prison population: 'An ordinary prisoner who watches the postal distribution every day and sees a political prisoner receiving letters and parcels asks him: "Who's sending you this stuff?" "Comrades." "Who are they? Your friends, your relatives?" "No, people I don't even know."'[97] As this activity involved frequent contact with dozens of left-wing prisoners, it gave investigating magistrates a perfect pretext to accuse Rame and Fo of involvement in the many jail riots which occurred at that time.

An equally disturbing facet of their political involvement, for the authorities, was the connection with left-wing conscript soldiers. *Lotta Continua* in particular had encouraged a network of conscript activists who would often leaflet barracks and occasionally organise strikes. Uniformed soldiers, albeit wearing dark glasses, would also sometimes march in major left-wing demonstrations.[98] When Fo performed in towns where big barracks were situated, hundreds of soldiers would attend his performance as any Fo show was also a left-wing meeting place.[99]

Touring was now a big problem, as so many theatres were being leaned on not to hire out their premises: most performances took place in remote suburbs of towns and cities. Judge Viola took action against Fo for the poster used to advertise performances of *Knock! Knock! Who's There? The Police!*[100] The run was extended in Milan only because they felt forced to occupy the theatre, as the owner suddenly announced he was going to cancel the original booking.[101]

Real attempts at bombing their performances, and much more frequently bomb threats, presumably carried out by neo-fascists, were a dual method of both demoralising Fo and Rame, while also attempting to frighten their audience away. For example, three sticks of TNT were found near the *Palazzina Liberty* in June 1974,[102] while a small bomb exploded and caused minor damage to the building in December.[103] On another occasion the police opened fire on an escaped calf in the park outside the *Palazzina*, wounding a passer-by. They felt threatened even in their personal life; Rame has stated on more than one occasion that for many years she opened the front door of her flat with her hands over her face, as she expected to be greeted either by an assailant or a bomb blast. In February 1972 a petrol bomb was thrown into the first floor of their villa at Cernobbio, but luckily it didn't explode and neither Fo nor Rame was at home at the time.[104] A member of *The Commune* recalls how the group were forced to take Fo's personal security very seriously during the early 1970s:

At the *capannone* we had lots of comrades doing the stewarding. They were volunteers, so every evening a group of 10–20 people took it upon themselves to act as stewards. So everyone who was coming in was checked for weapons, we looked in bags too.

We took precautions because it was clear that he was in their sights ... After the shows he always went home with one of us, with one car in front and one behind. We were very careful.[105]

As the mass movement started to decline the establishment became bolder and bolder. By October 1974 senior police officers were deliberately releasing false information concerning arrest warrants about to be issued against Fo and Rame, just to test their nerves and see whether they would try to escape.

One of the early symptoms of the mass movement's decline, which would become much more stark and tragic in later years, was the emergence of terrorist groups such as the Red Brigades, who kidnapped Judge Mario Sossi in April 1974. Before releasing him unharmed, his kidnappers insisted he dropped libel charges against Fo, a fact which the judge played up for all it was worth when he later persevered in taking Fo to court.

Even more serious were journalists' insinuations that Rame in particular was in close contact with active terrorists; quite frequently the description of terrorist actions included the phrase 'a blonde-haired woman was seen in the vicinity'. Or as in this case – the arrest of suspects for the firebombing of a factory – the accusation was made explicitly: 'The two people arrested were 47 year old construction engineer Francesco Rolla, of 20 via Spiga, who is in close contact with Dario Fo and Franca Rame ...'[106]

On 9 March 1973 the worst act of all occurred: while walking towards her hairdresser's in a street in Milan Rame was suddenly bundled into the back of a van by five men. They then proceeded to rape her, and when they had finished they stubbed their cigarette butts out on her body, as well as cutting her breasts with a razor. Her assailants knew perfectly well who she was: from their comments and insults it was also clear they were neo-fascists.

In his weekly magazine column the writer Umberto Eco looked back at the last few years of official harassment and repression:

Perhaps Dario Fo, Franca Rame and their friends are politicians who say more than just the funny things comedians say ... Fo and Rame had been annoying people for a variety of reasons. Apart from their frequent presence inside factories in dispute, there is the network of solidarity which Franca Rame had launched to financially help political prisoners ... There are many legal and illegal ways to silence indiscreet voices. Especially when they run the risk of being isolated, as is happening to Fo's group. Never more than in this moment do democratic audiences have the right to hear Fo's voice.[107]

The Actors' Union quickly proclaimed a month of anti-fascist activities; a mass meeting not only condemned the attack on Rame but also made it clear that this attack was part of a much wider campaign of far-right forces. A huge number of actors and directors supported this move, among them: Gino Bramieri, Vittorio De Sica, Federico Fellini, Paola and Vittorio Gassman, Giancarlo Giannini, Nino Manfredi, Mariangela Melato, Mario Monicelli, Franco Nero, Ettore Scola, Ugo Tognazzi, Paolo Villaggio, Monica Vitti and Gian Maria Volontè.[108]

Incredibly, Rame was back on stage after just two months in a one-woman show entitled: *Stop the Fascists!*[109] A few years later she would perform a thinly disguised monologue entitled *The Rape*, clearly based on her experience.

Twenty-five years later, in 1998, a definitive verdict on the rape was given by Judge Guido Salvini, mainly based on the confessions of one of the rapists. 'The action was suggested by some *Carabinieri* officers of the *Pastrengo* division, in the context of the co-belligerency which essentially existed at the time between some sectors of this division and right-wing extremists, and their struggle against the danger of communism.'[110] Because of the short distance between their flat and the hairdresser's, Rame and Fo had always thought that the attack was highly organised, and their suspicions were aroused even further in 1974 when it was discovered that their phone was bugged.[111] Following this chilling verdict, a *Carabiniere* who had been a captain in the *Pastrengo* division in 1973 recalled: 'The news of Rame's rape was greeted with euphoria within the barracks,' and the divisional commander General Palumbo 'was really happy. "It was time," he said.'[112] A new word has since been introduced into the Italian and English vocabulary concerning violence against women: state rape.

Chile: The End of the Parliamentary Road to Socialism

People's War in Chile was first performed in late October 1973, just six weeks after the Chilean coup. In the introduction to the play it is stated that the Chilean coup was an example 'of the fact that the ruling class do not relinquish power peacefully, that as soon as Capital feels threatened it turns to massacres'.[113]

The left-wing government of Salvador Allende, including both the Chilean Socialist and Communist Parties, had been elected in 1970, and from its inception had been a guiding light for parliamentary socialists throughout the world. Its very existence and reforming policies were used by parliamentary socialists against revolutionaries to argue that real and significant reforms could be made through Parliament. Two of Allende's most popular reforming policies were a degree of land redistribution to peasants and the nationalisation of some major foreign companies. Yet it should be borne in mind that reforms were quite limited; although 90 firms were nationalised and 1,400 landed estates subject to new legislation the overall scale of reform was not particularly sizeable: many of these firms were close to bankruptcy, and land reform affected just 7 per cent of the rural population.[114] In any event, Allende's government enjoyed widespread support outside Chile as well, as voiced 18 months before the coup by a PCI activist who argued against a preceding point made by Fo in the 'third act':

> Why is there this denial of the validity of a strategy of reforms for the building of socialism? We can say that a strategy of reforms can have a very large revolutionary content. We can say that Allende has taken power in Chile through democratic means ... it is certain that Allende is the beginning of an answer for a socialist strategy ... Why do we have to refuse this hypothesis of the building of a solution?[115]

These views were echoed around the world; for example, in Britain the veteran left-wing Labour MP, Eric Heffer, claimed that the new Chilean government 'can demonstrate a new way which will go beyond all the old wrangles about reform versus revolution'.

In any event, according to the extradition warrant presented in London in late 1998, Spanish authorities have estimated that during Pinochet's 1973–90 dictatorship 200,000 people were tortured, 3,000 assassinated, 1,000 disappeared and up to 6,000 people were buried in unmarked graves.[116] All of this was supported by the US and its secretary of state, Henry Kissinger, who once told CIA staff to save Chile 'from the irresponsibility of its own people'. Shortly before the coup he had written to the CIA: 'It is firm and continuing policy that Allende should be overthrown by a coup.'[117] And in 1976 Kissinger reiterated to Pinochet: 'We are sympathetic with what you are trying to do here. I think that the previous government was headed towards communism. We wish your government well.'[118] He had not changed his view in December 1998, stating: 'What's 6,000 people dead in two years? Maybe ten a day?'[119]

The drowning in blood of Allende's government now placed the whole notion of a parliamentary road to socialism into severe doubt as Fo explained, speaking as 'Dario' in the script:

> 'Look at Chile! Look at Chile!' How many times did we hear this phrase repeated last year, almost obsessively, when we were debating with the leaders of the Communist and Socialist Parties? 'Look at Chile; Chile is proof of how the proletariat can take power through free elections, through democratic institutions, through reforms, agreements, alliances with petty and big bourgeoisie, a few compromises ... There's no need for working-class violence any more.'

Then suddenly there was a massacre: the incredible violence of Capital, the army, the bourgeoisie. And it's not as if these leaders of the PCI and PSI have revised their positions as a result of the coup. You could have expected they might say: 'By God! So it's right what Lenin was always saying about the bourgeoisie being hypocritical and criminal ... that when Capital is losing power it kills, it commits massacres! ... It's useless: the proletariat's only saviour is revolution!' No! They haven't said this.[120]

For parliamentary socialists the coup in Chile starkly raised the following issue: what political strategy should be followed if big business and the armed forces would not allow socialism to be created through parliamentary reforms? The essence of the debate was that there were two different roads which could be taken: that of adopting a strategy of a revolutionary working class ultimately seizing power and destroying the existing system – as argued by Fo at the time – or that of adopting a more cautious strategy of government coalitions with parties of the centre-right. The PCI took this latter road, calling for a 'historic compromise' with the Christian Democrats. As PCI leader Berlinguer put it, 'Fifty one per cent wasn't enough' to form a government: a much broader government coalition was needed to avoid the possibility of bloody repression. As he wrote soon after the coup: 'Anti-democratic reaction tends to become more violent and ferocious when popular forces begin to conquer the fundamental levers of power in society and the state.'[121] The proposal implicit here is the end of any notion of the PCI making any fundamental change, therefore from this point on the PCI began to drop policies which talked about 'communism'; and by the late 1980s it became increasingly rare to hear any systematic discussion about a PCI government even intending to build 'socialism'.

The first major performance of *People's War in Chile* was held at the Turin sports stadium, where the play itself was part of an eight-hour event with songs, readings and other initiatives. One very significant item was the reading of a letter from 'Proletarians in uniform', an organisation of far-left conscript soldiers closely linked to *Lotta Continua* – a very relevant development given the central role of the Chilean army in the coup. The political weaknesses of Allende's government were also put under the microscope. At one point a film was shown which featured Allende's daughter stating the previous spring that 'Our army will not intervene in the political life of the country'. Fo had explained during rehearsals that on the basis of their research *The Commune* had wanted to deal with the nature of the Chilean army 'which somebody has tried to pass off as "democratic", with a tradition of "neutrality" and defence of democratic institutions. The historical reality demonstrates that this is a load of rubbish'.[122]

As ever, 'Dario Fo and Franca Rame were [also] physically involved in organising the show. The microphones need sorting out, as does stewarding, as well as the script. The order of the speeches needs to be decided, and boards placed to support the stage.' The show also had a practical purpose: the profits were donated 'to the Chilean people's armed struggle'.[123]

The show was written in a great hurry and consisted of a series of separate pieces such as Chilean songs, the reading of a transcript of the last few minutes of a left-wing radio station broadcasting in Santiago, as well as historical and political sections on both Chile and Italy. Fo had also decided to create during the performance the impression that a coup was taking place in Italy. As one of the singers recalled, the disjointed nature of the performance 'served to create the structure for the radio interference, the girl who came in and said that the phones had gone dead and the policeman who appeared'.[124] The 'fake coup' constructed by the cast and described in Appendix A worked successfully in many cities. But it was also criticised for being too provocative, whereas Fo argued that it was staged 'to overturn the rules of the theatre, which are always considered similar to those of the Parthenon'.[125] One of the reasons the play was criticised was because it embarrassed the leaders of left-wing parties. In some cities the actor playing the police chief announced that the 'only people who can leave are those who can show membership cards which show that they belong to government, or quasi-government, political parties'. At least one PSI official in Bologna asked to leave the hall (leaving everyone else to their fate, which was presumed to be arrest and interrogation by people launching a military coup) by showing his party card, and as he did so he turned to Fo and Rame and made the astonishing claim: 'You have have ruined Italy.'[126]

By mounting a fake coup Fo was not only making the point that the possibility of a coup was something which could not be dismissed in Italy at the time, but he also wanted to give some kind of explanation as to why this could come about. The point he made at the climax of his provocation was that under capitalism the bourgeoisie is in control of a crazy and anarchic system which periodically enters into massive social and economic crises, which in turn threaten the bourgeoisie's ability to maintain its control and subsequent privileges – and in order to maintain its control it will be prepared to support a bloody military takeover.

And if a coup was to be viewed as a possibility, Fo wanted people to learn some lessons from what had happened in Chile: 'It is not correct to prepare ourselves for a coup as Chilean leaders have said, but for revolution – if you want to avoid any possibility of a crazy coup d'état.'[127] For Fo the Chilean tragedy illustrated the dangers of parliamentary socialism as opposed to revolution: 'Workers understood well before the politicians where a reformist "dialogue" and limitless compromises will inevitably lead you. It means you are continuously disarmed, above all ideologically, when you face up to the bosses ... the only really serious way to support the struggle of the Chilean people is to act on the lessons learnt.'[128]

The play was another huge success, and Fo was performing to a mass working-class audience again. But the subject matter also touched a raw nerve among the authorities: before the show was even performed journalists had reported various examples of senior Italian military officers toasting to the success of the Chilean coup. This is not very surprising perhaps, as most of these officers had been educated and had begun their careers under fascism – indeed many of them were probably sympathetic to the idea of a military coup in Italy.

Consequently, Fo was bound to face some form of resistance from the authorities in view of both the content and the popularity of his shows, and the most notorious example occurred when he toured Sardinia. The following events will be discussed in some detail, as they are an eloquent testimony to Fo's huge popularity. More important, however, is the fact that the massive spontaneous support which erupted in Fo's defence meant that in future the authorities largely desisted from trying to interrupt or challenge his performances.

On 3 November the police chief in the small town of Nuoro banned a performance of *People's War in Chile*; indeed the local newspaper that reported on the controversy was unable even to inform readers as to where his shows were due to be held. This was far from being the first time that the authorities had harassed Fo, but his patience was wearing thin: 'If senior levels within the police continue to insist on banning the show it will take place anyway, even in the streets.'[129]

In the larger town of Sassari the police chief had insisted that firefighters had to check up on safety measures before a performance could be given, that a cinema could not be used as a theatre and that the selling of membership cards for a private theatre performance could not be allowed as they were being sold to third parties.[130] Fo unusually made the conciliatory gesture of allowing known policemen to be in the audience during the show on the first night. On the second evening Fo was due to perform *Mistero Buffo*, and *The Commune* decided to resist the police's entrance by resorting to an argument they had already used many times: that *The Commune* was in effect performing a private show to members of their private association. Fo and 15 members of *The Commune* apparently then lined up to stop the police entering, with Fo allegedly telling the head of the Flying Squad: 'You're not coming in. Charge at us if you like, do what you want.' The head of the local Flying Squad replied, 'If it's the last thing I do as a policeman, I'm going to arrest that man.' Fo was then arrested for 'resistance to and violent behaviour towards a public official'. Most of the crowd of 1,000 people who were arriving and intended to watch the show quickly decided to march to the town centre in protest.[131] A meeting was held at the students' union, and 2,000 people marched through the town, pushing the police back three times until they reached the main square.[132] By the time Fo was taken from the police headquarters to the local jail at 8.30 p.m. there were already 100 students chanting outside.[133]

According to Fo, when he was arrested and taken into custody, 'It seemed from the level of excitement at police headquarters that they had captured Liggio.' (Luciano Liggio was reputed to be the head of the Mafia at that time.) He also claims that one of the policemen who escorted him to the jail told him: 'I'm sorry. I agree with many of the things you stand for.' Apparently a prison warder also asked him to sign a photo of his son; these claims are perfectly feasible, given Fo's general popularity and the level of support which was being demonstrated outside the jail.

What seems beyond doubt, as it is confirmed in various sources, is that many inmates responded enthusiastically to Fo's presence within the prison walls. Along with those outside, inmates also started singing *Bandiera Rossa* through the bars of their windows and got a note to Fo asking him to 'show us the way to defend ourselves'.[134] Meanwhile, a delegation of local PCI MPs and trade unionists went to the local Prefect's office to demand his release.

A group of young people stayed outside the jail all night, and early the next morning a strike was organised by students which quickly saw thousands involved – including a contingent of 4,000 who returned to the jail to sing *Bandiera Rossa* and to chant 'We're not going to leave until Dario is released'.[135] Some demonstrators even improvised scenes from *Mistero Buffo*, the show which had been stopped by the police.[136] A demonstration was also called for later in the day by local trade unions, the PCI and far-left organisations.

The local electricians' union passed a motion condemning 'the attack on the freedom of popular culture to express itself, and therefore demands his immediate release'.[137] The Film Directors' Association defined his arrest as the latest repressive act against 'a culturally and politically committed man of the theatre'. The Theatre Writers' Union called on 'public opinion to protest against the arrest of Dario Fo', while the Society of Italian Actors announced it was holding an emergency meeting to discuss the issue.[138] Telegrams of protest began to arrive from the mainland, questions were asked in Parliament in Rome. The previous evening Rame had phoned her theatrical agents throughout the world, and foreign journalists and TV crews were on their way to Sardinia.

Meanwhile, Rame and other members of the cast improvised a rudimentary show in front of the jail, made up of songs and sketches attacking the police and fascists, with Rame incredibly managing to perform from the top of a tiny FIAT 500 car. Sassari was now being criss-crossed by marches, as striking bakers had decided to join in the protests for Fo's release.

While inside the jail Fo recounted that when he was let out for exercise 'as soon as the inmates heard that I was in the courtyard they started to sing *Bandiera Rossa* and raised their clenched fists through the bars of their cells'.[139] Shortly before his release Fo received a telegram from Pietro Valpreda, an anarchist who had been the victim of a much more serious frame-up and long-term imprisonment concerning the 1969 bombing in Milan: 'We are all close to you. Soon you and your comrades will be among us again.'[140]

When he was released at 2 p.m. Fo was greeted by Rame and crowds chanting 'Long live revolutionary artists' and 'Comrade Fo, you've been freed by the strength of the working class'. Interviewed outside the prison gates, he was unrepentant: 'The police had no right to stick their nose into our affairs.'[141] With people greeting him from their balconies, he then marched with his supporters through the town to the Trades Council building, from where he phoned his son Jacopo. In the afternoon a demonstration of over 1,000 was held in one of the main squares of Sassari to celebrate his release. In his speech Fo called the action of the police 'arbitrary, provocatory and illegal' – indeed the charges against him were quickly dropped. His speech was followed by that of Nino Manca of the Sassari CGIL union federation. Fo then performed *Mistero Buffo* in the square, the very show the police had stopped him performing the previous evening.[142]

In Cagliari, Sardinia's main town, the local branch of *The Commune* defined what had happened as 'the latest act in a series of attempts to stop the performance of the theatrical shows which the collective intended to bring to Sardinia'. After leaving Sassari in the afternoon, Fo had time to reach Cagliari and perform to a crowd of 2,500, several hundreds having been turned away from the theatre.[143]

In a press statement released a couple of days later Fo drew strong parallels between Chile and Italy: 'The struggle which followed my arrest has clearly shown that no substantial difference exists between the Chilean Christian Democrats – who are discussed in *People's War in Chile* – and the Italian Christian Democrats, and that Christian Democrat governments are enemies of the most elementary freedoms.' But the most important lesson to be learnt was that 'it is possible to unite, isolate and defeat them. The essential element is the unity of working-class people in struggle, united in their profound desire for liberation, for a new world'.[144] As a regular spectator at Fo's performances describes, the authorities had by now understood that direct harassment

produced the opposite effect. These actions made him more popular, they gave him the halo of someone who was being persecuted. The echoes of attempted censorship increased his opportunities of success ... in order to stop him presenting himself as a victim, or creating anti-censorship resonance, or indirectly providing him with publicity, they just let him do what he wanted.[145]

Although the performances were fairly rudimentary and the script not particularly sophisticated, the show was again a great success, because in political terms it had struck while the iron was hot, that is, it had created an opportunity for people to digest and discuss the implications of events in Chile. *The Commune* travelled 6,000 kilometres and performed to a total audience of about 70,000 people. Moreover, all the profits were sent to Chile: at 1999 prices £32,612 was sent to the political organisation MIR. As a financial report from *The Commune* noted: 'Economic support is important. A machine gun costs more than £330,' so in other words nearly 100 of these weapons could be bought. A further £6,522 was sent to the *cordones* of Santiago – a rudimentary form of workers' councils which had first emerged in late 1972.[146]

Palazzina Liberty

In March 1974 Fo rented the *Palazzina Liberty* from the Milan council. This had been the canteen for Milan's old fruit and vegetable market but had been empty since 1967 and had an audience capacity of about 600. However, once the full council found out what had happened all hell broke loose, with the Socialist Party suddenly becoming hostile in order to placate their Christian Democrat allies. The council rapidly brought forward proceedings to obtain an eviction order.

In the meantime *The Commune* quickly placed a huge red flag on the roof, but they were forced to buy a diesel generator to provide electricity, because the council refused to supply power. In order to demonstrate the level of support he enjoyed, Fo performed *Mistero Buffo* to a huge crowd of 15,000 people in the gardens outside the building on 7 April.[147] Various eviction orders were served in later years, but the building stayed under Fo's control until 1981.

Meanwhile, Fo and Rame's relationship with the far left had now changed. Further political divisions and expulsions had riven *The Commune* in both 1972 and 1973, and from 1974 onwards Fo and Rame made no real attempt to increase the collective's national organisation. Even so, membership of the Milan *Commune* had risen to 33,000 just a few months after the occupation of the *Palazzina*.[148]

Publicly Fo generally kept a disciplined and diplomatic silence on these internal political disputes, often to avoid a journalistic focus on his own individual situation. However, in an article published in 1976 he was scathing about the political in-fighting:

In the first *Commune* branch in Rome the cultural representatives of the various groups were simultaneously the treasurers of the same organisations. This illustrates that they were only interested in the takings, they didn't give a damn about the cultural content. This isn't even deviousness, it's obtuseness. It's real contempt for the masses. The audience is treated like a bunch of morons who are made to pay for the pleasure of feeling like revolutionaries ... 'they can be the artists and bring us a bit of money in, and then we'll think about giving out the right line'.[149]

The first new play performed at the *Palazzina* was *Can't Pay? Won't Pay!* in October 1974. Six months after the building's opening it also hosted, apart from *The Commune*, a theatre school, a photographers' collective, an art school and a medical school. A European conference of Eritrean migrants was hosted free of charge for three days; sacked workers used the building for meetings. A library with hundreds of volumes was also being organised.[150]

By this time his shows had become so popular that it is widely believed that the huge success of his next play, *Fanfani Kidnapped*, dealt the decisive blow in the failed presidential campaign of the veteran Christian Democrat leader, Amintore Fanfani. It was written, rehearsed and premièred in under two weeks, and scenes from the first version were presented as part of PDUP's party political broadcast in the regional and local elections of June 1975.

Fo, who is over six foot tall, played the part of Fanfani, who is about five foot tall. He did that by standing in a trench cut into the stage. It was a humiliating experience for the top politician who was then very much in the limelight, conducting a campaign against proposals to legalise abortion.

In the plot, Fanfani is kidnapped by some henchmen of his Christian Democrat rival, Giulio Andreotti, in the hope of gaining more votes for the party across the board. Fanfani then confesses to decades of misdeeds by the Christian Democrats. He has an ear amputated and is taken dressed up as a woman to an abortion clinic, where he has a Caesarean section and gives birth to a puppet in a fascist uniform. Fanfani then dies and ends up in heaven being put on trial by Mary and Jesus, who have made common cause with the wretched of the earth. Suddenly he wakes up from his nightmare, but the relief is only temporary as real kidnappers suddenly come in, ending the show.[151]

The third play to be staged at the *Palazzina Liberty*, in March 1976 – *Mum's Marijuana is the Best* – was his least overtly political play for many years. As a major biographer of Fo has commented: 'For many months Fo appeared to be blocked, undecided between a script on China or one on slum dwellers ... A precise and easily identifiable target against which an attack can be launched is probably missing, which is necessary for

Fo's comedy.'[152] Drug abuse was a new and relatively unknown phenomenon: in 1974 only eight people died of an overdose in Italy, and police seized just 1.5 kilos of heroin. A few years later the problem had mushroomed: by 1980 there were 200,000 addicts and hundreds of deaths per year.[153]

Perhaps it was the very novelty of the problem which led Fo to repeat a very common theme of the time: that the system encouraged drug use in order to distract and divert some of its fiercest opponents. At a certain point he indulged in outright conspiracy theories: 'We use drugs like you use napalm. And with this napalm of pills and packets we've got rid of all the black movements in America! And now we want to try it out in Europe.'[154] Other opinions have stood the test of time far better, as Fo wrote in the preface: 'Finally a new "other" has been discovered who can be persecuted: the *drug addict*. Once upon a time it was the "Jacobin", then "the Jew", the "subversive" or the "anarchist" – now it's the "long-haired drug addict!"'[155]

What has remained highly topical are the references in the script to deaths from other drugs, such as 70,000 from cirrhosis of the liver.[156] More important still is a clear statement on the longer-term causes of drug-related deaths:

> It's not the stupefying effect of the drug that kills you, it's what lies behind it! It is the fact, for example, that over the last two years 65 per cent of young people, male and female, still haven't found their first job ... it's the desperation in discovering you don't have a future, the understanding that all the so-called sacred values on which the system is built, the nation, the family, honour, good manners, are a load of rubbish![157]

Despite the lower level of overt politics in the play, during rehearsals Fo made it clear that even drug-related deaths should be looked at from a class perspective:

> In every thousand drug-related deaths there is just one rich person, and this is normally due to an accident – like someone who chokes because a fish bone gets stuck. Because for rich people drugs are something extra, an explosion, another extra pleasure on top of all the other ones. For youth in rundown suburbs, for poor people, it's everything.
>
>   These are the ones who die in cellars, in suburban parks – or maybe in the police vans which are taking them from a police station to a youth detention centre.[158]

Although the farcical nature of the plot makes for comical entertainment, the play has a bitter undertone that probably reflects the crisis of the revolutionary groups. Rather than attacking the evils of capitalism or the failures of reformism, Fo essentially conducts an internal debate within the far left on the growing issue of drug use. In some senses the problem was becoming generational: those who had been radicalised by 1968 had noticed that the number of activists had fallen, and were becoming frustrated: 'Last Monday, and yesterday as well, we had to decide about the nursery, and you weren't there ... And to think that once upon a time you were always up the front! I bet you don't even know that the Council's given the order for an immediate eviction from the eight occupied buildings.'[159] Although the play revolves around the issue of activists getting more and more involved in drugs, some political groups – due to a Stalinist heritage and sheer desperation – were beginning to condone widespread violence instead. At one point a character had been beaten up by left-wing activists committed to combating drug dealing physically, and another character comments: 'Ah, dialectical comrades, educators! Educators with an iron bar! They're putting the right ideas over ... they're putting the ideas right here: thump! (He mimes hitting *Luigi* over the head).'[160]

Despite the implosion and disintegration of the revolutionary left, Fo's activities were not particularly inward-looking during this period. His shows remained as popular as ever, and through local *Commune* branches he frequently performed 'intervention shows' at short notice in a variety of situations.

For example, the show described in Appendix B was held in direct response to a fascist bombing in the town of Brescia in June 1974; the bomb exploded without any warning at a trade union rally killing nine people.[161] The town's newspaper managed to capture the genius of Fo's performance style. On one level, 'People went to listen to Dario Fo like you go to visit friends, where you talk about the things you care about the most.' On another level the theme of the show revolved around what political attitude the working class should take towards fascism, and Fo

> says things that made your hair stand on end, but with his typically irresistible talents of communication ... He accused the entire system ... A nervous recollection of a period we thought was dead and buried ran through the crowd. The partisan spoke, the Sicilian storyteller spoke, workers from Brescian factories spoke ... They were all saying the same thing: stop the fascists. People have got clear ideas.[162]

Fo's commitment continued through the gathering political gloom; for example, New Year's Eve benefit performances inside occupied factories started to become a regular event: in 1975 he performed at the *Mammut* factory in Savona, in 1976 at the British Leyland *Innocenti* car factory just outside Milan and in 1977 at the *Motta* food factory in Corsico.[163] In

October 1977 Fo claimed that over the last year *The Commune* had given £243,613 to occupied factories at 1999 prices.[164]

Perhaps it was with some justification that in early 1978 Fo could comment: 'Even without counting the Molotov cocktails thrown at my house, the bomb at the *Palazzina*, the innumerable court trials that await me, I feel that during this last decade we have lived at least 200 years.'[165]

Accidental Death of an Anarchist

Fo claims that *Accidental Death of an Anarchist* has been the most performed play in the world over the last 40 years.[1] Its pedigree certainly is impressive: productions in at least 41 countries in very testing circumstances: fascist Chile, Ceausescu's Romania and apartheid South Africa.[2] In Argentina and Greece the cast of early productions were all arrested.

Within Italy it has been his second most popular play (*Mistero Buffo* is by far his most popular) – it has been estimated that in four years of touring across the country *The Commune* performed the show to about a million people. What is beyond doubt is that this play in particular demonstrates both Fo's skills as a writer, and the sensibilities of translators.[3] For example, the 1980 British edition contains references to General Pinochet's 1973 coup in Chile, developing one of the major themes of the original – the impossibility of substantially reforming the state. Fo's tradition of rooting his plays in the politics of his time was replicated in the play's first run in London's East End in 1979, when collections were made for a campaign which unfortunately failed to secure the conviction of the policeman or policemen responsible for the murder of Blair Peach, killed at an anti-fascist demonstration in Southall the same year.

The translators of the 1991 version referred to perhaps the more obvious and topical theme of British miscarriages of justice, such as the Guildford Four and Birmingham Six. Indeed Paul Hill, one of the Guildford Four, was asked to go to the rehearsals of a major production staged in London in 1991. Performances in Australia have referred to police attempts to frame left-wing activists for a bombing at the Sydney Hilton in 1978, as well as to the very high number of Aboriginal deaths in police custody, and so on.

The Strategy of Tension

The real-life events recounted in the play were partly a response to the
'Hot Autumn' of working-class struggle of 1969. For example, on 15
October there was a demonstration of 50,000 workers, in Milan against
the high cost of living.[4] On 19 November a hugely successful 24-hour
general strike took place to demand changes in government housing
policy. Rents were high – often for appalling accommodation – while
many flats were left unrented. Much of the explanation for this state of
affairs was the government's lack of interest: public house building had
decreased from 40 per cent of the housing market in the 1950s to 6 per
cent in 1969.[5] In the course of the strike a police officer was killed during
disturbances in Milan, although the immediate explanation given at the
time was that he had been killed by demonstrators – in reality it is more
likely that his death was the result of a driving accident involving another
police vehicle. On 28 November a law legalising divorce was passed in
Parliament, and on the same day a national demonstration of engineers
saw 100,000 marching in Rome.

On 11 December a Labour Charter between the government and the
unions was signed. As the historian Paul Ginsborg has argued:

> It represented a significant victory for the trade unions and for the new
> militancy. Equal wage increases were to be granted to all, the 40-hour
> week was to be introduced in the course of the following three years,
> and special concessions were made to apprentices and worker-students.
> The trade unions also won the right to organise mass assemblies at the
> workplace. They were to be held within the working day and were to
> be paid for by the employers, up to a maximum of ten hours in each
> calendar year.[6]

The following day a bomb exploded without warning in Milan at the
National Agricultural Bank in *Piazza Fontana*, killing 16 people and
wounding 90. The 'strategy of tension' had started and it marked the
beginning of modern terrorism in Italy.

A few hours after the bombing senior police officers were telling the press
that the bomb had originated from anarchist or far-left circles. At the
same time police squads were rushing around Milan's State University
looking for anarchists to arrest – without any evidence yet available the
police had already decided who was responsible.

Two anarchists whose names will always be associated with the *Piazza
Fontana* bombing (although they were both innocent of any involvement
in it) were arrested soon after the bombing. Pietro Valpreda, a ballet
dancer, was arrested three days after the outrage and was immediately
accused of being part of an anarchist conspiracy to organise a whole
campaign of bombings. He was never convicted, yet he spent three years

in jail and since his release no one else has ever been definitively convicted of the massacre. Nowadays the vast majority of Italians believe that the massacre was in fact perpetrated by neo-fascist groups who were encouraged and protected by the secret service, and one therefore presumes that there was also a degree of government collusion.

The thinking behind the strategy of tension, whether it be the neo-fascist groups who planted a whole series of bombs in those years or their accomplices and protectors within the secret services and the state machinery, was to halt the growth in the strength of the working class. The placing of bombs at random targets, generally with no warning, was bound to create severe tension within society. It was vital for these forces to create the impression that it was anarchists, communists, trade unionists and so on who were behind the bombs, just as they had unquestionably been behind numerous strikes and demonstrations in recent years.

This impression was to be created by the judicial system in particular and the state machinery in general, with the help of a compliant media. Once people had accepted that the left was to blame, and the bombs continued, they would demand a clampdown on the left. On the first anniversary of the *Piazza Fontana* bombing the Christian Democrat committee for the province of Milan passed a motion which called on the government to ensure 'a modern, correct and well-managed use of the security forces' in order 'to bring to an end the climate of disorder and violence which could undermine the credibility of democratic institutions'.[7] The leader of the right-wing Liberal Party, Giovanni Malagodi, went even further:

Milan is living through hours of disorder provoked by violent and seditious minorities who are creating obstructions and generating tension and fear. Milan's schools are 'picketed' by extremists who are stopping classes from taking place. Leaflets are being distributed which openly defy the law, inciting violence and insulting democratic institutions. Small marches are continuously criss-crossing the city and it seems that the only goal is to paralyse public life even further. The authorities appear to be dormant during such a grave moment, while a climate of fear is spreading among public opinion. It is not possible that a serious and democratic city such as Milan can be left at the mercy of an irresponsible and subversive minority who are, in fact, not protesting against the government but against a free democratic system.[8]

It was hoped that the overall situation which would be created would be one in which it was unclear who was *specifically* responsible, so in order to stop the chaos and the bombings the left had to be repressed *in general*. In the climate of fear and revulsion created by the bombings it was assumed that it would be relatively easy for the state to justify the suspension of normal democratic procedures and the repression of the left – a political climate would hopefully be created in which the left would be marginalised electorally in any case. Apart from an immediate weakening of the left, the final objective was the creation of a political system akin to fascism, hence the involvement of neo-fascist groups and elements within the secret service, many of whom had fascist sympathies. The attempt to create a witch-hunt of the left was initially successful: in order to avoid any 'guilt by association' with those apparently responsible for the bombing, many unions signed national contracts the day after the explosion in *Piazza Fontana*.

All of this is far from being an outlandish conspiracy theory, however. A week before the Milan Christian Democrats and Giovanni Malagodi made the statements outlined above there had been an attempted coup in Rome led by Prince Junio Valerio Borghese, although the news did not emerge until four months later. Even though the attempt was rather farcical, it was part of a tradition among senior military leaders, as witnessed by far more serious preparations for a coup in 1964.[9]

The essence of the strategy of tension is outlined by the character played by Fo in the play, *The Maniac*, while talking to a character who roughly embodies the ideas of the PCI, a journalist named *Maria Feletti*:

> the main intention behind the massacre of innocent people in the bank bombing had been to bury the trade union struggles of the 'Hot Autumn' and to create a climate of tension so that the average citizen would be so disgusted and angry at the level of political violence and subversion that they would start calling for the intervention of a strong state![10]

Apart from the play's overwhelming critical acclaim and popularity both in Italy and around the world, the immediate political success of *Accidental Death of an Anarchist* was the fact that it played a major role in exposing the thinking of those who were organising the 'strategy of tension'.

The Genesis of the Play

The second of the two anarchists, Giuseppe Pinelli, associated with the bombing was arrested before Valpreda: he was picked up a few hours after the explosion when he arrived at an anarchist centre during a police raid. He was a 41 year old railway worker, married with two daughters, and was to die just over 72 hours later in the Milan police headquarters, where he was being held illegally.

A few basic facts suffice to raise doubts in any rational mind as to how he met his death. Pinelli 'fell' from a fourth floor window to the courtyard below. The room he was being questioned in was just 13 by 11 feet; and there were five experienced officers in the room when Pinelli 'flew' from the window (which opened inwards) with a 'cat-like jump'. The first police explanation was that Pinelli had committed suicide by jumping; indeed police chief Marcello Guida (*The Superintendent* in the play) immediately stated on television that his suicidal 'leap' was also proof of his guilt.[11] The newspaper *Lotta Continua* commented: 'Similar suicides occurred in Italy during fascism'.[12]

The lack of any injuries to his hands – which would have been caused by the instinctive reaction of cushioning his impact – caused immediate disquiet. A lifeless body suggests an unconscious or dead body. A journalist in the courtyard looked up in the dark when he heard some noises and remembered thinking: 'What the hell are they doing up there? Why are they throwing a big box out of the window?'[13]

The other hypothesis which began to be discussed was that Pinelli's death was genuinely accidental and that the police were trying to cover up their own shortcomings, including intimidation, which led to his death. As the months wore on many people began to believe that his death was the result of oppressive interrogation techniques, often used by the police, which had gone slightly wrong. This is a variation on the hypothesis that he was effectively murdered by the police, which again, is by far the majority view today.

As investigations began, one of the most worrying elements was that none of the police officers under suspicion was suspended, thus giving them the opportunity to tamper with evidence. The first investigation into Pinelli's death by Judge Giovanni Caizzi concluded in late May with the ambiguous verdict that it had been 'an accidental death', thus giving Fo the title. A mood was growing throughout the country that a huge cover-up was in operation, even an ex-Prime Minister, Ferruccio Parri, was moved to comment at a public meeting: 'The judiciary is insisting on creating a legal verdict which saves the police, because the police are the state. If the police crumble into pieces so does the state.'[14]

However Judge Caizzi's verdict was released on the first day of a week-long newspaper strike, so it was 'old news' by the time the presses started to roll again.[15] And despite his verdict, this public prosecutor then strangely requested that the case be dismissed. Nevertheless, a second investigation was held by Judge Antonio Amati who reached a verdict of suicide in early July.[16]

The newspaper *Lotta Continua* was the most prominent in a widespread press campaign which strongly doubted the police's explanations and the judicial verdicts. On 20 April 1970 Luigi Calabresi, one of the policemen probably present when Pinelli left the police headquarters via the window, took out a lawsuit against the editor 'for continuous slandering aggravated by attributing to him a specific deed.' The reading of these events was that *Lotta Continua* had been deliberately provocative in order to force the issue out into the open. Yet Calabresi's move was similarly seen as an attempt to muzzle the press.[17]

The origin of the play illustrates Fo's close relationship with this growing movement, as he explains: 'During the spring of 1970 the comrades who were coming to see our shows – workers, students and progressives – were asking us to write a full-length piece on the Milan bombings and the murder of Pinelli, a piece which would discuss the political motives and consequences of these events.'[18]

Sympathetic journalists and lawyers gave them background material and unpublished documents and a first draft was quickly completed. Fo then continues: 'We were informed that we might be running the risk of legal proceedings, with trials and charges being brought against us. Nevertheless, we decided not only that it was worth the effort to try, but also that it was our duty as political militants. The important thing was to act and to act fast.'[19]

When the libel trial against *Lotta Continua* opened on 9 October it was the first public hearing of the events surrounding Pinelli's death. Fo later recalled that during the trial hearings, 'The roles were completely reversed: *Lotta Continua* no longer played the role of the defence but became the prosecuting counsel against the police. All the policemen's lies were uncovered, one officer contradicted another, they were hypocritical and fell into incredible traps.'[20]

These hearings provided Fo with much of the dialogue for the play. The testimony of police officers was full of inconsistencies and ambiguities; at one point an officer was asked whether he had heard Calabresi utter a key phrase during Pinelli's interrogation:

> I'm not able to rectify or be precise about whether I heard that phrase because it was repeated, or because it was mentioned to me. As I believe I've already testified to having heard it, to having heard it directly; then, drawing things together, I don't believe that I heard it. However I'm not in a position to exclude that it may have been mentioned to me.[21]

The first two hearings saw hundreds of demonstrators inside and outside the courthouse. During the proceedings the singing of *The International* and *The Ballad of Pinelli* could be heard. There was also scuffling between the police and people who wanted to reach the public gallery.[22]

The fact that *The Inspector* (or *Sports Jacket* in one version) in the play is instructed to wear a sports jacket and roll-neck sweater is directly related to the fact that it was Calabresi's favourite way of dressing during the libel trial. In the script the instruction that he should often be rubbing his right hand refers to the suspicion that Calabresi had struck Pinelli violently. And *The Inspector*'s nervous tic also corresponds to a tic which observers noted in Calabresi during the libel trial.[23] Anybody who had been following the trial closely and went to see the play would therefore have no difficulty in presuming that *The Inspector* was based on Calabresi. By the time he gave testimony, Calabresi's normally confident and at times aggressive demeanour had changed:

> Calabresi is no longer the prestigious person he once was, in front of the judges. Yes he's still got his roll-neck sweater under a striped gangster suit, his sideburns are well groomed, but at tense moments an unstoppable tic makes him massage his firm jawline. He has lost his normal air of superiority (also because as soon as he appeared rhythmic chants began: 'Mur-der-er! Mur-der-er!').[24]

Fo's play opened in early December, exactly a year after Pinelli's death. Yet it was presented without any real publicity. A journalist who met Fo at the state university of Milan during its first week observed:

> To look for information about Fo's play outside of this building would be pointless. Here, everyone knew that *Accidental Death of an Anarchist* was being performed in Milan, and they knew the street name and the time. Normal channels of communication are blithely ignored, but even so yesterday evening at least 500 people had to go back home because the theatre couldn't fit any more inside.[25]

It is important to remember that the political motivation which led to the play being written went far beyond the exposing of one particular scandal. Fo explains that *l'Unità*, the daily paper of the giant Communist Party, limited itself to sporadic and at times even-handed comments such as 'The matter is disturbing' or 'Just as Pinelli's death is murky, the massacre at the bank remains shrouded in mystery'. The subtext here is that as the scandal revealed the blackness at the heart of the state machinery, a machinery that the PCI one day hoped to operate, the PCI preferred to not pursue the matter.

In a document written by *New Scene* two months before the first performance, the kind of effects to be both avoided and created were spelt out:

> The most difficult issues related to this case will be confronted in order to avoid the piety, emotions and responses of 'the petty bourgeois enraged by the horrors of capitalism' (Lenin, *Left-Wing Communism, An Infantile Disorder*).
> We're not going to cry for Pinelli. If we did that we'd risk putting up with anything. Because he is a comrade fallen by our side we have to absorb strongly the meaning of his death. And we're not going to get emotional because that would let us 'digest' the show and make us feel we had an incredibly clear conscience. We should never forget that he

ended up on the fourth floor because of his political ideas – which we can criticise – but they guided him together with us in a common struggle to overthrow a social order.[26]

A decision to present the 'real Pinelli' on stage would obviously have increased the audience's compassion, so this was avoided. All of this is to not deny the amusing and farcical nature of much of the play. Yet the hilariously incongruous explanations given by the policemen as regards the anarchist's death become increasingly interspersed towards the end with more general observations made by *The Maniac*, many of which are cited below.

Smashing the State

The fundamental dividing line between revolutionary and parliamentary socialists is that the former believe that socialism cannot be created through Parliament whereas the latter maintain that the parliamentary system can create socialism. For revolutionaries, socialism comes about through a working-class revolution, one result of which is that the existing state machinery is destroyed.

This argument is played out in detail in the final stages of the play, where *The Maniac* outlines the hollowness of a reformist parliamentary strategy:

> The people are demanding real justice? And instead we'll make sure they're happy with a slightly less unjust system. The workers are calling for a halt to the outrage of vicious exploitation? And we'll act to make it a little less vicious and concentrate above all on making sure they don't feel outraged again, as long as they stay exploited ... They want to stop dying in factories? We'll install a few more safety measures and increase the payments for widows. They want an end to the class system? So we'll reduce the gap, or even better make sure it isn't so obvious!
>
> They want revolution? And we'll give them reforms ... loads of reforms ... we'll drown them with reforms. Even better, we'll drown them in the promise of reforms, because we won't even give them any reforms!![27]

As has been seen in Chapter 2, this political argument was by now familiar territory to Fo. The difference with this play was not only the fact that Fo had successfully returned to the format of farce, but that all the underlying political arguments found an echo in a crisis-ridden society. Fo made his views explicitly clear in a performance note at the end of the script:

Underlying the text ... is a Leninist view of the theory of the state and its workings. The judiciary and the police which the play attacks are not institutions to be criticised or modified, upon which pressure should be exercised to stop their malfunctioning: they are the most direct expressions of the bourgeois state, the class enemy to be smashed.[28]

In opposition to ideas such as these, the general reformist reading of the events surrounding Pinelli's death, and the strategy of tension as a whole, was to concentrate on the specifics of each particular scandal. But as Fo pointed out in the introduction: 'We insist on treating the anarchist's death as a "work-related accident", and not at all as an exceptional event.'[29]

One of the fundamental political purposes of the play, therefore, was the need to draw general political conclusions from each individual scandal. At one point *The Maniac* outlines the normal sequence of events: 'A huge scandal ... A lot of right-wing politicians arrested ... A trial or two ... A lot of big fish compromised ... Senators, members of parliament, colonels ... The social democrats weeping.'[30]

Yet *The Journalist*, who represents parliamentary socialism, thinks this would be a good thing: 'I believe that a scandal of that scale would actually do credit to the police. It would give the average citizen the sense of living in a decent society for once, where the system of justice was just a little less unjust ...'[31] As parliamentary socialists want to gain control of the state machine, in the final analysis existing state institutions must be defended.

The Maniac also clarifies why a society obsessed by scandal furthers bourgeois interests: 'You see, your average citizen doesn't actually *want* all the dirt to disappear. No, for him it's enough that it's uncovered, there's a nice juicy scandal and everyone can talk about it ... As far as he's concerned, that is real freedom, the best of all possible worlds.'[32]

The Journalist starts to agree with him: 'When there aren't scandals, they need to be invented, because it's a good way of maintaining power and defusing people's anger.'[33]

The Maniac then spells his views out in greater detail:

You remember the 'Profumo' scandal in England? A Minister of Defence, caught up with drugs, prostitution and spying ...!!! Did the state collapse? Or the Stock Exchange? Not a bit of it. If anything they came out of it stronger than before. People thought: 'The rot's there, so let it float to the surface ...' We're swimming about in it – even swallowing some of it'.[34]

The Superintendent also follows his drift: 'That would be like saying that scandal is the fertiliser of social democracy!'

The Maniac continues:

Spot on! Manure! ... scandal is the best antidote to the worst of poisons – namely when people come to realise what's really going on. When people begin to realise what's going on, we're done for! ... people can let off steam, get angry, shudder at the thought of it ... 'Scumbag generals!' 'Murderers!' And they get more and more angry, and then, burp! A little liberatory burp to relieve their social indigestion.[35]

The play was immediately a smash hit in Milan, as Fo recalls: 'Every evening the theatre was sold out half an hour before the performance began, and we ended up performing with people on the stage, in the wings. Despite the provocations; the usual phone calls from unnamed callers telling us that there was a bomb in the theatre; the interventions of the Flying Squad'.[36]

The tense atmosphere of police harassment or infiltration of the shows was also put into the script. At one point *The Superintendent* states that police agents are in the theatre and suddenly claps his hands at the audience, after which voices shout out 'Sir...? Yessir...!' *The Maniac* immediately 'reassures' the audience: 'Don't worry – they're all actors. The real ones sit tight and don't say a word.'[37]

The intention of making the public reflect calmly on the scandal also seemed to have worked, given that the only criticism made in the PCI's *l'Unità* review was that 'something seemed absent to us: a sense of moral outrage, indispensable when dealing with such a controversial issue'.[38]

Perhaps the success was also due to the fact that, after his more recent 'serious' political plays, the form here has returned to farce. There are many gags, mistaken identities and the use of props – and *The Maniac* frequently changes his appearance.

Fo's play couldn't have been more topical. The first performance took place just a few hours after a demonstration to commemorate the first anniversary of the bombing in *Piazza Fontana*, which ended with a student named Saverio Saltarelli being killed by a tear gas shell fired by the police from very close range.[39] Such was the climate of activism that students went to Milan's two most prestigious theatres, the *Lirico* and the *Piccolo*, and were able to read a brief statement to the audience, who responded with one minute's silence in honour of the dead student.[40]

The following day, a Sunday, *New Scene* hosted a debate, with 700 participants in their theatre, on the ramifications of the student's death; and on Monday a meeting of 3,000 people in the main hall of the state university voted on how to commemorate the first anniversary of Pinelli's death the following day. Mass pickets were organised, and tens of thousands of people marched again in Milan to commemorate the anarchist's death, bringing the city centre to a standstill for the entire day. The largest demonstration was led by a huge banner with the slogan: 'Repression harms workers – reformism disarms them.'[41]

Problems continued on the tour, with police chiefs often leaning on theatre owners to refuse any bookings; indeed this was another reason why Fo ended up playing to audiences outside the conventional theatrical circuit, that is in public squares and occupied factories.

The circumstances of a continuously growing popularity necessitated frequent technical changes:

> When we found ourselves performing under the roofs of occupied factories ... we started to put three or four microphones in a row in front of the stage ... When we started using sports arenas for the *Anarchist* we were facing audiences of 6–7,000 people, we had to go even further: so we started to copy the electrical equipment of pop groups, who were the only people who performed in those places.[42]

In a postscript to the play in 1974, Fo perceptively comments on the underlying political appeal of the play:

> What has been the real reason for the show's success? ... It has been above all the way it deals with Social Democracy and its crocodile tears, the indignation which can be relieved by a little burp in the form of a scandal; scandal as a liberating catharsis of the system ... The indignation of the good democratic citizen grows and threatens to suffocate him. But he has a sense of satisfaction when he sees, in the end, these same organs of this rotten and corrupt society, pointing the finger at this selfsame society, at its own 'unhealthy parts', and this gives him a sense of freedom throughout his whole being. With his spirit suitably decongested, he shouts, 'Long live this bastard shit society, because at least it always wipes its bum with soft, perfumed paper, and when it burps it has the good manners to put its hand in front of its mouth!'[43]

However, it was not just Fo and newspaper critics who declared the play a success, for its popularity was just as great on tour. At a debate in May 1971 a worker drew some very wide-ranging conclusions:

> The Pinelli affair gives us a chance to make a general criticism, a profound argument aimed at making all of us aware that it is impossible to go on living in this society, where for all of us – as long as things carry on as they are – any authentic freedom or humanity is impossible.[44]

As the play was performed night after night, the libel trial continued, revealing the police cover-up and thereby providing Fo with more material. However, the trial was suspended in June 1971 when a judge was removed from the bench for alleged irregularities, not uncoinciden-tally, soon after he had agreed to exhume Pinelli's body for further examination.[45] In the same month Calabresi was promoted from deputy inspector to inspector. The public outrage was immense, and Fo typically related to it and worked the latest developments into the script.

Attempted Obliteration of an Anarchist

The success of Fo and this play has contributed to a lasting awareness of the real issue, that is, the fact that the bombers have never been convicted. While anarchists were initially arrested for the bombing and then released, there have been a series of trials involving neo-fascists which have not secured a definitive conviction. In 1994, 25 years after the bombing, 10,000 people marched in the morning to commemorate the bombing and demand justice, while 3,000 attended the official ceremony in the afternoon.[46] Thirty years later, nobody has been convicted of one of Italy's most notorious acts of terrorism.

In 1987 the Socialist Party Milan Council led by Paolo Pillitteri, the cousin of Socialist leader Bettino Craxi, announced that it intended to remove the plaque commemorating Pinelli from outside the bank in *Piazza Fontana*. The reasons were twofold: the first was rather banal – apparently some people felt offended by the inscription on the plaque which reads 'To Giuseppe Pinelli, an innocent anarchist railway worker killed in the Milan police headquarters on 16 December 1969'. The second unstated reason had a broader intent: the Italian state, or what Fo calls 'power', wanted both Pinelli's death and the failure to prosecute the people who had organised the bombing to be totally forgotten.

What happened next was almost identical to what happened in 1970, as Fo recounts: 'It all started when the papers reported that Pinelli's plaque was to be moved from *Piazza Fontana* into a museum. Many angry comrades contacted me, several of whom had helped us in 1970 to get hold of documents for *Accidental Death*... so straight away we thought that the show should be revived.'[47] The show's revival would remind people that the system still had many skeletons in the closet.

In order to contribute to the campaign against the council's intention to rush the proposal through, the show was organised in just one week, so the first performances had fixed lighting and prompters visible on the stage. The opening night saw the theatre packed, mainly with young people, including Pinelli's two daughters. Fo's introductory speech was typically sarcastic: 'For a long time the police headquarters have been pressurising various mayors to remove the plaque in *Piazza Fontana* which commemorates the death of Pinelli. Then Pillitteri arrived ... and tried to convince the council to grab the plaque and maybe throw it out of the window as well.'[48]

Again, the show was a great success. The only negative review, not surprising in the circumstances, came from the Socialist Party daily, which defined Fo as being 'tired and repetitive' and invited him to go back to working on television.[49]

In any democratic country those individuals running the political and judicial systems are occasionally found out to be responsible for favouring gross miscarriages of justice, and even when the scandal has emerged, the arrogance which derives from their position of privilege is rarely absent either. For example, following the quashing of the convictions of the Guildford Four and the Birmingham Six in the early 1990s, sections of the British establishment and the judiciary continued a whispering campaign, hinting that these victims of injustice must still be guilty of something. Lord Denning once notoriously remarked: 'We wouldn't have all these campaigns to get the Birmingham Six released if they'd been hanged.'

The same occurred in Italy. Despite the issue of Pinelli's highly suspicious death and the fact that he has never been posthumously convicted of any crime, the establishment still refuses to admit its mistakes. In 1992 the Socialist Party leader, Bettino Craxi, claimed: 'I think Pinelli may have had a role of logistic back-up. But once he understood what had happened he committed suicide out of remorse.'[50]

Despite these repeated attempts to besmirch the name of a victim of injustice, the establishment has not succeeded in criminalising Pinelli. Soon after Fo's revival of *Accidental Death...* the council withdrew its proposal and the plaque commemorating Pinelli can still be found in *Piazza Fontana*.

The Frame-up of the Anarchist's Friends

Apart from the death of Pinelli, there have been at least five other murders associated with this case. The most notorious one, that of Luigi Calabresi, the officer most people suspected of killing Pinelli, occurred in May 1972. Just a few months after Pinelli's death a huge piece of graffiti was painted on the front wall of Calabresi's house: *Pinelli's murderer*. Many of the main streets of Milan were also painted with the graphic statement: *Calabresi is a murderer.* [51]

The killers made a clean getaway, and as Calabresi was due to be tried for the manslaughter of Pinelli and was also under investigation concerning a possible murder charge, the response of the revolutionary left was to suspect that his murder had come from the right and not the left. As an article in *Lotta Continua* argued at the time: 'This attack has got rid of a man who for the bourgeoisie was better dead than alive. Calabresi and his group of officers were the weak link in the whole conspiracy of the *Piazza Fontana* bombing; there was a constant risk they would give the game away.'[52]

Fo made these suspicions crystal clear in a play which at least thematically was the continuation of *Accidental Death...: Knock! Knock! Who's There? The Police!* During the second act a senior figure in the Home Office refers to Calabresi by name and describes how he is feeling in the light of the accusations made against him: 'He's gone mental. He says that the Home Office is dumping him ... that it's now become obvious that the state wants to use him as a scapegoat.'[53] A few minutes later in the same act Calabresi's death was announced, along with the reasons why several police chiefs were threatening to resign: 'They're saying they accept that they can end up being killed as officers of the state ... but they won't accept being killed on the orders of the state by other plain-clothed policemen.'[54]

No real progress was made on Calabresi's murder until 1988, when a former member of *Lotta Continua*, Leonardo Marino, accused Adriano Sofri (who in 1972 was editor of the newspaper *Lotta Continua*), along with two other men, of having organised and committed the murder of Calabresi. As a result, Sofri and these two other men are currently serving a 22-year sentence for Calabresi's murder, purely on the basis of Marino's testimony. The issue has now become known as the 'Sofri case', as he is the best known of the three. With the three men now in their fifties, the behaviour of the judiciary towards these men smacks of the establishment's revenge against the powerful revolutionary organisations which challenged the system during the 1970s.

With no other legal recourse available to them, the three have often threatened to start a hunger strike. Immediately after winning the Nobel Prize in October 1997 Fo condemned this scandal in his first press conference and announced that a substantial amount of the prize money would be donated to the campaign for their release. And his first play after winning the Nobel Prize dissected and ridiculed the sole 'evidence' for their conviction; although in many ways the text is more of a public lecture than a theatrical performance.

Free Marino! Marino is Innocent!

The first section is probably a consequence of Fo's experience at press conferences and theatre performances in the weeks and months after his Nobel award, in which the issue of the Sofri case emerged continuously. As he explains in the opening of the play:

> Above all among young people we noticed a frightening misinformation about the atmosphere and the political issues of that period. As we recounted certain details, certain events, they looked at us with bewilderment and we were amazed when we discovered that these

young students knew nothing about the bombs, the massacres, and the state's judicial cheating which took place 30 years ago.[55]

He continued in similar vein during his acceptance speech for his Nobel Prize in early December 1997:

> I understood that I was shouting in the dark because people knew nothing of the background ... they knew nothing about the state's massacres in Italy, of trains which were blown into the air or bombs placed in big public squares, or of the trials which were conducted as farces. The terrible thing is that to talk about a contemporary event I have to recount history starting from 30 years ago.

Fo has calculated that Marino has told at least 120 lies during his accounts of the events surrounding Calabresi's murder, and they form the basis of the text.

Firstly, during the many trials which have been held over the case, it has emerged that before Marino's first official 'confession' he spent 18 days in the company of the *Carabinieri* prior to being questioned by an investigating magistrate.[56] When Judge Pomarici found this out at one of the trials he shouted at the officers concerned because they had not revealed this highly significant detail in previous hearings. They then answered: 'We didn't want to tell you because we were afraid that somebody would suspect that during those days we wanted to train Marino in his confession!'[57]

What is even more worrying is that Marino has never denied that he was involved in organising an armed robbery a few months before his confession; the suspicion naturally arises that his apparent confession was in exchange for more lenient treatment for his involvement in a number of crimes in the late 1980s. Furthermore, Marino never even mentioned to his wife that he was going to confess.

Since the death of Pinelli in December 1969 the revolutionary left in particular had largely come to the conclusion that Calabresi had the greatest responsibility for the death of the anarchist. This is the rational basis upon which Marino makes the claim that *Lotta Continua*'s (LC) leadership decided to order Calabresi's murder in the early months of 1972. A three-man group composed of Ovidio Bompressi, Giorgio Pietrostefani and Marino were supposedly entrusted with the murder. However, they needed some firearms training, and Marino claims that they sometimes went up into the mountains to engage in target practice against some rocks. Yet as Fo notes: 'If there is one really crazy thing it is target practice ... anybody who knows anything about it can confirm this: if you shoot against a rock the bullets bounce back at you.'[58]

The decision of the LC leadership to kill Calabresi was apparently made more urgent when in early May an anarchist student named Serantini died from wounds inflicted by the police in Pisa. According to Marino, LC decided to bring forward the killing of Calabresi in revenge for this but Marino started to say he didn't want to go through with it, and at this point Pietrostefani allegedly told him: 'The only thing is for you to go to Pisa where tomorrow there'll be a demonstration for Serantini. Speak with Sofri, and you'll see that he'll persuade you.'[59] Sofri was the main leader of LC and was convicted on the basis that he instigated the murder of Calabresi.

It was pouring with rain that morning in Pisa, there are many photographs which show dozens of unfurled umbrellas at the LC rally, but Marino testified that he didn't remember any rain. Yet the judge incredibly backed him up: 'If Marino has stated that it wasn't raining then without doubt the Meteorological Office has made a mistake ... or rather it was raining but only in certain areas, as often happens in May. It was raining here and there, but in *Piazza Santo Stefano*, where the LC rally took place, there wasn't a drop.'[60]

If that line of reasoning seems absurd, it is nothing compared to what emerged in a cross-examination between Marino and a defence lawyer. It begins with Marino stating that Pietrostefani was also taking part in the conversation between him and Sofri. The strange thing was that the demonstration was full of plain-clothed policemen, acting both as detectives and photographers, as there was an arrest warrant out for Pietrostefani at that time. Not only are there no photographs of Pietrostefani in either police or press photographs, but neither are there any of Marino, who claims he had a lengthy conversation with Sofri. Marino develops a very curious argument concerning the presence of Pietrostefani:

Marino: 'Well, we could say he wasn't ... right beside us ... on top of us ... but a little further away.'
Lawyer: 'And from a little further away he listened, he took part in the discussion?'
Marino: 'Yes, but without getting himself noticed ... with a few gestures ... a bit surreptitious ... there were a lot of trees around, you know.'
Lawyer: 'But was he underneath or in the trees? Maybe swinging from one to another like Tarzan?'
Judge: 'Counsel for the defence, please don't engage in excessive irony! And you, Marino, concentrate a bit more! Let's see, you first stated that Pietrostefani was beside you, then he was a little further away but listening and taking part through gestures – with policemen all around – but from behind the trees!'
Marino: 'No, in fact he was much further away ... we almost couldn't see him.'
Judge: 'Think again Marino: was Pietrostefani there or not?'

Marino: 'Well, maybe I got confused ... I was sure he was around ... but in all honesty he wasn't there. Neither here nor there!'
Judge: 'Ah, that's better!'[61]

One of the things that Marino claims Sofri told him was that the LC leadership had had a meeting in which they had voted seven to three to kill Calabresi. LC was undoubtedly a revolutionary organisation, and subsequently well known and monitored by the police. But if it had ever had such a vote and taken steps to murder Calabresi, it is clear that in legal terms it would have been a subversive or terrorist organisation. So once Marino had made this accusation concerning the leadership, two of the leaders at the time, Marco Boato and Guido Viale, went to see the investigating magistrate but he declined to interview them. And in one of the many sentences handed down in this case a judge wrote: 'Yes, our intention would be to arrest and charge all of the leadership group, but unfortunately we have not been able to discover their names.'[62]

This is absolute nonsense. Given the nature of an organisation such as LC, 'Everyone has always known their names! All of them, including their profession, the road and the number of the house they live in, their telephone number, bank account number, shoe size, number of real teeth and dentures!'[63] Fo's convincing argument is that putting all these people on trial for terrorism, that is, for the equally serious charge of instigating Calabresi's murder, would mean putting Marino's testimony under the microscope again.

There is a mass of contradictions as regards the build-up to the murder as well. For example, Marino has claimed that he stole the car used for the murder from the opposite side of the road where it was actually stolen. He said that he forced the side window on the left whereas it was the right-hand side one which was forced. He said that the car was beige though the real one was blue, and so on.[64]

There are many other suspicious facts linked to the car: when it was found by the police it contained no fingerprints whatsoever, not even those of the owners – yet Marino claims that he never cleaned it and ran from the car in a great hurry leaving the door open and the motor running.[65] His explanation for the lack of fingerprints was that he wore gloves, but he also states that he had to hotwire the car by connecting wires underneath the dashboard. He admits though that his accomplice, Bompressi – one of the three convicted – did not wear gloves, but Marino explains that he opened and shut all doors and windows for him.[66]

Not only is Marino's testimony highly suspect, but many other matters cannot be forensically tested either. For example, the bullet fragment found in Calabresi's head was destroyed a long time ago, as was a bullet found in his clothing. Not only is this highly unusual for the unsolved murder of a police officer, but the car in question was also destroyed in

December 1988 for non payment of road tax, *after* the arrest of Sofri and the others.[67]

Furthermore, two eyewitnesses identified the driver as a fair-haired woman,[68] and indeed for 16 years the police were looking for a woman, until Marino came forward and said he was the driver. As Fo ironically comments:

> Here is the metamorphosis after 16 years. Marino appears with his black bushy hair, with no breasts or a limping gait, but to compensate he's got a big moustache: 'I was the woman driving the car!' The police, the investigating magistrate, the prosecuting counsel and the president of the court exclaim: 'There's no doubt, it's her! Sorry, it's him!'[69]

One of the most shocking things is that Marino's testimony is not only doubted by Fo and many others, but it was also questioned by the judge who wrote the definitive sentence. Yet he turned this problem around in a truly perverse fashion: 'Yes, it is true Marino often contradicts himself, he frequently reveals imprecisions and inconsistencies, but this is incontestable proof of his sincerity.'[70] The judiciary's defence of Marino began at the first of many different trials and appeals, when the judge argued at the very end of his sentence: 'Marino was educated by the Order of Salesians, and it is known that whoever has been through the Salesians does not ever lie!'[71]

What becomes clear is that there is a judicial collusion in favouring Marino's account. At one point during the cross-examination it was revealed that Marino's description of the escape route he had taken was exactly the opposite direction from that taken in reality. A judge then intervened to save Marino from giving some ludicrous explanation: 'I created the misunderstanding, I gave Marino the map upside down so I led him to make a mistake.'[72]

It has not been easy for the judiciary to maintain a conviction which is essentially based on Marino's testimony alone. At their first trial Bompressi, Pietrostefani and Sofri were convicted and then given a 22-year sentence, and Marino an 11-year sentence, a verdict that was upheld at their first appeal in September 1991. The issue then ended up at Italy's highest court, the Full Cassation Court, which threw out these first two sentences on the basis of Marino's behaviour and testimony. As Fo comments: 'Marino isn't credible even when he sneezes.'[73] The judges then ordered a retrial, cancelling out the previous two.

A second Appeal Court decided on the acquittal of all four in December 1993. These courts are one of the few in Italy to have a jury, in fact there are six ordinary jurists and two judges – and in this case all six jurists and the president of the court decided on acquittal. However, each court is required to issue a written sentence, and inexplicably they asked the remaining judge to write the sentence.[74] In order to understand what happened next, Fo suggests, 'We have to leave the world of Dickens and Orton and enter the world of Lewis Carroll.'[75]

This judge went on to write a 'suicide sentence'. Fo explains: 'The technique is this; when you want to undermine a trial verdict you write a mad, impossible sentence. So the Court of Cassation is forced to reject it and the trial is held again.'[76] Fo then argues that in October 1994 the Cassation Court duly followed the script, indeed it was

> like the sheet music of a comic opera. The Cassation judges perform in chorus, with melody, counter-melody and falsetto: 'But this is impossible! What a mess! How can one accept such a crazy sentence! No way, the sentence that frees all of them has to be stopped, everything needs to be done again ... This isn't how things are done! Tra-la-la, tra-le-le!'[77]

The issue then went back to another Appeal Court, another six jurists and another two judges. This time the judges were far more insistent upon conviction, and as soon as they retired to the jury room the president of the court, Judge Della Torre, began by saying: 'So, we all agree they're guilty?'[78] Four jurists, half of the total jury, argued for a verdict of 'extenuating circumstances' which would free them all and end the trial. The judge wouldn't hear of it, but nevertheless promised that he would call for an amnesty in his sentence. Eventually two jurists changed their verdict and the three were convicted, but in the final sentence handed down in November 1995 Marino's crime is struck out.[79]

One jurist named Giovanni Settimo took legal advice about what he felt had been the undue pressure applied by the judge in the jury room. One of the lawyers told him: 'Now you realise how justice works in Italy'.[80] Settimo, backed up by another jurist, went public with his accusations. A court from another city then appointed an investigating magistrate, Judge Salamone, but in line with a script which has been followed many times, the judge's brother was suddenly very publicly placed under suspicion by Parliament's Anti-Mafia Commission. Soon after that Salamone himself was told that he was under investigation for involvement with the Mafia, and he dutifully kept to the script and ended his investigations.[81]

One very important fact concerning this trial is that Giovanni Settimo, the brave jurist who stood up to the judge and spoke out publicly, was in the 1970s a neo-fascist activist and a sworn enemy of *Lotta Continua*.

Fo's play was just one personal response to an issue which many people viewed as a miscarriage of justice. Soon after their imprisonment in February 1997 a demonstration of 15,000 people was held outside the jail in Pisa, which was supported not only by Fo, but also by the film directors Bernardo Bertolucci and Gabriele Salvatores, as well as 80 MPs. In October 105 senators sent an appeal to the President of the Republic asking him to use his powers of pardon. At the same time a petition with 160,000 signatures – organised by a former president of the Constitutional Court – was presented to the President of the Republic, again asking for a pardon. Shortly before the petition's delivery the president announced he would not grant them a pardon – something the three had refused to request as they declared themselves innocent. And when Fo's play was due to be broadcast on television in March 1998, the President of the Appeal Court bench, which was handing down the eighth sentence on this case, phoned the secretary of the Milan Magistrates' Association asking them to apply pressure to get the programme stopped.[82]

In the latest twist in October 1998, the Appeal Court decided to reopen the case. Fo characteristically commented: 'After my intervention many people said that it could have been harmful and that I should have kept quiet. They were intellectuals with reactionary souls, who prefer silence to words.'[83]

Conclusion

If one compares the conclusion of *Free Marino! Marino is Innocent!* to that of *Accidental Death of An Anarchist*, it appears very weak. *Accidental Death...* denounced the entire police force and the whole legal system, and made the point very strongly that the details of one particular scandal should be generalised to understand and illustrate the common patterns according to which the state normally works.

Yet Fo avoids making these generalisations in *Free Marino!*:

Personally I can assure you that I'm indignant. And I want you to be as well. Because if you haven't understood what kind of trap has been sprung in all this story then it is useless that I'm here performing an entire show for you. My words ought to stop, I've got nothing more to say to you! If you haven't understood that this is a huge swindle and that these three characters have been imprisoned unjustly, after having been freed, then it is pointless for me to carry on! I don't want to speechify. I want each one of you to think about it and draw your own conclusions.[84]

Fo comes close here to the moral indignation over one single issue he criticised so mercilessly nearly 30 years before. Despite all the details he gives about police and judicial manoeuvres essentially to pervert the course of justice, he doesn't bring them all together and make the same general points he made in *Accidental Death*.

Indeed in the version of the play broadcast on television he even made a short declaration in favour of Italy's various police forces which had harassed him and Rame for years: 'It must be made clear that our criticisms are certainly not directed at those thousands and thousands of members of the security forces, the *Carabinieri* above all, who every day risk their own lives guaranteeing the security of every citizen, and their right to freedom and justice.'[85]

The reasons behind such a massive shift on Fo's part are to be found in the vastly different political situations in which the two plays were written, namely 1970 and 1998, which will be outlined in Chapters 4 and 6.

Can't Pay? Won't Pay!

Upturns, Downturns and *Autoriduzioni*

Non si paga! Non si paga![1] was the first show performed in the *Palazzina Liberty* on 3 October 1974.

Following the working-class militancy which exploded in 1969, and then continued at a very high level for several years, many employers were forced to concede significant wage increases. Another characteristic of those years of working-class rebellion was defiance of the law, both within factories and outside them in everyday life. For example, non-payment of rent rose from 9.7 per cent in 1968 to 21 per cent in 1971.[2]

Within factories speeds on production lines were often reduced by workers on the spot, or alternatively production would be sabotaged. One of the first examples of what became known as *autoriduzione* (literally 'self-reduction') took place in the *Pirelli* factory in Milan in August 1968, with workers dropping production speeds by 10 per cent.[3] During the 1969 'Hot Autumn' there were cases of *autoriduzione* in which production speeds were lowered by up to 45 per cent.

Such was the atmosphere of militancy that even the normally legalistic PCI congratulated workers on what they had done: 'It is as if an orchestra had managed to play a difficult symphony harmoniously without the conductor and at a tempo agreed upon and regulated by the players of the single instruments.'[4] Among all the new methods of struggle which were emerging, *autoriduzione* really captured some workers' imagination, and the following year another left-wing paper reported that the same factory 'functioned with the regularity of a clock, but the tick-tock is more spaced out in time; it has a slowness that exasperates the bosses, who protest about the "irregularities" of this form of struggle. The workers ... make the bosses dance to the tune of their music.'[5]

The very fact that workers took such action meant that the authority of factory foremen, and management as a whole, was severely weakened. Indeed, management were often subjected to intensive questioning, and blatant absenteeism was also widespread. Perhaps it is not surprising that at one point the managing director of FIAT, Gianni Agnelli, temporarily decamped to Switzerland, despairing of ever being able to control his factories again.

In December 1969 engineering workers signed a new contract which gave them significant wage increases, a 40-hour week and parity of wages between white and blue collar workers. Unions were allowed to hold ten meetings per year within the workplace, in work time, and were given official noticeboards and the right to issue information.[6]

As part of this explosion of rank and file activity, new delegate-based factory councils were thrown up to coordinate these actions: there were 8,101 of these by 1972 made up of 82,923 elected delegates, growing to 32,000 in 1975 and nearly 250,000 delegates.[7] Apart from significant wage increases, another major improvement obtained was the passing of the Workers' Statute in 1970, which gave all workers the right to meet within the factory, as well as instituting the crime of 'anti trade union behaviour'. The first law giving limited rights to divorce was passed in December 1970, and following a general strike in 1969, a fair-rents scheme became law in October 1971. During these years, a banner which once opened a demonstration of FIAT workers – *We want the lot* – did not seem at all out of place.

Struggles continued at a high level over the next few years, both of workers against bosses and of workers against trade union bureaucracies. One event in late 1973 indicated the turning of the tide, however: the decision by OPEC countries to raise the price of crude oil by 70 per cent in autumn 1973 hit Italy particularly hard, as oil constituted 75 per cent of Italy's energy needs – and it must be remembered that Italy is a country with virtually no indigenous energy resources.

Inflation soon reached 20 per cent and remained very high throughout the 1970s. Consequently, in line with IMF policy, the Bank of Italy introduced severe deflationary policies and restricted the money supply.[8] In January 1974 Prime Minister Rumor said that the increase in the price of oil had created a 'grave' situation which must not be worsened by problems 'produced by our own behaviour'. The rationing of energy and certain foods was introduced.

The following month big increases in the cost of petrol, food and oil products were announced. Upon hearing this news many factory workers walked out spontaneously and stayed out for a week. All of this produced a political crisis, with the Republican Party opportunistically resigning from the coalition government on 1 March in protest at the huge cutbacks in public expenditure insisted upon by the IMF as part of its loan conditions.

A major recession was therefore taking place by mid-1974. By June, wholesale prices were 41.8 per cent higher than in the corresponding period of the previous year. One of the long-term economic consequences of this period was industrial decentralisation and the growth of the 'black economy'. A more short-term response was widespread recourse to indefinite lay-offs.[9] In these circumstances Fo argued that the classic response, strikes, 'were ineffective to a certain extent, because if the owner is affected at all it is only minimally.'[10]

These were the circumstances in which the *autoriduzione* movement of consumers as opposed to workers – the central theme of the play – began. One of the first episodes occurred in Turin, where two local bus companies raised fares by between 20 and 50 per cent. As the historian Paul Ginsborg has described:

> In August 1974 groups of workers at FIAT *Rivalta* refused to pay the 25–50 per cent increases demanded by the private bus companies which took them to work. Instead, they offered to pay at the old season-ticket rate. The local metalworkers' union quickly organised the protest and elected 'bus delegates' who collected the season-ticket money at the old rate and sent it to the bus companies. The example of the FIAT workers was then taken up throughout Turin and Piedmont. 'Autoreduction' also spread from transport to electricity. The local electricians' unions organised the paying of bills at the old tariff (some 50 per cent of the new), and promised that no one would have their supply cut off for taking such action. As a result, an estimated 150,000 electricity bills were 'auto-reduced' in Piedmont. During the winter of 1974–75 the movement spread rapidly to other cities of the Centre and North; telephone charges were also brought under attack.[11]

The national electricity company, for example, did not take all this lying down. They sent out thousands of letters demanding payment – otherwise supplies would be cut – but the unions called on their members not to plunge people into cold and darkness.[12]

In a period of such rapid inflation, and a situation in which workers' bargaining power with management had declined sharply due to economic recession and lay-offs, such forms of protest were a limited but unifying response. But they were also essential to defend living standards against growing inflation. On 29 August, pasta – which most Italians eat at least once a day – disappeared from supermarket shelves as a 50 per cent price increase was announced. Over a two-month period milk and sugar prices rose by 50 per cent, and meat by 18 per cent. On 14 September it was discovered that in order to cut costs inferior flour had been used to make spaghetti, thus making it soggy when cooked.

Despite working-class resistance, it was now clear that a full-blown recession was destined to bite even harder. In late October it emerged that meat consumption in Rome was 30 per cent lower than in the previous year, whereas bread consumption had increased by 20 per cent. Unemployment had also risen by 6.1 per cent in the twelve months to

September 1974.[13] A few days later it was announced that mains electricity would be cut for 30 minutes every day, despite the fact that night-time temperatures were already at zero degree.[14]

Fo's play, *Can't Pay? Won't Pay!*, emerges from this period and is centred on the *autoriduzione* of a group of working-class housewives. This entailed the refusal to pay the artificially high price increases established by supermarkets, or occasionally – as featured in this play – to reduce the price to zero by not paying at all.

These *autoriduzioni* were therefore a working-class response to a scheme to claw back the real wage increases which had been granted in previous years. This tendency was most prevalent in the northern working-class cities of Turin and Milan, but also in Rome. However, there was also another manoeuvre on the part of employers: firms declared they were experiencing an economic crisis and laid off workers indefinitely; they then received most of their wages through a state-funding system.

As well as being the first show performed in his new theatre, it was also Fo's first play since the end of his bourgeois period that saw 'farce' mentioned in the subtitle. And in fact it contains all the classic ingredients: women pretending to be pregnant to hide their stolen goods, fake dead bodies that fall out of cupboards at the wrong moment, the husband who unwittingly prepares a soup using bird seed and so on.

The plot highlights the *autoriduzione* practised by *Antonia* and *Margherita*, as well as the instinctive militancy of a young southern worker named *Luigi*. Piero Sciotto, who played *Luigi* in both the 1974 and 1980 versions, gave them the following political definitions: 'The wife understood things better ... the young worker was a kind of rebel without any broad political understanding or direction.'[15]

The real political target of the play was the moderatism of the PCI, as represented by *Antonia's* husband, *Giovanni*. The play was both written and set in the period of the 'historic compromise' launched by PCI leader Enrico Berlinguer in October 1973. Although this was initiated primarily in response to the military coup in Chile and as such was a political initiative, it also had an economic element, primarily the call for PCI members and supporters to follow a 'policy of sacrifices' or 'austerity' in the 'national interest'. In concrete terms this meant accepting a lowering in working-class living standards and was a prominent element of the PCI's programme for several years, as Berlinguer argued to cadre members of the party in January 1977: 'A more austere society can be, and must be, a more equal, better ordered and more just society, which is really more democratic and free, and definitely more human.'[16]

In effect this policy is the primary but unstated political target of the play. In a speech which is essentially lacking from the very unsatisfactory English translation[17] *Antonia* tells her husband near the end of the play:

I'm fed up with your hot air ... your speeches about responsibility, about sacrifice ... about the dignity of tightening your belt, about your pride about being working class! And who are these workers? Who is this working class? It's us, didn't you know? ... But you can't see a thing because your eyes are tied up like you were playing blind man's buff ... and you sit around like god knows what mouthing off your slogans.[18]

The comedy and dramatic tension of the play are driven by *Antonia's* increasingly farcical statements and actions aimed at hiding her illegal activity from her strongly law-abiding communist husband. Yet in a precursor of a major theme of Fo's plays during the 1980s, both *Antonia* and *Margherita* are far more active, quick-witted and imaginative than their rather slow-witted and politically cautious husbands. The plot is largely driven forward by these two female characters whose actions and arguments force *Giovanni* in particular to re-examine his ideas. *Antonia's* efforts at hiding the stolen goods are coupled with a growing frustration at her husband's unwillingness to fight back. One of her most telling comments which refers to his (and in real life to the PCI's) moralistic statements about sacrifices and obeying the law – again missing from the English translation – is when she tells her husband: 'You're not even a communist any more ... You've become a left-wing verger.'[19]

By the end *Giovanni*, pushed beyond endurance by the police arriving to evict him and other tenants who are behind with their rent, ends up supporting illegal and militant action in a speech unavailable in translation:

You can't just say to the bosses ... 'Excuse me, could you just move over there; we need a bit of a breathing space. Please be a little kinder, a bit more understanding ... let's come to an agreement.' Oh no, the only way to get that mob thinking straight is to stuff them down the bog and pull the chain! Then things would be great. Maybe there would be a few less illuminated window displays, less motorways ... we've always been rushing around to keep them going ... now we'll keep ourselves going ... we'll build our own houses ... make a new life for ourselves![20]

Using the political transformation that *Giovanni* undergoes in the course of the play, Fo urges PCI members and supporters to reject the policies of their party.

However there is an important difference in *Can't Pay? Won't Pay!* (*CPWP*) compared to many of the plays which preceded it: collective action such as the *autoriduzione* in the supermarket is only referred to, and essentially we remain within the walls of a flat. Indeed, during the final moments the main protagonists look out of the window down into the street, where a higher level of action is taking place – part of a whole section that is missing from the English translation entirely.

In Italy the play was criticised by the far left for being too much like his old-style comedies. Fo responded:

> I had never abandoned farce. In *Can't Pay? Won't Pay!* we have above all followed the method of verifying the text with an audience of workers and local people. We performed it in front of them and this obliged us to 'correct' certain characters because they made some observations about them, as well as changing the entire finale.[21]

Life Imitates Art

Right-wing critics soon discovered they had far more powerful ammunition than normal to use against Fo. As he explained in the prologue to an updated version performed six years later:

> The audience followed the play in some confusion, they looked at us as though we were a bit mad. We were talking about women who had gone shopping on the outskirts of Milan and had found that prices had been increased massively. Furious, they decided to pay half the price of what was indicated on the goods on display, exactly half price. Our story was a total invention.[22]

Yet two weeks after the play's first performance the very events recounted on stage were taking place in Milan supermarkets. Even a week after the play's première, there were scuffles in one supermarket between staff and left-wingers, in which the latter unsuccessfully attempted to create a situation of *autoriduzione*. The following week two supermarkets were successfully 'raided'; at one of these 40 demonstrators entered the aisles and two of them gained control of the cash registers and allowed shoppers to pay at 'old' prices. The police quickly arrived and arrested eleven people, also impounding a car with a speaker system. Apparently £13,100–£16,370 of goods were stolen in the general confusion.

There were more people – about 100 – involved in the almost simultaneous raid on the second supermarket. Demonstrators cut the phone lines and then proceeded to announce their actions over the supermarket public address system. Again, about £13,000 was 'lost', and by the time the police arrived the demonstrators had left. However, in this case leaflets from a Maoist group (*Servire il popolo*) were left behind, which justified their action thus: 'The goods we took were already ours, just as everything else is ours because we have produced it through our exploitation.' The leaflet also argued for greater civil disobedience: 'Let's get organised in working-class areas – rip up the gas, electricity and phone bills. Tear up the rent book. Don't pay for public transport any more! Let's take all we need, let's reappropriate our lives!'[23]

While it is unlikely that Fo had anything to do with these actions, it is understandable that right-wing newspapers would accuse him of being an instigator. In any event, a trial was quickly held, and Fo commented triumphantly on its outcome in the prologue to the 1980 version:

It emerged during cross-examination that the prices fixed by the supermarkets were out-and-out robbery. In the end all the women who had been charged were freed because 'there was no case to answer'. To put it simply, the court decided that those shoppers had paid the correct value of the goods. Consequently, you can deduce that the owners had arbitrarily increased the prices, doubling them. The bosses were the real thieves.[24]

But in responding to these accusations he also made more general points:

With workers being laid off[25] and not being able to struggle within the workplace, for what reason are they going to go on strike when they're already at home? Strikes are an important process of growth, to gauge your strength and to go outside and leaflet, speak to people, get them to understand workers' dramatic situation. But some people within the trade union movement only understand strikes as being a group of people picketing in order to damage the bosses.
   Today, in this situation, this is no longer useful. There is a reduction in workers' pay packets: they are worth half of what they were a year ago, and to add on to that there are the lay-offs which on paper mean £100 less a month, but in reality it is much more than this. It's also certain that there are more than 70,000 workers affected by FIAT's decision: how many families, how many other workers is that? All of this is to explain that we haven't instigated anyone to do anything.[26]

The overall economic situation bears out Fo's analysis, and indeed the circumstances surrounding the ensuing tour brought into focus the fact that such a severe economic crisis had dented the militancy of workers. Piero Sciotto has recalled:

After having put on a show to 4,000 in Padua to support an occupied factory ... we were forced to return to Milan because of a trial against the *Palazzina*. During the tour we had sensed the violence of the attack that the bosses were preparing, using the opportunity of the economic crisis. In Milan we held a meeting with militant workers of the *Fargas*, *Pirelli* and *Alfa Romeo* factories. Nobody had any clear idea of the scale of the crisis, so we launched a survey in the Milan area and identified 150 small factories in occupation: tens of thousands of workers were defending their jobs in total isolation, with the trade unions who were very careful about not mentioning the whole issue.[27]

Even in this specific detail the signs of working-class defeat begin to take shape: the government was attempting to lower living standards, the factory owners were trying to lower their costs by either sacking or laying off workers, and workers themselves were forced into the defensive move of occupying their factories. Another revealing indicator was that union leaders now felt strong enough to ignore some of the crucial concerns of their rank and file.

Six days after its première the increased confidence of the ruling class became clear at the end of a performance. Persistent rumours had circulated during the day that Fo and Rame were due to be arrested and held in jail for aiding and abetting the left-wing terrorist group, the Red Brigades. Consequently, as Fo explained at the end of the show, there would not be the normal debate as the cast wanted to leave the theatre along with the audience. Although they were never arrested or charged, Fo pondered on the reasons behind such rumours: 'Perhaps they don't want to just frighten us. Maybe they're trying to discredit *The Commune* as well which, with its thousands of members, is becoming an increasingly awkward phenomenon.'[28]

The Continued Success of the Play

CPWP represented the beginning and the end of the *Palazzina Liberty*, as it was Fo's first and last play to be performed there, with a new version opening in September 1980. Fo stated that the motivation behind this new version was 'that the suggestion for this came from abroad – *Can't Pay? Won't Pay!* is currently my most performed play in Europe'.[29]

The widespread success of this play undoubtedly has a broad political explanation: it deals with a form of civil disobedience, of working-class resistance, which is not centred on the workplace. The years between the two different versions, that is, 1974 to 1980, both in Italy and elsewhere, were years in which this change in social protest became more and more pronounced. In other words having talked about offensive actions centred around workplaces for many years, together with the need to reject the road of parliamentary socialism, in *CPWP* Fo developed a comedy that reflected some of the new realities of working-class life.

This is probably why it has entered the everyday language of political protest. In the late 1990s the subject matter of the play – the inability of working people to be able to afford basic foods – means that the most appropriate cities for its performance have become Bangkok, Kuala Lumpur, Jakarta and Moscow. Because Fo does not possess a religious reverence towards his scripts, he has no theoretical objection to his scripts being substantially adapted to local circumstances: 'I view scripts as living and adaptable material. For example, a few years ago in England *Non si paga! Non si paga!* was focused on Thatcher's vicious cuts in social services.

They had called it *Can't Pay? Won't Pay!* and it became the main slogan of the anti-Thatcher campaign.'[30] It is unclear whether he is referring to the massive protests against the Poll Tax in the early 1990s, but what is beyond doubt is that the title of this play became the main slogan of the campaign – and it is likely that many of the participants had no idea where the slogan had originated from.

As ever, Fo used the 1980 version to talk about current events, and as the play premièred in Milan a huge strike was breaking out in FIAT car factories against a planned wave of redundancies, so Fo went to perform outside the gates of a blockaded FIAT factory in Milan. Inside the gates were 6,000 FIAT cars waiting to be despatched throughout Italy, along with railway carriages loaded with another 460 cars destined for Germany. Not only were car workers on strike, but train drivers refused to go through the closed gates as well. Fo's performance was in the open air, and the council had refused the use of chairs for the performance: 'throughout the afternoon Dario Fo and Franca Rame's show – a mixture of their most "abrasive" pieces, such as *Tale of a Tiger* and *All Home, Bed and Church* – had been publicised through megaphones and leaflets.' Collections were held for the Turin workers who had been on all-out strike for nearly a month: 'As people fell silent you could hear the whistles of the trains which passed through the nearby station, and Fo moved into top gear. Children who were asleep in their mothers' arms woke up, and the old women who had unusually come out of their houses started to pay more attention.'[31]

But the epicentre of these struggles was at the FIAT factories in Turin over a plan to sack 24,000 workers. Workers blockaded the factory gates for a month while negotiations were taking place between unions, management and the government. Rame often went to Turin, for example, performing pieces of *All Home, Bed and Church* at the gates of the *Rivalta* plant, which were adorned with a huge banner which read 'We're not going back indoors'. The significance of this was that a large number of *Rivalta* workers were women.[32] She also visited the *Lingotto* factory near the end of the strike, where a high proportion of women had been selected for redundancy. It was a largely improvised performance, with several women workers invited on to the stage to perform a pantomime about assembly-line work.[33]

Although Fo and Rame could not have been aware of this, it was to be a turning point for industrial relations in Italy. One of the smokescreens which both the FIAT boss, Agnelli, and politicians threw up was to accuse workers of aiding and abetting members of the left-wing terrorist group, the Red Brigades, in order to weaken the political following of these militants, who very rarely had any connections with terrorism at all. By the end of the new version *Giovanni*, the PCI member driven to rebellion by the worsening conditions detailed in the script, begins to see through the smokescreen which was being created:

For years now we've been stuck in a rut, waving our hands around, frightened: 'Whatever you do, don't move, don't start struggling! This isn't the right time, you'd play the terrorists' game because they could say we're supporting them.'

Terrorism? Who's the terrorist these days? What do you call this kind of massacre that Agnelli is organising? Look at it – 24,000 lay-offs, isn't that a real massacre?[34]

As in so many of Fo's plays, the fictional plot involving invented characters is mixed in with real life. The main inspiration for FIAT workers during their month-long strike was the occupation at the Gdansk shipyards in Poland which led to the creation of the *Solidarity* trade union. Not only among bureaucrats in Eastern Europe, but also among many observers in the West, there was a deep level of shock and confusion as they tried to comprehend the fact that Polish workers were suddenly holding what had seemed to be an all-powerful regime to ransom by occupying their workplace.

Initially *Giovanni* laughs at these workers, obsessed by the involvement of the Catholic Church in their struggle. But when he speaks the very last lines of the play it is clear that now he understands that, while contradictory political influences are important, what really matters at the end of the day is that workers understand the huge power they wield when they take mass action. In essence Fo is arguing that individual battles may be lost or won but the struggle between workers and bosses will go on:

It's all a bit like Russian roulette, sometimes there are jobs, sometimes there aren't. But we don't like this game. We prefer to play another one.

To be honest us workers really have been ground down, we've practically got our arse on the ground. But beware, maybe slowly we'll rise to our knees, and then we'll get up on our feet. And we warn you: standing tall we always make a lovely impression! Oh I can see you smiling. But nobody expected Gdansk, did they?[35]

Regardless of this upbeat conclusion, the FIAT workers were defeated. In October an agreement was reached which 'laid off' 23,000 workers for a 30-month period at 93 per cent of their normal wages. Trade union activists and left-wingers were disproportionately selected by management, and in any event very few of those selected ever worked for FIAT again. The generation of workplace activists which had turned industrial relations upside down since 1968 was either effectively sacked or deeply demoralised. Productivity at FIAT factories rose by 30 per cent almost immediately, and over the next year absenteeism and lost hours declined tenfold. By early 1982, 12,000 workers had taken voluntary redundancy packages, union membership declined steeply and several factories were closed.[36]

Such a stark defeat for the working class had profound implications for Fo's work, an issue that will be taken up again in Chapter 6.

Mistero Buffo[1]

Mistero Buffo in History and in Theory

No book about Dario Fo can avoid talking about *Mistero Buffo* (*MB*) at length. Not only is it his most performed show – it has been estimated that up to 3 million Italians have seen him perform it – it is also the one in which his more theoretical ideas about theatre come into focus.

Franca Rame has stated that Fo began to collate pieces for *MB* as early as 1963, translating and rewriting many medieval texts from Latin and Provençal. However, even his first major work – *A Poke in the Eye* from 1953 – contained reworkings of stories such as Cain and Abel, Samson and Delilah.

Despite some rather wide of the mark criticisms, Fo has a consistent record in stating that he has elaborated these original texts, which often have a prominent religious content, for the purposes of his performances.[2] It is the exception rather than the rule for Fo to stick closely to an ancient text.

As has been seen in Chapter 1, Fo's theatrical traditions were rooted in popular storytelling and variety rather than classical or avant-garde theatre. This interest later encouraged him to research popular medieval theatre in Italy, and he became particularly interested in the role of the *giullari*, the travelling players who performed to townspeople or peasants in public squares.[3] This was a common art form throughout European society, given that similar figures can be identified such as the French *jongleurs* and Spanish *juglare*.[4] This was an earlier tradition to the better-known *commedia dell'arte*, which tended to be a performance art practised solely within a major court of nobles. Indeed many of the court performers were former *giullari* who had agreed to perform at a prince's court.

The *giullari* did not generally perform for the aristocracy or the Church, indeed they repeatedly criticised them and were often executed by being burnt at the stake, or alternatively had their tongues cut out; even when they died many were refused religious burial. According to Fo the *giullari* were particularly popular among the peasantry, as they frequently criticised the fact that peasants' lands had been seized by greedy landowners. Due to widespread illiteracy, the *giullari* also had a role in bringing news to local people; indeed Fo has repeatedly defined one of their functions as being 'the people's spoken newspaper'. Overall, perhaps, they could be considered as the 'illegitimate' or popular theatre of the period.

Fo recounts that *giullari* generally 'used to turn up in the streets of the town and reveal to people their own condition'.[5] This brief statement brings into focus a fundamental theoretical concept in all of Fo's work, which is derived from the Italian Marxist, Antonio Gramsci. It was no coincidence that the introduction to the first edition of *MB* contain a lengthy quote from Gramsci concerning the importance of working-class consciousness:

> It was through a critique of capitalist civilisation that the unified consciousness of the proletariat was or is still being formed, and a critique implies culture, not simply a spontaneous and naturalistic evolution ... Consciousness of a self which is opposed to others, which ... can judge facts and events other than in themselves or for themselves but also insofar as they tend to drive history forward or backward. To know oneself means to be oneself, to be master of oneself.[6]

Just like a *giullare*, Fo is attempting to make audiences become aware that their position in society is a consequence of the privileges and oppression perpetrated at their expense by another group in society, the ruling class. In a way this is the basic tenet of Fo's political theatre: opposition through knowledge, together with real understanding – not just a spontaneous explosion of outrage against injustice.

To return to the historical role of the *giullari*, people gathered around in the square and 'would set up a kind of make-believe trial of the noblemen, the rich, the powerful, and bosses in general. In other words, merchants, emperors, grasping moneylenders, bankers ... all of which anyway amount to more or less the same thing. Bishops and cardinals were also included.'[7]

Many of the performances of the *giullari* were based on their reading of the Bible and the Gospels, but the written versions, which were generally commissioned by either the Church or local princes, tended to omit the critical content and irreverent tones which dominated these performances. Therefore, Fo has not only tried to recreate the genuine nature of the performances that were given, but he has also attempted to reinstate the real content of the original scripts.

However, he is equally aware that such distortions of history and culture were not unique to Italy:

If we take for example Shakespeare's *Hamlet* and how they have familiarised us with it at school and in the theatre: he is blond, elegant, tall, romantic, someone who fights and with whom women fall in love ... this is how the bourgeoisie has introduced us to this author and character. But if we go and look at him as Shakespeare did, then you get a real people's reading of it. When you look at the original edition, the Jutland edition, you realise that Shakespeare said: 'Hamlet is plump, sluggish, a simpleton with his face full of freckles. He is a mummy's boy who always wants to be close to her. He lives for this and would always like to return between her legs.' Impotent ...

In the end his duel is a suicide, it is not a moment in which he fights. He is a man who lets himself be killed because he doesn't know how to struggle. This is the issue, if you start to read Shakespeare like this and perform it like this in front of people, there's no doubt that workers and everybody else will understand the meaning.[8]

This last point also illustrates the underlying basis for some of the criticisms which Fo has encountered: he is frequently thinking about a working-class audience and how any performance should try to relate to their experience which, particularly in the early years of *MB*, was one of massive and path-breaking struggles – often in opposition to union bureaucrats and Communist Party leaders. *Mistero Buffo*, and the political ideas underlying the plot, were also a weapon to be wielded against the cultural policy of the Communist Party:

The PCI always tends to put forward an inter-class position as it doesn't see culture as a class weapon. It more or less says the following: 'Today Shakespeare isn't revolutionary, but it's good that workers go and see his plays because he's a great artist.' Fine, but you have to read him in a revolutionary sense. What I mean is that if you use him for the proletariat he has one angle, if you use him for the bourgeoisie he has another. Culture isn't something neutral which everybody uses in an indiscriminate fashion: for example, you can make revolutionary use of Shakespeare and reactionary use of Brecht.

Then there is the question of 'who's in control'. If control means the intervention and the creative input of the working class, you produce alternative culture. If on the other hand your work arrives from on high then it's a conservative activity.[9]

One thing that Fo never tried to do was to create any sterile definition of popular or working-class theatre, or as he put it in a debate following one of the early performances of *MB*: 'People's culture doesn't just mean taking back the things which are obviously of the people – but also all the things that the boss has taken from this culture and developed in a particular way. We should tell people how these things were created and developed.'[10]

While Fo is perfectly happy partly to follow and acknowledge classical theatre, he is far from uncritical with regard to its origins and perspective: 'They've always told us that classical theatre is above everything and everyone, that it has nothing to do with class struggle. No, classical theatre is fundamentally a class theatre, planned, written and developed by one social class to defeat another.'[11]

So many of Fo's critics have been unable to grasp the simple notion that dominant ideas and ideologies are the product of struggles within society, that is, class struggles, and therefore they end up missing many of Fo's points. Moreover, their frequent lack of familiarity with and hostility towards working-class life simply increases their incomprehension. Today's cultural gurus attempt to locate culture beyond the tensions and conflicts of present or past societies; as Fo argues: 'Culture has always had a class basis. What is culture? It is a political vision of the world: a way of speaking ... it is choosing one thing rather than another, creating one form rather than another.'[12]

In reworking ancient texts Fo's intention was far from that of simply bringing unknown historical documents into the public domain. As he once explained, the mixture of past and present contained within *MB* made it a very potent work:

> I didn't want to conduct an archaeological exercise with *Mistero Buffo*. No. What I, and the other comrades with whom I conducted the research, were concerned about was the need to show that *another* culture exists. It is true that ruling-class culture exists, but this doesn't mean that there isn't another valid culture you can work upon in order to reappropriate it, to carry forward the idea of a proletarian culture.
>
> There are those who say, 'Because bourgeois culture is dominant, you need to start from that.' I say, 'Fine, we've got to be familiar with it, but it would be wrong if we based ourselves upon it.' We must start from the production of an autonomous culture of the oppressed classes, which is made up of criticism and struggle.[13]

Fo's dialectical and historical understanding of culture is naturally reflected in his use of language in *MB*, which in performance frequently involves almost incomprehensible medieval dialects, onomatopoeic sketches in various 'languages' called *grammelot*, as well as lengthy historical introductions. A linguistic content of this nature, performed to a working-class audience, could easily give rise to what Fo calls 'lexical terrorism':

> Words are used to terrify people. Some people employ lots of annotations or use little known words or mention scarcely known historical figures,

so as to virtually create a division among the audience. The result is embarrassment for the majority and the prestigious elevation of those few who know the origin or the synonyms of these words into a congregation, a gilded ghetto.[14]

The solution to these difficulties is quite simple: explain the meaning of these terms or use simpler words alongside the more obscure ones. This is something that Fo does throughout *MB*, which makes what is at times a linguistically complicated performance comprehensible to people who may not even be fully literate.

In practice Fo's theoretical intentions provoked a passionate response.

Mistero Buffo in Practice

The first public rehearsals of *MB* took place in May 1969 at the state university in Milan, in support of the student movement and its newspaper *Movimento Studentesco*,[15] with the first official performance being held on 2 October in a *Casa del popolo* just outside Milan. Fo recalls that a huge debate followed the performance: 'The question was raised as to whether the effort of rehabilitating popular culture was part of class struggle, whether it was worth it ... Some people thought I was right, others thought I was wrong. We carried on arguing until four in the morning.'[16]

Early performances were a real tour de force, with Fo using slides which illustrated medieval paintings, sculptures and miniatures, as well as performing for three and a half hours.[17]

Rame outlines both the first performance and how *MB* has evolved over the years:

> He did it as a reading, because he hadn't had time to learn it all by heart, but he improvised a great deal, and people were enthusiastic – the subsequent debates on popular culture were very heated.
>
> Gradually Dario worked out the right rhythm and structure through public performance, and began to perform individual pieces, talking about where he had found them, the significance of popular theatre, popular culture, and popular language, and how it had been continually stolen and mystified by the powers-that-be ...
>
> Besides being a play, *Mistero Buffo* is also a living newspaper, continually incorporating current news events and political and cultural satire into performances.[18]

Even right-wing newspapers, in this case the Turin-based daily, *La Stampa*, owned by FIAT, had to grudgingly admit the impact of *MB* at its Turin première:

A show that due to its deliberately educational structure (but not professorial nonetheless; difficult words are 'translated' immediately, philosophers or writers are never mentioned without explaining who they are) would appear to be a lesson or a lecture – or due to his frankly overt Marxism it could even be a speech at a rally. On the contrary: it is a real show, extremely lively and entertaining.

The audience were initially fearful and uncertain, but they gradually grew in courage and more and more comments were made. Discussions developed, rotating around Fo, who thunders against left-wing intellectuals (who in his opinion believe, or pretend to believe, that they are smashing the 'system' by eating away at it like woodworm, while all the time they are strengthening it); it all ended at nearly two in the morning.[19]

Given the lack of a fixed and permanent structure to *MB*, it was the part of Fo's repertoire best suited for the 'intervention' shows mentioned in Chapter 2 which, particularly in the period 1975–85, were generally held inside factories. It required no scenery or props, and generally Fo was the sole performer. As can been seen in Appendix C, requests arrived from a variety of sources, as Piero Sciotto recalls: 'It could be a representative of the factory council, or it could be a representative of one of these revolutionary groups which was particularly active in that factory, in that area, or in that struggle.'

The next step Sciotto took was: 'You made an appointment and you went there. You saw what the place was like.' As regards publicity, 'We had our own *Mistero Buffo* posters. So we put on a strip which said "Thursday 28 January" at the "Electrolux factory" in "Novara". But as soon it was known that Dario Fo was coming there was no need for posters.' Given the circumstances, preparations did not always go smoothly: 'Sometimes if there was no time we turned up without having made a visit beforehand. When we arrived they would say, "We're doing it in the canteen." You knew that the canteen was a place – whether the factory had 500, 1,000 or 6,000 workers – without very high ceilings. You adapted things to the situation.'[20]

Fo has sometimes proudly defined himself as a modern *giullare*, or the *giullare* of the working class. And it is not hard to see why: he would sometimes perform *MB* in medieval Italian inside an occupied factory full of modern machinery. Here he recalls one particular performance:

It was amazing to perform there, between all that machinery and using a truck as a stage. In one occupied factory somebody – maybe the police – had cut the power by throwing an iron bar into the generating station. Some workers then turned up with two lorries and they illuminated the stage with their headlights. But that wasn't enough, so they brought a small car on to the stage.[21]

In these performances Fo would regularly move from a medieval monologue about a Pope or a peasant uprising, to discussing the reasons behind the factory occupation, to the latest example of government corruption. It is not only the question of the lack of a fixed script which makes *MB* so original: Fo's performance is unique because he jumps in and out both of specific characters and of the Middle Ages. He explains the history of that period, but then talks about today as well. In a very tangible transposition, Fo is a modern *giullare* and his contemporary audience the equivalent of the peasants of the Middle Ages.

Following in the tradition of the *giullari*, Fo ensures that the audience has a role to play in the performance: 'The public is included in the performance because Fo believes in their intelligence. He speaks to them with a direct and candid simplicity that transforms spectators into Fo's co-conspirators against injustice.'[22]

Not only were factory occupations illegal, so too were theatrical performances inside them. The authorities, however, decided not to intervene, as Piero Sciotto explains:

Going inside factories and making trouble about the presence of actors, or Dario Fo, would only have aggravated the situation. An 'unacceptable act of censorship' would have occurred and the struggle would have become more visible. It was already difficult for them, because if Dario went there it all became more visible anyway. But if you then added on an act of repression it became even more visible – because it wouldn't have just been repression aimed at a factory, but also at Dario Fo! And they couldn't do this without paying a price. These events occurred in a kind of no-man's land. It's not as if they gave you permission to go and do the show, but there was nothing they could do about it.[23]

The unprecedented popularity that Fo enjoyed and the massive support shown when he was briefly arrested in Sardinia meant that 'Dario became untouchable – at least publicly'.

Even the Catholic Church, caught up in the social and political whirlwind of Italy during the 1970s, was not totally immune to the lure of *MB*. In June 1973 *The Commune* branch in the village of Vispa, near Savona, managed to get Fo invited to perform *MB* inside the local church. The village priest had agreed to the proposal, influenced by the fact that he had chosen to work in the local plastics factory, the major employer in the area; not surprisingly in Vispa the PCI gained 70 per cent of the vote at elections. The priest simply commented: 'The church is not only a house of prayer: above all it is a place where you can develop free men. And it can host anything which contributes towards that, even a show by Dario Fo.' Although the population of the village was just 600, over 1,000 people squeezed into the church, with many more being turned away.[24]

The Vatican's Response to *Mistero Buffo*

As long as Fo was performing *MB* to a left-wing working-class audience the Vatican was not particularly concerned. When the state television channel RAI decided to broadcast *MB* in April 1977 the Vatican became far more vociferous, as Fo would then reach a far wider audience, an audience that would in part probably agree with many of Fo's criticisms of the Church – indeed it would be the first time that many of them would ever encounter such criticisms.

Even before the end of the first 'episode' of *MB* the telephone of Giovanni Benelli, the Vatican's deputy secretary of state, was ringing. And the following Sunday an emergency meeting called by Secretary of State Jean Villot was held, which was also attended by Benelli and Agostino Casaroli, the Vatican's foreign minister. A proposal had emerged within the Vatican to provoke a diplomatic issue with the Italian government by threatening to break off relations if the following episodes were transmitted, but the meeting quickly discarded this hypothesis.

Instead they fell back on a series of long and harsh articles in *L'Osservatore Romano*, in which they accused Fo of 'encouraging the disintegration of the whole of Italian society'. One of the most frequent demands was to stop all future broadcasts. The Vatican's allies in the Christian Democrat party also carried the attack forward. A senior RAI (and Christian Democrat) manager, during a meeting of its monitoring committee, called Fo 'an ideological swindler, a liar, Jacques Tati's mongoloid brother, the true expression of the arrogance of television's power'.[25]

The Vatican's chief cardinal, Ugo Poletti, sent a telegram to the then prime minister Giulio Andreotti: 'Representing innumerable Roman citizens and organisations, expresses pain and protests against the television broadcast of Dario Fo's *Mistero Buffo* as blasphemous and anti-cultural, in addition profound humiliation for the inconceivable vulgarity of a public broadcast which degrades Italian nation in the eyes of the world.' In addition, the secretary of state called on priests to devote their sermons to condemning *Mistero Buffo* the following Sunday, and dozens of Catholic organisations tried to take Fo to court for blasphemy.[26]

The Vatican's press officer defined the programme 'as the most blasphemous show ever broadcast in the history of world television'.[27] Fo's immediate response was unrepentant: 'This is the best compliment the Vatican could have paid me.'[28]

However, Fo understood that there was far more at stake here than censorship, and in another interview he went on to explain the 'religious' aspect of *MB* further:

When I started to study the history of theatre a long time ago, and to do research into its origins, I realised that the majority of its texts were based on religious stories, and that it was impossible to bring the theatre of the *giullari* back to life without coming to terms with Christianity, its protagonists and its temporal power.

So bit by bit, year after year, I put together this show which has Christ, the Apostles and the Madonna as characters, and where saints, miracles and the Gospels are talked about. This is not because – as many people have asked me – I had suddenly become a Christian. I have always been a convinced atheist and Marxist and continue to be one.

But in researching medieval texts I came across this Christ figure far too often for me to ignore it. He had been transformed by the people into a kind of hero in opposition to the powerful and ecclesiastical hierarchies, who had on the contrary always tried to monopolise and keep him far away from the people. It's sufficient to mention that until well after the year 1000 people were not allowed to read the Gospels, and that their translation into the vernacular took place very late.

Yet the people did not accept their exclusion and had given life to a vast number of apocryphal Gospels, from which a different Christ emerged, he was more human and always on the side of the weakest. He had a lot of pagan, almost Dionysian, joy inside of him, for love, parties, beauty and earthly things. And at the same time he was full of hatred and violence towards hypocritical priests, the aristocracy who wanted to dominate the weakest, and a triumphant Church and its temporal power.[29]

Put simply, Fo's subversion of the traditional Christian message undermines some of the basic tenets of Western civilisation. What Fo puts in the place of a submissive Christ to some extent is the culture of ordinary people or, as a worker in another of Fo's plays once said: 'The people have a vast culture. Most of it has been destroyed and buried by the Church, the aristocracy, the bourgeois system.'[30]

For the Vatican what was probably the most worrying aspect was not the heavy irony and disrespect shown towards various popes and archbishops; it was the underlying message that the Bible's version of history was not accurate. As one senior official argued: 'One cannot see any reason which could possibly justify the authorisation of such a vulgar mystification of historical truths.'[31] To lose its monopoly on the interpretation of religious history would be a terrible blow for the Vatican.

Despite these arguments, which filled the front pages of newspapers for several days, the full series of broadcasts went ahead. Fo's understanding of this decision was purely political: 'We haven't been called back to television because someone's changed their mind, or because of a sudden gesture of generosity by television bosses.' The real reasons were 'the pressure of a current of thought, the struggles that the left has fought in recent years – also those that have carved out a cultural space. We're going back on television because we're one of the strongest cards that the left can play'.[32] Yet when the broadcasts were due to be repeated five years later, in the spring of 1982, RAI refused to do so. After criticising the decision, Fo announced he would partially make amends by performing extra shows of *Mistero Buffo* in Rome.[33]

The controversial reputation of *MB* also followed Fo to Argentina in May 1984. Even before Fo and Rame had arrived the archbishop of Buenos Aires had written strong condemnations of their work, with phrases such as: 'I would rather see the cathedral burn down than see the values of the Church and its teachings wounded.' Consequently, Catholic demonstrators often arrived at the theatre wearing T-shirts of Jesus and prayed in the foyer; disturbances broke out when the word '*Papa*' was used on stage (the word for 'Pope' is the same in both Italian and Spanish).

There was an even more disturbing presence alongside Catholic activists, however: that of fascists in leather jackets who repeatedly threw stones at the theatre's windows, up to third floor level. On the worst night of violence hundreds of actors and technicians from the major theatres in Buenos Aires abandoned their performances and came to do the job that the police were refusing to do: defend the theatre from attack. And the following morning 1,000 actors and technicians held a demonstration outside the theatre in support of Fo and Rame's right to perform.[34]

During one performance of *Mistero Buffo* there was absolute pandemonium when a demonstrator in the audience threw a bomb towards the stage; however, when it exploded it transpired it was 'only' a military tear gas canister. The many mothers of the *Plaza de Mayo* who were at the performance protected the demonstrator from a severe beating, saying: 'Don't hurt him. You should get angry with those bastards who gave him the order to chuck this bomb.'[35]

On Writing and Performing

Over the years different sketches have been inserted and discarded, and in a single *MB* performance Fo can play the role of dozens of different characters. Furthermore, all sketches are introduced by historical and theatrical explanations which are often longer than the sketch itself. Then there are the references to contemporary events, which can often constitute a significant part of the whole performance too. Because *MB* has no permanent form, no fixed script or precise period during which the events take place, what it has come to embody is the necessity for improvisation and the constant interplay between performer and audience. All in all, as one critic has observed:

By presenting a kind of fragmented iconicity – fragments of characters, fragments of actions and interactions – Fo has shaped a dramatic montage in which the shifting perspectives force a sense of community. There is no time to identify privately with one character or point of view; the spectator is too busy in every given moment, working on the collective creation of the event, an event which is tossed back and forth through the time and space of the theatrical protoplasm like Brecht's atomic particles of humankind.[36]

While Fo is quite happy to acknowledge his debt to Brecht and many other dramatists among whom he often mentions Ruzante and Molière, it is not enough to compile and debate a list of famous dramatists who have influenced him in order to understand his work fully. This is because Fo is probably motivated more by questions of performance than by the techniques and traditions of dramatic writing. As one expert on Fo has commented, the writers and performers he respects the most 'are more frequently regarded as purveyors of mere entertainment – strolling players, clowns, variety performers, farceurs and scriptwriters for various popular carnivals and fêtes.'[37]

As Fo explains, *MB* is not conventional or literary theatre: 'In a basically literary theatre ... The spectator is reduced to a voyeur: someone who is there to steal a naturalistic event that is proposed time and again as if it were real life.'[38] The structure of *MB* is clearly at odds with bourgeois or classical theatre, both as regards its performance style and its conception of the relative importance of following a script.

Fo had been developing these attitudes several years before first performing *MB*, even before leaving the rigidity of the bourgeois theatre. After the première of *I'll Think About it and Sing* in 1966 he said: 'I don't like wrapping a show up in cellophane straight after the first performance – it's the death of theatre. This is the very moment when you should make corrections, perfect it, maybe even start all over again.'[39]

Because of his conception of writing many Italian authors in particular have never viewed Fo as a dramatist, that is, a writer of theatrical texts. They therefore found it hard to hide their irritation when he was awarded the Nobel Prize for Literature. And Fo later joked that in the days immediately following the announcement, 'It seems that there were extra-ordinary sales of medicines for severe spasmodic abdominal pain. I know that many people were desperate, and somebody said that it was now pointless to continue writing.'[40]

Naturally enough Fo fundamentally disagrees with the viewpoint of these actors, writers and critics: 'These gentlemen who breathe forth the works of Shakespeare forget that his texts were outlines as well. Shakespeare said: "Words are theatre," and I think this Nobel Prize is a recognition of the value that words have on stage. Words can be written only after they have been used and chewed on stage on many occasions.'[41]

Again, Fo's concern about an audience's reaction to a performance is nothing exceptional in terms of theatre performances in Shakespeare's time, as one Shakespearian scholar has argued: 'The audience was an active participant in the collective experience of playgoing, and was not in the habit of keeping its reactions private.'[42]

Apart from monitoring audiences' reactions to various comic moments and taking note of what is said in debates, Fo here explains what other factors cause his texts to be always open to change: 'If we compare the first draft of every play with the final version we always notice a big difference. In some cases they are almost unrecognisable. These variations are also created from the fact that we feel we need to change things due to the pressure of current events, scandals and new political situations.'[43] The constant dialogue with a critical audience has meant continuous rewriting, but in turn this has contributed to an increase in a show's efficacy and also a sharpening of his political message. Writing and performing occur at a given moment in time, in a specific political situation; Fo has never intended his theatre to become an immobile monument of modern drama.

The problematic nature of theatrical texts and their relation to theatrical performances should not be viewed as particularly surprising. After all, as one critic has stated, theatre 'is a living, dynamic art whose completed form is the performance, an ephemeral product that changes with each audience. No performance lasts beyond its duration'.[44]

Indeed Fo doesn't just take this position as regards theatrical writing, but both writing in general and writers, who 'write in the silence of their rooms and their work remains a black mark on a page. They don't know how to communicate what they have written, the word dies with them. When I hear a poet read his poems I could shoot him'. And he goes on again to comment on what he thinks his Nobel Prize for Literature represents: 'They decided to award what lies at the origin of writing. Homer never wrote a line, he remembered and recited his poems. I know from experience that in theatre the act of writing comes late, after outlines and drafts.'[45]

Breaking the 'Fourth Wall'

One of the fundamental components of Fo's work has been an attempt to break down the 'fourth wall' of the theatre. While it is difficult to perform theatre without 'three walls' – the backdrop and the two sides, it is not essential that there should be a metaphorical 'wall' between the stage and the audience. Yet Fo argues that this is the case for most theatrical performances: 'People find themselves following events unfolding on stage as though they were themselves on the far side of a curtain, or of a fourth wall which permits them to see – while remaining unseen.'[46]

Consequently, during a Fo performance a deliberate effort is made to avoid creating an artificial barrier between actors and audience.

Because of his popularity and the fact that many of his shows are performed outside the commercial circuit at reduced prices, his performances are normally crowded, and he often spends the first few minutes of his shows directing people to empty seats and areas. He frequently has a drink in the foyer before the show, or talks with friends or striking workers in the audience, before walking on to stage from the stalls. Not only for many years was there a 'third act' of general discussion, but alternatively a striking worker or the victim of a miscarriage of justice was often given the microphone to explain their situation and ask the audience for support, with Fo either taking part in the discussion or just letting people speak for themselves.

Furthermore, for much of his career Fo has been against 'naturalism', the use of lots of objects on stage. The 'fourth wall', however, can also be made up of an extremely sophisticated lighting system and coloured filters, which according to Fo can 'create an aquarium atmosphere in which actors and props are immersed'. And it can also be the 'deathly pale make-up on actors' faces', so that the end result is that 'spectators find themselves in a situation in which they are voyeurs, spying on a tale which is nothing to do with them'.[47]

Fo frequently talks to the audience as Dario Fo – you are not 'at the theatre' in the bourgeois sense of the word. Indeed, during many of his performances in prestigious theatres it is often the middle-class members of the audience who end up feeling uncomfortable in familiar surroundings – whereas normally it is working-class people who don't feel at home at the theatre. He has often said that during his shows he tries to create an atmosphere in which the audience feels as if they were guests in his home.

The following description of a 1984 performance is a good example of Fo's relationship with an audience:

Lots of people have bought a ticket anyway, even though it means watching the show sitting on the floor. Half an hour before the start, and the protagonist is having a drink in the foyer bar.

Suddenly many people decide they're thirsty and go to the bar as well and we lose sight of him for a short while. A few minutes later he's on the stage talking with some technicians. Sitting in the stalls, we look on and wait – has the show already started? No, because Dario Fo begins, taking off his jumper and saying: 'All right let's begin, even if we're a bit early ...

'But please, make yourselves comfortable, we were all waiting for you,' he says, directing his remarks at some latecomers. 'Eh, I know how people who have booked over the phone think: I'll stay in the foyer

a bit longer because I've got a seat anyway ... and can you imagine the pleasure in making 19 people get up simultaneously?'
Inevitably the audience starts laughing.[48]

Alternatively, here he is using a more irreverent tone as he starts a show in 1976: 'You can still find spaces on the sides ... I mean you've left spaces beside your bums so you should all move a bit closer together. Sometimes people get on really well together and become close friends ... Get them in quicker, will you, Franca, otherwise we'll never get started.'[49]

A frequent definition of his post-1968 work used by both Fo and others has been 'throwaway theatre' in the sense that his work not only needs to be constantly updated, but that if you are to break down the 'fourth wall' then you should comment on recent events. As one writer observed in 1975:

> Since most of the plays deal with contemporary events and situations, they are given a certain run – usually a few months – and then discarded. History moves too fast, *The Commune* would say, for theatre pieces which require a lengthy job of interpretation, careful laborious construction, staging and rehearsal. New political issues are constantly arising, and the theatre has to keep up with them.[50]

Consequently, Fo frequently departs from the script and improvises some comments or sketch about current events; this is often done during an introductory monologue in which Fo outlines the show, which can sometimes last half an hour.

Apart from Fo's own identification with the tradition of the *giullari*, one of the reasons behind this concept of performing a 'throwaway theatre' was the fact that for many years after 1968 he no longer had large theatres and their resources to rely on – costumes, lighting engineers, a stable scenic structure and so on. And therefore, he says, 'It was in those years that I learned to work without stage sets or costumes, and rely on completely different resources such as sounds, gestures and words, which can be used to illustrate a situation.'[51] In other words there was no refinement, no aesthetically pleasing scenery, but just a straightforward message. Looking back on his pre-1968 theatre in 1974 Fo commented:

> Good heavens, if I think of the care I put into staging certain shows such as *The Lady is for Throwing Away* – 55 days of rehearsals, all the actors professionals, all of them learning to do somersaults, backward somersaults, to walk on their hands, to do the splits, to use their voices in falsetto like a clown, a training that never ended, I say to myself, 'How you've deteriorated in terms of technique and art.' But in terms of politics, in terms above all of changing ideological and cultural perspectives, I believe that this has been a step forward.[52]

While Fo's one-man shows, principally *Mistero Buffo,* have maintained the characteristics of being 'throwaway theatre' along with an effective demolition of the fourth wall, from the mid-1980s his ensemble pieces started to increasingly resemble the format of his pre-1968 period. This reversion has not taken place because Fo has ever rejected the usefulness of breaking the fourth wall or developed a critique of 'throwaway theatre'. The real explanation lies in the changes in the political situation, which have led to changes in the social nature of his audience, their political opinions, the disappearance of an alternative theatrical circuit and, most importantly, the sharp decrease in large-scale working-class struggles. Just as Fo has insisted that theatre is influenced by surrounding political ideas, so too has his own theatre evolved according to changing political circumstances.

The Power of Laughter

One of the stereotypes ascribed to Marxists and revolutionaries is that they have no sense of humour. It should be clear by now – and this becomes much clearer upon watching a Fo performance – that laughter is an essential part of his work. However, he also makes a political point as well as a theatrical point over its usefulness:

> If you can only believe in the revolution if you keep a straight face, with no irony, no grotesqueness, then I don't believe in it. But if we want to be 'illuminated' and negate the importance of the *giullare,* of making people laugh about the conditions they are subjected to ... well, we're not even Marxists, because what Marx says about the potentials of human civilisation is something completely different.[53]

Indeed Fo has often made the point that the level of public laughter, or satire on display in society, is closely related to the level of democracy. Speaking in 1979 he said:

> I don't understand this fear of laughter. I think we should look closely at one of the results of this fear – if you go to Russia today you notice there's not a single satirical play on there. Not a single one ...
> The end of satire is the first alarm bell signalling the end of real democracy. The person who said that really knew what he was talking about. That was Mayakovsky. He was censured to begin with, then he was banned, and then he was driven to suicide. And don't forget that Lenin was very fond of satire. He said, 'I'm no theatregoer, but I do understand the importance of Mayakovsky's satire.'[54]

In political terms, the objects of his satire are generally the rich and the powerful, or alternatively the political ideas of the left that he thinks are mistaken. He consciously avoids some of the comic targets 'of traditional bourgeois theatre, which always laughs at the weak or the marginalised'.[55]

Apart from the sheer artistic entertainment value, the purpose of laughter also has a mental and political use for Fo. While other emotions such as pity, anger or sadness can be psychologically liberating, Fo has often taken the view that 'laughter is a reflex of reason. Laughing at custard pies is obviously mechanical, but we don't do custard pies'.[56] Behind the buffoonery and hilarity of a Fo performance there lies a serious intention. Comedy must exist alongside tragedy: that is, together with themes such as hunger, injustice and the quality of daily life. As Fo explains: 'The moment you forget to use laughter, reason starts dying from suffocation. Irony is the irreplaceable oxygen of reason.'[57] The comic, the grotesque, turns things upside down, changes perspective, shows things differently.

Part of the genius of Fo, and the emotional appeal of much of his work, is that he discusses politics and teaches us while at the same time making us laugh.

The Downturn Period

Due to Fo's close involvement with the working-class struggle, the severe downturn in struggles was to mean a profound change in both the subject matter and circumstances of his theatre from the late 1970s onwards. Both Fo and Rame started to develop more and more interest in themes such as women's oppression in society as opposed to the 'collective' issues of working-class struggle. Furthermore, many of their shows were now written by both Fo and Rame, such as *Let's Talk About Women* and *All Home, Bed and Church,* and were performed as monologues by Rame.

An emblematic short play which touches upon very personal issues was Fo and Rame's partly autobiographical *Open Couple,* dating from 1983. Fo says of *Open Couple*:

> It is a grotesque story about a marriage which is collapsing. He, who is an unrepentant *Don Juan,* tries to persuade her that the modern thing to do is build up a store of different relationships. But when his wife takes him at his word and a finds a lover – who is also handsome and intelligent – the husband goes crazy and after various escapades blows himself and his house to pieces.[1]

Fo continues: 'For me writing *Open Couple* was an exercise in autobiography. Although certain dialogues were obviously transformed into a grotesque register, they reflected the discussions and arguments between me and Franca.'[2] This private tension later emerged publicly when Rame announced her separation from Fo in late 1986, a move which only lasted a few months.

The importance of such a subject matter is not so much that it has to do with the personal lives of Fo and Rame, but rather that the plot is emblematic of a variety of responses to a downturn in working-class struggle. Some activists began to experience crises in their relationships, others discovered drugs, religion or a totally different lifestyle or ideology. What was common to many people's experience was a feeling of disorientation, as *The Man* character (the one loosely based on Fo) says at the start of the play: 'I didn't dream up the downturn, it's something real. Isn't it true that with the defeat of so many struggles we've felt a bit frustrated, as if somebody's pulled the carpet out from under our feet? Look around and what do you see? Passivity, cynicism!'[3]

Not only had the hope which had characterised the post-1968 years substantially declined in political terms, but in terms of a theatrical audience there was a decrease in the receptiveness of a sounding board. In essence, to talk about a militant working class no longer seemed relevant or appropriate to as many people as before. One regular member of his audience recalled the political mood of Fo's public: 'The theatre was always full, but the audience was more and more depressed.'[4] Furthermore, the disappearance of the three small revolutionary parties of the 1970s was also a strong contributing factor in the decline and virtual disappearance of an alternative theatrical circuit in any stable or national sense.

Therefore, the underlying explanation – for both the different subject matter and a return to bourgeois theatres – was the decline of the working-class struggle: the audience Fo had fed off since 1968 – a militant working class – was now demoralised and politically confused. As one worker at the FIAT *Mirafiori* factory – the epicentre of many of the struggles of the 1970s – said in 1988: 'The last time we tried to put a picket line there was the during the renewal of the wage contracts of 1983. It cost us 20 names denounced to the police and one sacking. After that we stopped trying.'[5] Workers had started to lose confidence in their ability to change the world and increasingly they started to delegate the solution to their problems to trade union leaders or leaders of the PCI. Struggles were now much smaller and defensive than the mass struggles brimming with innovatory tactics which occurred a few years earlier. Instead of performing to thousands of workers on strike for higher wages, better conditions and so on, Fo and Rame's contact with workers became much more mundane. One example was their visit to three Alfa Romeo workers who had locked themselves in their union offices in protest at being sacked.[6]

Fo didn't resign himself quickly to these changed circumstances. For example, at the key turning point, September 1980, he was arguing:

> I'm not saying that there aren't reasons for thinking there's a crisis: it is perfectly clear and obvious that there's a crisis – but the problem is those people who turn laments on the downturn and defeat into a way of life. I'm reminded of how Sartre defined this attitude: 'the pleasure of shit'. Shit exists, but then there are those who sing about – *oh how lovely it is to swim in shit* – they write out long lists of all the different types and shapes. This isn't my approach: we try to connect with

workers, students and ordinary people. And we find that every time we raise these arguments they always respond positively.[7]

However, the continuing popularity of Fo's performances and his stubborn refusal to be overcome by a sense of demoralisation could not change objective reality.

Disorientation was such that in June 1980 Fo even felt obliged to convince people of the need to vote – 'We weren't given the vote as a gift by politicians, judges or multinationals' – while at the same time calling on people to vote for the far-left *Proletarian Democracy* party.[8] A few months later at the première of Fo's new play on terrorism a journalist wondered: 'Perhaps many want an "answer" from Fo.'[9]

The difficulty of this political and industrial downturn was that it didn't arrive with peals of thunder and bolts of lightning, but rather it gained ground surreptitiously. And similarly, Fo didn't suddenly and dramatically 'break' with the revolutionaries, the revolutionaries simply declined as a national force. As a former student activist of that period commented, a Fo performance was one of the few occasions where political despondency and abandonment were not the dominant mood: 'People weren't going to see him because he had sold out, or because his plays showed that he had sold out.' By the mid 1980s the most enjoyable part of his shows for a political audience were his lengthy unscripted intro-ductions, in which Fo would often improvise and comment on contemporary political events:

> Even if people went back home saying, 'Well, Fo has created something pretty mediocre,' they forgave him the weaknesses of the text which had been written and performed and said, 'What about the first bit? He's the same as he always was, a great actor engaging in militant criticism, laughing at the powerful.'[10]

Similarly, Fo's return to the commercial circuit took place without any ideological explanations or justifications. Circumstances slowly forced it to happen.

Initially this occurred in early 1981, and then more comprehensively during the 1981–82 season. The first play performed in these circum-stances was *Trumpets and Raspberries*, which premièred at the *Cristallo* theatre in January 1981, with full price tickets costing £3.25, *Commune* members paying £2.75 and students £2.15. Low ticket prices were the essential condition for Fo's return to the commercial circuit. Later in the year the owner of the *Odeon* theatre, the scene of many of his successes during the 1960s, invited Fo and Rame back. Again, one of the essential conditions of the agreement was the lowest prices in a major theatre: £5.40 (with a £1.10 discount for group bookings). As Rame, who was due to perform *All House, Bed and Church*, explained: 'Believe me, Dario and I are tired of performing in places which are difficult or dangerous. Above all we're tired of making people uncomfortable.'[11]

On a broader level *The Commune* had applied to return to playing the major urban theatres under the control of the *Ente Teatrale Italiano* (ETI), the Italian Theatre Board. In autumn 1981 contacts appeared to lead to some kind of agreement, although in October a dispute erupted over pricing. If ETI's policies were to be followed, season ticket-holders would pay £9.75 and non-season ticket-holders £13, whereas *The Commune* wanted lower prices. ETI also insisted on what *The Commune* defined as a very harsh percentage contract: 70 per cent of takings would go to *The Commune*, and 30 per cent to the theatre.[12] All of this was a far cry from what Fo was saying about the management of national theatre in 1975: 'Everything depends on the same old swindles in smoke-filled rooms, on what contacts you've got, whether you're part of the "club" or not. This big merry-go-round, which essentially decides whether you live or die, is called ETI.'[13] What is revealing here is *why* Fo had returned to the wheeling and dealing of the commercial circuit: it was simply because the alternative circuit had died. Although he would still perform in occupied factories and at other political events, the sizeable revolutionary milieu of the early 1970s now had very little organisation on the ground, the PCI was less and less interested in the kind of politics Fo represented, but most of all millions of previously radical workers were either politically disoriented, cynical or unemployed. By the early 1980s the networks and audience Fo had worked with during the 1970s had essentially disappeared.

In the first few years of Fo and Rame's return, low ticket prices certainly were guaranteed for their shows. Yet in early 1982 the price for their show in Bologna had risen to £5. It has to be said that this was still a low price in relative terms, as Fo explained: 'We increased tickets to £5 when we realised that we were worth less than two *Coca Colas*, an ice cream and a *cappuccino*.'[14] But over the years prices crept up as the mass movement continued to decline. One typical complaint in late 1982 – and these complaints often emerged because *The Commune* would talk to the press about the details of their negotiations – was from a cultural association in Padua, who protested that tickets cost £5.75 and that Fo and his company demanded 40 per cent of takings plus £1,865.[15]

During this period Fo made the point that it wasn't just ticket prices that led him to leave commercial theatre in 1967, it was also the season ticket system: 'It sometimes happened that we performed in theatres that were empty, despite the "sold out" signs in the windows outside. How come? They were seats reserved for season ticket-holders.'[16] Yet the season ticket system, which obviously allows theatres to make financial plans, was essentially upheld for Fo's performances. So Fo would sporadically insult these season ticket-holders, who were normally rich middle-class people who would simply come to a performance because they had already paid for their ticket: 'Season ticket-holders are ordered, forced, they go to the theatre because they get their call-up papers.'[17] Generally they made up the first eight rows of the stalls, and in press interviews Fo would sometimes really go to town about this: 'The first eight rows are a sea of mediocrity. We're performing for the ninth row backwards.' A non-season ticket-holder recalls: 'They would often not realise Fo was poking fun at them ... He wasn't able to perform a show without laughing at them, he had to unburden himself of the disappointment of performing to season ticket-holders.'[18]

Essentially, in political terms, Fo was shouting in the dark: to reach a mass audience he now had to make compromises he had refused to make since 1968. There is nothing very surprising in this change of venues: Fo was first and foremost a man of the theatre with left-wing ideas, so when a mass left-wing movement declined it was only to be expected that his theatre changed both as regards its performance environment and the subject matter of his plays.

As theatrical performers, Fo and Rame no longer felt duty bound to respond to the demands of a movement which was now a shadow of its former self. Looking back in 1983 at the preceding years of political activism, Rame put things quite graphically: 'We had Mao Zedung shoved up our backsides, Gramsci stuffed up our noses, Lenin coming out of our ears.'[19] As a result of all these changes, as Rame explains: '*The Commune* is no longer a theatrical collective. It has returned to being actor-managed. Formally it is the property of Dario and myself.'[20] Two years later Fo placed this new arrangement in a broader context: 'There was an evolution, determined by external conditions and circumstances – the reality of the political situation for example.'[21]

Nevertheless, Fo and Rame kept faith with their beliefs and supported causes which experienced far lower levels of support than in earlier years and campaigns which were often defensive or symbolic. In June 1981 he performed to 4,000 people in Pisa in a benefit show for the newspaper *Lotta Continua*.[22] Another example among many which illustrates his continued commitment was a performance at a 4,000-strong festival in Milan organised by *Proletarian Democracy* in 1987, called in opposition to the massive power of the FIAT car company, which had managed to sack five workers at the Alfa-Lancia factory. Fo arrived at 11 p.m., after having performed in the revival of *Accidental Death of an Anarchist* earlier in the evening.[23] When factories were in dispute Fo and Rame would now perform outside the factory gates rather than inside an occupied factory.[24]

While the main explanation for a general decline in left-wing ideas lies in a far lower level of working-class struggle, alongside this was the disorientation caused by left-wing terrorism – very much a symptom rather than the cause of the decline.

Left-wing Terrorism and *Trumpets and Raspberries*

One of the political undercurrents thrown up during and after 1968 was an idealisation of political violence. Not only would young activists praise the military commitment shown by individuals such as Che Guevara, but the war of national liberation being waged in Vietnam was also subject to something verging on hero worship. This uncritical attitude has now become a constant of the Italian far left: moving from the Vietcong to the PLO, the IRA, the ANC, the Sandinistas in Nicaragua, the Zapatistas in southern Mexico and since the collapse of the Eastern Bloc, Castro's regime in Cuba. As each movement is defeated, or slowly mutates into a party openly managing national capitalism, many activists blindly move on to the next campaign without ever understanding the political weaknesses associated with such movements.

Italian history also suffers from a further complication: the successful anti-fascist Resistance movement of 1943–45, largely led by communists. No serious Italian politician or historian would deny that armed resistance played a vital role in bringing about the end of fascism and the creation of democracy, hardly an insignificant political movement in anyone's books. This heady mixture of recent Italian history (also embodied by many of these activists' parents, often long-term PCI members) and ongoing national liberation struggles was a constant source of inspiration for young activists. However, their enthusiasm for these movements was largely uncritical; and at times the political objectives and practice of these struggles were overlooked in favour of the moralistic praise of military courage.

All of this was a harmless undercurrent in the years following 1968 until some activists, frustrated by the lack of a revolutionary situation by the early 1970s, decided to take up arms themselves. Initially, these activities involved relatively low levels of violence, such as the temporary kidnapping and interrogation of hated factory managers; actions which many workers approved of. For several years the small revolutionary parties refused to distinguish themselves substantially from these tiny terrorist groups, defining the individuals as 'comrades who make mistakes'. For example, at the June 1974 *Lotta Continua* conference party leader Adriano Sofri referred to 'the exemplary actions of the Red Brigades'.[25] Members of terrorist organisations were therefore able to use the widespread political sympathy on the far left, and their shared activity in previous struggles, in order to gain some logistical help.

The moralistic exaltation of individual courage which sometimes characterised the far left meant that the basic tenets of revolutionary politics – which both the far left and terrorist groups claimed to follow – had not been understood at all: 'They all forget that workers, even revolutionary party members, will only take revolutionary action when *they* themselves feel that a transformation of society is necessary. It is not revolutionaries who *make* revolutions; it is the mass of workers. The task of revolutionaries is to lead these workers, not substitute for them.'[26] Essentially a few hundred individuals – and even in its period of major activity, that is 1970–82, the Red Brigades never had more than 500 members – decided to substitute themselves for the lack of activity of millions of workers.[27]

This substitutionism was to have disastrous consequences. The early collusion between the far left and terrorists in a period of relatively low levels of violence became far more of a concern when terrorism grew larger and more violent during the late 1970s, a period in which one of the state's responses was to enact a series of repressive laws that brought fear and demoralisation to much of the far left. The key law was the power to hold anyone accused of terrorism in preventative custody for up to eleven years, without any need to provide evidence.[28]

Fo and Rame had faced accusations of being linked to terrorists as early as 1972, probably as a result of their activity in helping left-wing prisoners. As the accusations became more and more frequent, a revealing exchange once took place between Fo and Rame at a press conference, when Fo stated that with many of these allegations: 'Their technique is that of shit-stirring – you insinuate, you insinuate, you do things in such a way that people see a newspaper headline about the Red Brigades and our photo underneath.' Rame then complained: 'It's not possible to go on like this. A month doesn't go by in which they're not attacking us.' Fo disagreed: 'Franca, this is an emotional viewpoint. You can't really respond to the idea of not carrying on. We're definitely carrying on, it's clear now what their game is.'[29]

For the left as a whole unsubstantiated accusations of involvement in terrorism were becoming increasingly commonplace by the mid-1970s. These accusations were then frequently followed by lengthy periods of imprisonment and long drawn-out legal cases. It is ironic that during these years, unknown to Fo and Rame, their son Jacopo was briefly a sympathiser of the left-wing terrorist group *Front Line*.

In any event, one early example of Fo and Rame's understanding of the debilitating effect of accusations of terrorism was to call a march in Piedmont in July 1975. It left the gates of the FIAT *Lingotto* factory at 11 a.m. on a Saturday morning to march to Fossano jail, to demand the release of Giovan Battista Lazagna, a PCI member, who had been a partisan commander during the Second World War and had been awarded a silver medal of the Resistance. He had been arrested nine months earlier because somebody had accused him of being a theoretician of the Red Brigades,[30] but throughout his period of imprisonment no proof had been presented – under this law no proof had to be presented, even though suspects could be held for eleven years.

The previous evening Fo had performed *Fanfani Kidnapped* to 11,000 people in the city, so perhaps it is not surprising that a crowd of 1,000 assembled to start the march. It had also been officially supported by the National Association of Italian Partisans, the far-left organisations PDUP, *Lotta Continua, Avanguardia Operaia* and the *Movimento Studentesco*. Furthermore, factory councils, democratic lawyers and French partisans had also given their support. One of the most famous marchers was Pietro Valpreda, the anarchist who had been framed and imprisoned for several years for the 1969 bombing in Milan.

Not only is this event significant as one of the first examples of protest against the witch-hunting of the left, but it is also a useful example of the drawing power of Fo and the political use he could make of his mass support. On the first evening of the march he and others performed folk songs for the marchers, while on the second night 3,000 people squeezed into the main square of the small town of Fossano to see him perform *Fanfani Kidnapped*. A local journalist observed that the square 'looked out over kilometres of the Cuneo plain, it was packed, there was no room for anyone else. Some people were perched up in trees, and only half enjoyed the show out of fear of falling off. Others followed the show sitting behind the stage'.[31]

Despite much of the far left's confusion over terrorism, Fo always took up a critical position against it: 'Terrorism never destabilises the established rule; rather it strengthens it, since it destabilises the opposition which is thus forced, in order to avoid being suspiciously drawn in as a cover to terrorism, to accept, support and allow those laws and those uncontrollable, violent acts which will in fact be used against citizens and workers.'[32]

Hindsight has proved Fo to be largely correct. The rise of terrorism facilitated the PCI's move to the right in the mid-1970s, and the party's close links with the working class meant that millions of workers started to head in the same direction. In the long term this strategic decision contributed to a slow but steady decline in PCI membership and electoral support throughout the 1980s. In the short term, as Fo argued in September 1977: 'If we understand this situation, we also understand that to put forward the idea of an "armed party" is madness ... it is mistaken and damaging. It is vital to understand the current situation and the balance of forces.'[33] In essence the situation was such that the working class was moving to the right, and yet the terrorists were acting as if millions of workers were moving to the left and were already revolutionaries.

An even worse consequence than the PCI's move to the right was the refound unity among the Christian Democrats and the opportunity given to the state to criminalise much of the far left. In one interview Fo defined this as the 'sandstorm method':

The important thing is the sandstorm, to raise hell, to dazzle, to create a scene. The newspapers and television do not even bother saying any more, 'They say,' 'It appears that,' 'There is a suspicion,' no: they say 'is' and 'it is certain!' Expect that the next day all is denied, in a hush, between the lines.

In this 'blizzard,' where everyone is screaming, '*He* has the plague,' power has freed itself first of all from the presence of the so-called front-line democrats, the intellectuals, the artists, the freethinkers.[34]

The situation had many parallels with the 'strategy of tension' employed about ten years earlier: there was an establishment campaign to associate hundreds of thousands of left-wingers with terrorism. In 1980, at the height of the hysteria and paranoia, Rame brought on to the stage the wife of an ex-student leader of 1968. The man was severely ill in jail, where he was being held on remand on charges of terrorism.[35] Such actions cost them dearly in other ways too; it appears to be one of the main reasons behind the refusal of American authorities to grant them a visa for several years.

Trumpets and Raspberries (in Italian, the word 'raspberries' refers to the rude noise and not the fruit) dealt with left-wing terrorism to some extent, but to a far greater extent it was a farce which had as its main theme the state's relationship to big Capital – what links the two themes together is the kidnapping of the FIAT boss, Gianni Agnelli.

This show represented a significant turning point in Fo's career: firstly, it was presented in a conventional Milan theatre in early 1981, as the *Palazzina Liberty* was by now in a bad state of repair, and it was also his first ensemble piece in five years, that is one involving both himself and a whole group of actors. Fo has hinted that the decline in struggle and the fear of repression induced by terrorism contributed to such a long silence; another contributory factor was the very speed and escalation in terrorist violence. The kneecappings of the early 1970s had turned to murders by the mid-1970s and culminated in the kidnapping and murder of Christian Democrat leader Aldo Moro in 1978, after he had been in a 'people's prison' for 55 days. There then followed widespread state repression, so that all in all, 'There was neither the time nor the possibility to decant the events, to create a synthesis from them.' And even after nearly a month of open rehearsals with debates Fo admitted: 'There are still very few certainties. But this is also the moment in which we can try to understand: up until what point has terrorism been exploited and used, by whom, and for what reason?'[36]

In the play the planned kidnapping of Agnelli by left-wing terrorists goes wrong, in that in a moment of confusion the identities of Agnelli and one of his assembly line workers at the *Mirafiori* factory, *Antonio*, are mixed up. A badly injured and facially disfigured Agnelli is rescued from the aftermath of a terrorist attack and is thought by everyone to be one of his militant workers. The comic vehicle of the play is thus one of mistaken identity: that of Agnelli being thought of as *Antonio* (although both characters are later referred to as *The Double*). The amusing nature of the mistaken identity is that Agnelli and *Antonio* are at the opposite ends of the social scale: the former being the most powerful capitalist in Italy and the latter a worker in what had historically been one of the most anti-capitalist workplaces in the country.

Due to his injuries Agnelli is unable to speak, and therefore to convince people of his real identity. Whereas once *Antonio* understands he has saved his hated boss he too has his reasons for pretending to be Agnelli: 'If my workmates at *Mirafiori* find out about it, when I turn up for work they'll greet me with a bulldozer! They'll push me up against a wall and execute me by spitting at me!'[37]

Towards the end of the play Agnelli starts to write letters identical to those written by Aldo Moro during his imprisonment by the Red Brigades in 1978, demanding his release in exchange for political prisoners. Although Agnelli's kidnapping was fantasy, Fo was making a direct comparison with this real-life kidnapping which occurred three years earlier. On this occasion Moro's party colleagues preferred to let him die despite the many pleas he made in letters released by his captors, in which he proposed to exchange his freedom for that of left-wing terrorists currently being held in jail. Agnelli's theatrical kidnapping allowed Fo to make the following point about the basis of the state: 'If Agnelli were kidnapped would the state's behaviour be the same as that of its major leaders during Moro's kidnapping? In essence – is the state that unitary and heroic thing they want us to believe – or is it rather a support for real power, economic power, Agnelli's power?'[38]

This is why in the concluding speech of the play *The Double* – about to reveal himself as Agnelli – explains:

> These days only we captains of industry study *Das Kapital* ... Especially where it says: 'The only true power is financial-economic power, in other words, holding companies, markets, banks, commodities ... In other words, Capital.'
>
> And then he adds a sentence, which children should memorise and sing in the playground: 'The sacred laws of this state ... the economic state ... are written on watermarked paper money. So government, state and institutions are nothing other than supporting services, for the real power, which is economic power.' Supporting services ... you see? So, Aldo Moro was sacrificed in order to save the respectability of the aforementioned financial state, not for the supporting services, for which nobody gives a damn! Get it into your heads: I am the state![39]

In essence Fo is arguing that the state is the representative of big Capital, and in the hypothetical case of the most powerful capitalist being kidnapped, it would react differently to the real-life case of Aldo Moro.

This central theme on the nature of the state was largely overlooked as the play also touches upon terrorism and, given the hysterical climate concerning terrorism at the time, reviewers and politicians concentrated on this issue.

The Christian Democrats and the right wing predictably attacked the play for condoning terrorism, or at least making light of it. As was the case with political violence in the north of Ireland for many years, the major parties demanded a ritual and absolute condemnation of it, often using this as a smokescreen to avoid a discussion about what was causing the violence in the first place. Fo was forced to explain patiently the links between the nature of the Italian state and the phenomenon of terrorism, or how hysterical condemnations of terrorism and the suspension of basic civil liberties helped to reinforce the state and the party at the heart of it. More than a year after the show's première he was still trying to explain above the clamour: 'People refuse to see the degeneration of the state. The mistaken response to terrorist lunacy is a child of the state.'[40]

The PCI too was equally hostile, entitling its review of the play 'It isn't Agnelli who's been kidnapped, but Fo's talent'. Fo was apparently using the play 'to speak about something else, to move on to the ground from which the most disturbing wounds of postwar history have emerged'. This insinuation – that Fo was a supporter of terrorism and justifying it in his play – was common to many other parties. The PCI felt particularly aggrieved, as Fo often combined the common definition of the PCI being the party of 'firmness' in its refusal to negotiate with terrorists, with it becoming a 'party of death' by condemning kidnap victims to be killed by terrorists. Again, the PCI's accusations were deadly serious, given the widespread use of preventative custody implemented purely on the basis of unsubstantiated allegations. The PCI's daily found that Fo was 'in harmony with that viewpoint which has oscillated between negotiations and even darker behaviour, and he brands the so-called "party of firmness" as the "party of death"'.[41]

Although the PCI had been strong on 'law and order' for many years, its hysteria in this case was also due to the political situation of the time. A month before Fo's new play premièred, the Red Brigades had kidnapped Judge Giovanni D'Urso, condemning him to death. Two weeks later a revolt broke out at Trani high security prison, where many terrorist suspects were held. Indeed, D'Urso was only released the day after the play's première.[42]

During D'Urso's kidnapping, however, the government had decided to allow negotiations behind the scenes, although all major parties called for a press blackout on statements made by terrorists – indeed two journalists who published an account of D'Urso's interrogation by the Red Brigades were arrested. This was the climate in which Fo and Rame's decision to allow three female relatives of those prisoners involved in the Trani jail revolt to take the stage at the end of the first night's performance occurred. Their reading of a statement which essentially demanded better living conditions in jails was a common enough occurrence in Fo's theatre, but in the atmosphere of that period Fo received the worst press of his career.

The PCI's reviewer was semi-hysterical:

> It is violent to have brought three women who were visibly upset, with tears in their eyes, on to the stage. The violence was also directed at the audience, who largely left the theatre in silence, something which appeared to us to be an extremely civilised demonstration of dissent which went to the very heart of this so-called 'theatre'.[43]

Undeterred, on some nights Rame would ask the audience to come up on to the stage before the show and sign a petition demanding the abolition of high security jails and better health treatment for inmates. Despite the press hysteria the play was a great success, with the 34 Milan shows totalling an audience of 50,000 spectators.[44]

The hysteria continued for months. Fo calmly answered the criticisms of the statement made on the first night:

> As far as it concerns me and my theatre nothing new happened ... to be honest after the show the problem of Italian prisons was discussed. Just as in the past we have discussed similar problems, such as strikes or occupied factories ... If providing people with information about everyday political events is holding a rally, well yes, we held a play and a rally.[45]

In his opening introductory monologue, which changed every night, Fo would attack a sacred cow of the Italian political system, Leo Valiani, a life senator. He was an 'untouchable' because he had taken part in the anti-fascist Resistance movement, but Fo attacked him for both being prominent in the refusal to negotiate the release of Aldo Moro in 1978, and his defence of eleven-year periods of preventive custody. Fo renamed him a 'death senator'.

The leader of PCI senators then attacked Fo in a parliamentary debate, describing his actions as 'belonging to the foulest fascist sub-culture' and expressed his support for Valiani, to thunderous cheers from the chamber.[46] The PCI daily then published a letter from Fo, which detailed the extreme conditions that both inmates and their relatives had to endure in certain maximum security jails. In responding to Fo's letter, the paper insisted that his action 'merits repulsion and disgrace'. In discussing his use of the prison relatives' anguish, the PCI daily again made the same insinuation, claiming it was 'only an alibi for inexcusable leniency, if not worse'.[47]

None of these revolting insinuations affected the popularity of the play. *The Commune* has calculated that 60,000 paying spectators saw the first 50 performances,[48] with a total of 25,000 attending in Turin, 24,000 in Florence, and 2,300 people per performance in Rome. In Naples the show was in such demand that ticket touts were operating outside the theatre.[49]

Obviously conscious of the public's support, Fo and Rame continued their campaign in favour of prisoners' rights. At a performance of *All House, Bed and Church* near Genoa in November 1981, a woman read out a document before the show attacking police harassment of people accused of links with terrorism without a shred of evidence. A PCI councillor, head of the council's cultural committee, immediately wrote a letter to the local police: 'As regards this incident I wish to make it clear that neither myself nor any of the organisers were aware of such intentions, as it amounted to a serious impropriety for which the company will have to accept all responsibility.' The councillor ended his letter expressing solidarity with the police's battle to defeat terrorism.[50]

Fo and Rame were among the few prominent Italians to question the actions of their government concerning terrorism, indeed these actions were so serious that Amnesty International began to investigate the Italian legal and penal systems during this period. As with *Accidental Death of an Anarchist*, in *Trumpets and Raspberries* the serious political point that Fo was making concerned the nature of the state. The play has very little to say about terrorism, which remains a background phenomenon. Indeed, there are no deaths in the play and the use of guns is merely farcical.

The Tale of a Tiger

The underlying difficulty that Fo was facing by the latter half of the 1970s was the downturn in struggle, which had made many of the political messages that had been central to his work since 1968 – the strength of workers' culture and struggle, and the creation of a fundamentally different society – appear more abstract and remote. And Fo's theatre had never been characterised by abstract subject matters and remoteness from current social and political issues.

Perhaps Fo's first attempt to grapple with this downturn in an explicit fashion was in his monologue, *Tale of a Tiger*, first performed in September 1977 in Bologna, with a more definitive performance later given at the *Palazzina Liberty* in February 1978.[51] In the introduction Fo explains: 'It's a hopeful piece, just at a time when negativity and a general collapse of ideals seem to be the dominant forces in our everyday lives.'[52]

The tale is an allegory taken from a Chinese folk tale, and even this is probably a revealing choice: Fo could no longer point realistically to real and inspiring struggles which were taking place in Italy at the time. This fact was not lost on a reviewer of an early performance who, while praising the performance, noted that for Fo it possessed an uncharacteristic 'lack of clear references to current politics'.[53] The seeds sown by terrorism had reaped a whirlwind of repression and disorientation. At the end of another performance a second journalist noted: 'Even Fo, although he reminded his audience about those who are struggling and those who are in jail, is worn out, his fire is waning. Even he, like many of us, feels the cold winds blowing.'[54]

These objective political difficulties were overcome by Fo's outstanding performance, indeed at 50 minutes this is his longest monologue. Although set in China, much of the subject matter – peasant life and family arguments – is strongly embedded within Italian culture. The monologue recounts the story of a member of the Chinese Communist Party's Long March of 1934–35 who is wounded and ends up being sheltered by tigers. But Fo again makes the explicit point that the purpose of telling the tale is to illustrate a broader issue:

> In China, the she-tiger has a very specific allegorical meaning: you say that a woman, a man, or a people 'has the tigress' when they make a stand. At a time when most people are running away, giving up, taking to their heels, ditching the struggle, getting cynical, in short, coming to the point where they run down both themselves, and all the acts of generosity they performed in the past ... the people who 'have the tigress' don't do this, they resist![55]

It is clear here that Fo is transposing a Chinese folk tale to the 1968 generation, many of whom had by now drifted out of the radical political commitment which had been the lifeblood of much of Fo's activities.

However, Fo's concerns were not perhaps just focused on the growing return to private life. In the following quote, again from the introduction, he comes very close to criticising the Chinese Communist Party and its recently deceased leader, Mao Zedung:

> The tiger also has another allegorical meaning and this is perhaps the most important. A person 'has the tiger' when they never delegate anything to anyone else, when they never expect other people to solve their problems for them even when the person to whom those problems might be delegated is the most valued of leaders, a leader who has shown his capacities on countless occasions, perhaps the most honest and trusted of party secretaries ... No! Never! People who 'have the tiger' are those who undertake to be inside the situation, to play their parts, to monitor and watch, to be present and responsible to the ultimate degree. Not out of any sense of suspicion, but in order to avoid

that blind fidelity which is a cancer, a stupid and negative element of the class struggle, the enemy of both reason and revolution.[56]

Sadly, Fo's criticisms of Chinese 'communism' – which was being increasingly revealed as a sham – never really went further than this. One reviewer noted that 'It invites us to reflect upon today's China, that of Hua Kuofeng and Deng Xiaoping',[57] but revealingly the journalist does not draw any conclusions from this reflection. However, Fo's muted criticism can only be expected: after all he was a theatrical artist who since 1968 had been deeply immersed in an enthusiastic but raw political movement – he never made any claims to be a political scientist or political leader. The important point is that both Fo and the movement he was part of, in a collective sense, failed to understand the nature of the Chinese regime from the point of view of 'classical Marxism' – that the creation of a socialist or communist society could only be achieved by the activities of millions of working-class people. Disorientation increased throughout the 1980s as it became clear that the Chinese economy was run along capitalist and not communist lines, and the lack of any democracy was starkly revealed in the Tiananmen Square massacre of 1989.

Despite the downturn in working-class struggle and the demoralising revelations emerging from China, *The Tale of a Tiger* still packed a political punch. Most of the monologue describes how the tigers help the wounded soldier to recover from his wounds and then all move down from the mountains, where some villagers use the tigers to see off the right-wing nationalist forces of Chiang Kai Shek. The concluding section of the monologue details the continuous demands from 'the party' for the peasants to return the tigers back to the forest, that is, not to use them any more. It begins with a party political commissar telling the peasants: 'They lack dialectics. We cannot assign a role in the party to tigers, and if they have no place in the party, then they have no place at the base either. They have no dialectics. Obey the party. Take the tigers back to the forest.'[58]

Yet the peasants disobey and hide the tigers, later using them to repel the Japanese invasion. Another party commissar then comes along and, in a clear parallel to the revelations which emerged in the 'Gang of Four' trial of 1980 and other public power struggles within the Chinese Communist Party leadership, tells the peasants: 'You did well to disobey that other party commissar, the last time, because, apart from anything else, he was a revisionist, a counter-revolutionary. You did well ...! ... But as from now on, you won't need them any more ... Take the tigers back into the forest now!'[59]

The peasants hide the tigers again and use them once more when Chiang Kai Shek's nationalists attack them with American weapons. The party arrives again, but in Fo's description its increasing bureaucratisation is clear: 'All the leadership, with their flags in their hands ... And the flags were waving ... and they were applauding us! The fellows from the party, and those from the army. And the higher coordinating intermediary cadres. And the higher, higher intermediary central coordinating cadres.'[60]

Fo's argument here is clear: the party leadership is terrified of the peasants' capacity for independent thought, their potential power – and by implication, the power of urban workers too. Yet, because they cannot convince the peasants to get rid of their tigers they make a fairly worthless concession, first saying they can put them in a museum, but then suggesting they be kept in a zoo so that visiting tourists can see 'the tigers of the revolution'.

The peasants rebel again, and the response of the leadership, which ends the whole monologue, develops into an excellent example of the bureaucratic mumbo-jumbo which had now become the norm for communist parties all over the world:

Obey! You don't need them now, any more. There's no need for the tigress now, because we don't have any more enemies. There's just the people, the party and the army. And the people and the party and the army are one and the same thing. Naturally, we have a leadership, because if you don't have a leadership, you don't have a head, and if there's no head, then one is missing that dimension of expressive dialectic which determines a line of conduct which naturally begins from the top, but then develops at the base, where it gathers and debates the propositions put forward by the top, not as an inequality of power, but as a sort of series of determinate and invariate equations, because they are applied in a factive coordinative horizontal mode – which is also vertical – of those actions which are posed in the positions taken up in the theses, and which are then developed from the base, in order to return from the base to the leadership, but as between the base and the leadership there is always a positive and reciprocal relationship of democracy ...[61]

The final act of the monologue sees the peasants releasing the tigers, which then chase off the party leadership.

Despite the popularity of the piece – which was one of his main monologues throughout the 1980s – given its failure to explicitly attack Chinese 'communism', Fo's condemnation of the massacre of Tiananmen Square in 1989 before a performance rings hollow in an ideological rather than personal sense: 'I dedicate this show and *Tale of a Tiger* in particular to the youth of Tiananmen Square; who have tried to make the world understand their desire to move towards a democracy which unfortunately does not exist in their country.'[62] Fo here is condemning the lack of democracy in China, yet even a brief analysis of Mao Zedung's rule leads one to conclude that it was a regime that *never* allowed democracy in the sense that Fo uses the word.

Maoism and Marxism

Initially, the implantation of Maoism into Italy had some positive aspects, in that much of the interest derived from a preceding rejection of the parliamentary politics of the PCI. In the early 1960s, when many of the activists who would lead the small Italian revolutionary parties were coming into politics, the Chinese leadership had decided to attack the Kremlin for its bureaucratic and conservative accommodation with the West, a verbally radical position which many young activists seized with enthusiasm. As the historian Paul Ginsborg notes, a distorted reading of the 1966–67 Cultural Revolution increased curiosity even more: 'In contrast to the hierarchical and centralized Russian version ... the Cultural Revolution was very widely interpreted in Italy as being a spontaneous and anti-authoritarian mass protest movement. Socialism was to be reinvented from the bottom upwards.'[63]

In the years which immediately followed 1968, that is a period of ever-increasing struggles, the harsh criticism of Maoists against the Soviet Union and parliamentary politics seemed to fit. The verbal radicalism of Maoism could comfortably exist in a climate of mass struggles which were apparently destined to grow remorselessly. Although it probably felt inspiring, ultimately it was meaningless to chant one of the most popular slogans of this period: 'Create 10, 1,000, 10,000 Vietnams!' Similarly, it was confrontational but completely inaccurate to call the Christian Democrat government 'fascist'. This superficiality was somehow buttressed by the belief in the existence of a powerful socialist homeland, that is, China, so a sense of political security and certainty was nevertheless created.

To a political animal such as Fo, who had been critical of both Stalinism in Russia and the PCI's lack of radicalism in Italy, the arguments put forward by Maoists must have found him in broad agreement with them. The myths which were beginning to be spread about China must have also appealed to Fo as an artist, as Chinese society was apparently extremely democratic, with masses of people participating in all facets of politics and the arts.

Yet the reality of China was that Mao had been a loyal follower of the Kremlin for decades before breaking with Moscow in 1961. Furthermore, the Chinese revolution of 1949 came about as a result of rural guerrilla warfare, led by a Communist Party with virtually no industrial workers. The prominence of guerrilla warfare during the 1960s was further enhanced by the success of Castro's 1959 revolution in Cuba, as well as the international prominence of figures such as Che Guevara. While these successful revolutions and military campaigns were celebrated by young Italian leftists, the central element in these struggles, that is, guerrilla warfare led by the peasantry – and its irrelevance to Italy – was an issue that was overlooked in the enthusiastic embrace of Mao as the 'Great Helmsman' of international communist revolution upon whom 'the sun never sets'. The key factor in building socialist societies would be the 'correct leadership' of Communist Parties, and not the active participation of millions of working-class people.

For Marxists who believe in one of Marx's most famous dictums, that 'the emancipation of the working class is the act of the working class', societies such as China and Cuba were aberrations as the working class played an extremely minor role in their creation. The number of industrial workers who were members of the Chinese CP, or Fidel Castro's rebel army – the key forces in the creation of these new societies – was miniscule. And the influence of workers over these new regimes remained negligible, in fact workers were denied elementary rights such as independent trade unions.

The creation of socialism was to be achieved essentially through the 'correct leadership' of a Communist Party. The building of socialism thus depended on having the 'right line', or alternatively on a form of idealism rather than practical action. Much of the rhetoric of these regimes naturally appealed to an idealistic mindset, that is, the tendency to act according to a set of political formulas rather than the nuts and bolts of everyday working-class struggle.

At key moments the same tendency surfaced in Italy; one good illustration of this was the decision by most revolutionary forces to abstain from involvement in the new factory councils which had arisen after the 'Hot Autumn' of 1969. As these had been set up with the consent of union leaderships and the PCI they were to be shunned as reformist manoeuvres and creations of bourgeois society, despite the fact that they were organisations involving the vast majority of newly radicalised workers. A few years later the growth of left-wing terrorism was influenced by the heroism of peasant guerrilla struggles and an obsession with a 'correct leadership' over the masses.

Furthermore, Maoism as a form of political organisation was very similar to the Stalinism of the Communist Party of the Soviet Union (CPSU), indeed the constitution of the Chinese Communist Party was based on the very hierarchical structure of the CPSU. Most of the small revolutionary parties in Italy, particularly *Lotta Continua*, modelled their own organisations on the top-heavy structure of the Chinese Communist Party.

Organisations such as *Lotta Continua* were also characterised to a large extent by extreme verbal radicalism and confrontational politics on the streets. Such a stance could find a mass resonance in the early 1970s, but by the end of the decade revolutionaries had to learn how to retreat, and those who couldn't often broke like straws in the wind.

For example, the emergence of a radical women's movement created a lot of difficulties within LC, who in a notorious example in December 1975 decided to send their male stewards to break into a women-only march, which also included female LC members.[64]

On a broader level, by the end of the 1970s Maoism was found to be severely wanting. One of the first damaging revelations was the arrest of Lin Biao for his apparent conspiracy to overthrow Mao in the early 1970s, and his subsequent death in a 'plane crash'.[65] Yet Lin Biao had been a senior communist for 40 years in China and, in the years before his arrest, was Mao's official successor. Following Mao's death in 1976 the leadership had another period of bloodletting in the shape of the arrest and conviction of Mao's widow and three other senior leaders who became known as the 'Gang of Four'. In this period the leadership backed Pol Pot's regime in Cambodia, 'As it established a Stalinism even more horrific than the Russian original.'[66] In 1978 'communist' Vietnam invaded 'communist' Cambodia, leading to 'communist' China declaring war on Vietnam. The same year saw the beginning of a new policy by the 'great moderniser', Deng Xiaoping: 'market socialism', that is, the open introduction of market forces into the economy. And despite the influence of Stalinism and Maoism within the Italian left, by the 1980s realistic accounts of the Cultural Revolution were now circulating, which defined the period as a virtual civil war within the country, with various factions of the leadership trying to manipulate millions of people to follow their own agenda. This contrasted sharply with the earlier rosy accounts which had defined the period as one of mass creativity and democracy[67]

Due to its verbal radicalism and its distinguishing feature, in Italy, of radical opposition in the streets, Maoism could be appealing and endure as long as the movement was growing: 'But as the torrent subsided the best of the revolutionary tradition has proved more durable than many of the better known ideological formations born of 1968.'[68] Artists such as Fo were grappling with revolutionary ideas during the 1970s, but during this period in Italy it was impossible to engage with a genuine revolutionary Marxism: Stalinism and, later, Maoism had either destroyed or distorted the heart of Marxism: the 'self-emancipation of the working class'. While the 'Marxism' of the PCI had become a single-minded drive to gain a parliamentary majority in order to manage Italian capitalism, Maoism in Italy existed as a purely propulsive movement unable to explain setbacks and relatively uninterested in complicated political questions.

Fo and Rame were influenced by Maoism as much as anyone else active in 'the movement'. In August 1975 Fo, Rame, student leader Mario Capanna and others went on a trip to China and loved what they saw. On his return Fo stated: 'There is a new man because there is a new philosophy.' Although he also made several critical observations, overall Fo's impressions were very positive: 'Everyone really does say what they think ... the openness of Chinese society, the huge creative possibilities it offers everyone, are a living reality.'[69]

Despite such glaring illusions, by the late 1970s the collapse of Maoism as an ideology, and the discrediting of China as a 'communist' country, contributed directly to the collapse of the semi-Maoist revolutionary milieu which had mushroomed in 1968. Both the existence of a 'socialist homeland' (China) and an alternative version of Marxism to Stalinism (Maoism) were slowly and painfully being revealed as illusions. Fo was affected by this collective sense of disorientation as much as anyone else, and given the political commitment that has characterised his theatre, it is not surprising that in later years he avoided placing working-class struggles or calls for revolution or communism as prominent themes in his plays.

Although Italian Maoism has been shown over time to be unable to cope with a downturn, and as a system of government in China it has been revealed as a gross caricature of Marxism, for Fo it has proved to have been artistically beneficial to be a Maoist during this period. Had he firmly adopted an ideology in opposition to Maoism he would, of necessity, have cut himself off from the mass movement and, therefore, would have felt less need to contribute to its struggles. This is not a defence of Maoism, but a recognition that artistic development is influenced more by artistic stimulation than by firm ideological allegiance.

As a result of these changes Fo and Rame's practical political stance shifted notably from the late 1980s onwards. After an absence of many years Fo returned to playing PCI festivals in 1988, and at the PCI's national festival in 1989 Fo publicly embraced Giancarlo Pajetta, a man very much of the Stalinist old guard, telling him, 'It's time to make peace.'

Very soon after the collapse of the Berlin Wall in 1989 the PCI leadership proposed to change the party name, in order to remove any remaining association with a discredited 'communism'. This move revealed the shift in Fo and Rame's politics further; essentially, they were now close to the PCI. Fo's response to the proposed name change was principled but perhaps ambiguous:

> I'm not happy that it's changing its name. What upsets me the most is the idea that you can solve everything by changing a name. So I say 'no', because PCI is the name of a party which fought against Nazism and Fascism, and which organised glorious struggles of workers and peasants. It would be like burying a precious memory. Changing name would be a marketing decision and, as such, vulgar.[70]

A few weeks later Rame was less ambiguous: 'There is no basis to feel ashamed of the PCI's name. I don't understand, I feel embarrassed.' She said that she might join the PCI again, which she left in 1971, 'to be able to express my ideas better'.[71]

Taken out of context, opinions such as these could lead one to believe that the 1970s, that is, the decade studied most closely in this book, had never happened. The complete rejection of the PCI – its Stalinism and parliamentarism – was no longer a point of principle: 'progressive intellectuals' such as Fo and Rame were welcomed back within the party's orbit. The PCI's rapid move from its official adherence to 'communism' to right-wing social democracy was reflected in two name changes: the PCI became the PDS (Democratic Party of the Left) in 1991, and then DS (Left Democrats) in 1998.

When the centre-left government coalition, which included DS as its major party, fell in October 1998, Rame criticised the radical left-wing party Communist Refoundation, which had voted against it: 'It has seriously damaged the whole country ... There are those on the left who defend Refoundation, but everything seems so confused today. People are fed up, bored. I flip from anger to desperation. I never imagined that at this point in my life I would be defending Cossutta.'[72] Apart from illustrating Rame's emblematic confusion, her support for Armando Cossutta is very revealing: he was deputy leader of the PCI for much of the 1970s, and for decades had been the PCI leader most closely associated with Stalinism.

While this mending of fences with the parliamentary left was certainly taking place at a formal political level, Fo's theatrical activities and the political content of his plays continued to display complete independence throughout the 1980s and 1990s.

Exit Stage Left?

Fo's ability to isolate himself from the political debris surrounding him was partly due to the way he responded to the increasing national and international recognition he was receiving.

In 1978 he was appointed director of Italy's most prestigious opera house, La Scala in Milan. As part of its bicentenary in that year, he directed a minor opera entitled Story of a Soldier, with music by Stravinsky.[73] Although he was an internationally acclaimed actor and dramatist, Fo had also been a director throughout his career and this production reflected his approach to theatre. A very big stage was used, the original libretto was rewritten by Fo, and the cast improvised their actions to some extent during both rehearsals and performance. It was undoubtedly a major production and marked a return to the official theatre before the return of his own company with his own plays. In late 1981 Fo produced an updated version of Bertolt Brecht's Threepenny Opera, but due to his rewriting of the script and music the Brecht family refused to co-operate, so in many ways this major production was closer in spirit to John Gay's Beggar's Opera, which was the original inspiration for Brecht's opera. In

February 1987 Fo produced *The Barber of Seville* in Amsterdam, as well as two comedies by Molière in Paris in 1990.

Another development was an increasing tendency to perform outside Italy. During the 1979–80 season Fo held performances in Denmark, France, Germany and Sweden, while Rame performed *All House, Bed and Church* in London for two weeks in May 1982, with other shows taking place in Amsterdam and Copenhagen.[74] In April 1983 they both returned to London to perform individually and to hold theatre workshops, with Fo performing in 1984 and Rame in 1986 at the Edinburgh festival.[75] Rame also gave performances in Canada in 1983 and Cuba in 1984. This level of frequent but brief performances outside Italy has continued up to the present.

In this period Fo and Rame were twice denied US visas: once in 1980 and again in 1983, the main reason provided was their activities in support of left-wing prisoners. However Ronald Reagan finally relented in 1984, granting them a six-day visa.[76] Two years later they were able to tour the eastern states of the US to great acclaim.[77]

Another sphere of activity was their increased television and film work. Both made a series of programmes for television: firstly *Good Evening with Franca Rame* in 1980 and secondly *Forced Transmission* in 1988. In the following year Fo starred in the film *Music for Old Animals* and in a film version of Manzoni's classic *The Betrothed*.

Apart from these 'diversifications' into directing, television, cinema and overseas, Fo maintained his regular rhythm of writing new plays throughout the 1980s and for most of the 1990s, and then of touring Italy and starring in them. For much of this period his plays were the most popular in the country and were generally performed in the most prestigious theatres. The financial circumstances of his company were also very different; for example, government subsidies in the 1996–97 season amounted to £18,711 – 5 per cent of the company's total income.[78] This is not to criticise the company for accepting finances from the government, which all companies had a right to receive, but merely an illustration of how the circumstances of Fo's theatre have changed over the years.

However, Fo and Rame had not lost their political and social commitment; they were simply living through times very different to those of the 1970s. The causes they now supported were often less controversial: for example, a show they performed in April 1995 provided half of the finances for the purchase of a minibus for mentally handicapped children. Another example was the profits from a show (£13,150) given by Fo and Rame in December 1997 being used to create a youth centre at Tuzlas in Bosnia.[79] On the other hand, the political downturn had not totally obliterated antagonistic attitudes from the authorities. In October 1993 the mayor of Milan wrote to Fo warning him not to perform a show which he defined as illegal, as it was to be held in a squatted ex-factory renamed *Leoncavallo*, headquarters of the far-left autonomist movement in Milan.

The End of the Regime

Notwithstanding these activities, Fo's political interest continued to be stimulated throughout the 1980s due to the stench of corruption around him. Even in the early 1980s Fo had anticipated the degeneration of politics which was to emerge ten years later.

However, referring back in this quote to a key concept of *Accidental Death of an Anarchist*, he also understood that a constant dict of scandal created theatrical problems:

> Nobody becomes indignant about scandals any more, they've become a digestive, 'the liberatory burp of social democracy' ... Before, when someone was caught with their fingers in the till, they made a great effort to explain they were innocent. If they're caught in exactly the same situation today they don't even bother defending themselves. They say: 'I'm stealing so what?' There's now a huge blackout on loads of things: terrorism, the Mafia, everyday crimes. There's no resentment or indignation any more, just passive acceptance ... My job is to defeat indifference. The most dangerous thing that could happen today is for people to abandon political and social commitment. Theatre is movement, it's never theory. What I've always been looking for is the right screw to fix people into their seats.[80]

His first main work relating to corruption was *Francesca's Abduction*, first performed in December 1986 but substantially rewritten in summer 1987, in which *Francesca* was played by Rame. There are other actors in the play wearing masks of Italian politicians' faces, like Giulio Andreotti, Bettino Craxi and Ciriaco De Mita, as well as Ronald Reagan. The tone is set early on, when *Francesca* steps out of character and addresses the audience directly with heavy irony:

> The quickest among you would have already understood that it is a play in defence of the rich ... In response to the crazy campaign that is being organised against them today, we feel it our duty to run to their defence ...
>
> All the newspapers talk about the rich, the front pages talk about the rich ... what time they eat, what they're doing, what they're thinking ... how they wear their watch ... at the same time there has been an outbreak of weirdness and hatred against the rich by some people – investigating magistrates, for example ... you can bump into terrifying prosecutors who are emerging from the lower classes, who,

in the role of avenging angels, are beating the drum of nobody being above the law – and they're chucking big landowners, bankers and industrialists into jail ...

Essentially the rich live in segregation ... poor things, they don't know what freedom is. From birth they vegetate in captivity, inside villas and palaces, surrounded by electronic alarm systems and video cameras ...

The rich mother doesn't ask her son: 'Are you wearing your woollen jumper, dear?' ... but: 'Have you put on your bulletproof vest, dear? Put it on, otherwise you're not going out!'... They won't leave themselves defenceless even when they make love, given that they don't trust each other... I can't tell you what a racket they make! Two tanks crashing into each other! To make love in a different way, rich young couples often shoot at each other ... For centuries they've been pairing off among themselves in order to maintain their purity and they've ended up with stupid dogs ... I mean really stupid ... nearly as stupid as the Windsors![81]

Francesca's Abduction clearly foresaw many of the scandals which were to emerge in the *Tangentopoli* investigations of 1992–94. Yet despite the biting irony in speeches as the one above, Fo's anger largely existed in a political vacuum. The 1980s were very much a decade in which the rich got richer remorselessly, whether the country was being run by Giulio Andreotti, Bettino Craxi, Ronald Reagan or Margaret Thatcher.

The Italian regime began to fall apart in March 1992, with the arrest of a corrupt administrator named Mario Chiesa. This was quickly turned into an avalanche of judicial investigations and waves of arrests over the next few months. In May Rame was interviewed by the *Guardian* and said of the judges: 'It's not enough just to applaud them; we must support them, help them, work with them.'[82]

One of their initiatives was to rewrite totally a play which was first performed in 1964: *Seventh Commandment – Thou Shalt Steal a Bit Less*. *SCTSSBL 2* premièred in late 1992, during an intense period of continuously emerging scandals, and consequently it underwent daily changes during its very popular tour. Arrests of the 'great and the good' were so common that one lawyer who stormed out of the theatre offended by all the insults was arrested at home two hours later for his own involvement in a scandal.[83] In many towns, through earlier announcements in the left-leaning magazine *Avvenimenti*, and interviews in local newspapers, Fo and Rame made it clear that a *bocca della verità* (mouth of truth) would be in the theatre foyer, in order for people to place in it their own reports of scandals, given that over a two-year period several if not dozens of scandals were emerging every day as 'whistleblowing' came close to becoming a national hobby.[84]

The 1992 performances no longer had to repeat the fictitious setting of a cemetery and lunatic asylum of the 1964 version – Franca Rame made no secret that she was recounting real-life facts. Essentially the 'play' was a public lecture by Rame, reading and extemporising from a series of public documents or investigatory books, such as the following:

> Parliament spent £1.1 billion on paper in '91 – they destroyed the Amazon basin! Meals and snacks: £1.9 million, £3.8 million on postage and telephone bills, more than £3.3 million on heating. Over £900,000 on removals and portering – within the Parliament building itself! From one room to another! £289,000 on toilet paper – £791 a day. We need to accept that our MPs eat an awful lot ... but they also have wonderful digestion.[85]

By late 1993 televised trials were taking place in which sitting MPs were forced to give evidence, and their testimony often verged on the surreal. One minister admitted to taking a bribe of £2 or £3 million, he couldn't quite remember how much because 'I didn't count it carefully. At seven in the morning you're hardly wide awake'. The reason that major businessmen gave him the money was solely because 'they agreed with our (Christian Democrat) political programme'. The minister eventually admitted that they were bribes and would be used for election expenses, but after sarcastic prompting from the public prosecutor, Antonio Di Pietro, he admitted that elections were seven months away. So, apparently these businessmen told him, '"It's better to get organised early ... the sooner you start, the sooner you reach your destination." You can't imagine how much they insisted! They were really overbearing!' Fo and Rame, along with millions of Italians, were indignant: 'Thieves like these can carry on calmly in Parliament, holding Ministerial positions, proposing and voting on bills. And then they regularly pocket, as if nothing has happened, their salaries, along with their expenses, allowances and gratuities. And people like us, who point out this disgusting situation, are immediately defined as extremists.'[86]

When the ruling politicians and their parties were exposed in 1992–94, because of the long decline in working-class struggle Fo and Rame could do nothing more than scathingly denounce their activities, as they were unable to point to a credible alternative.

In an interview during the tour Fo claimed rather grandly: 'This time we want to destroy even the slightest chance that this ruling class attempts to recycle itself. We're warning people to be careful, because underneath their new jackets they're still wearing the same smelly woollen jumpers.' Rame's assessment was perhaps more honest and realistic: 'Revolution? We wanted to make one, but the investigating magistrates have made one. It's a good thing.'[87]

Politically, this kind of response was quite a revelation. In order to effect political change, to reduce and potentially sweep away the party which had dominated Italian politics for 50 years, Fo and Rame were supporting the actions of a pillar of the Italian establishment, the judiciary. It was no longer mass struggles which were the conduit for their shows, but a segment of the Italian state – which for many years they had made no secret of wanting to destroy. Such a transformation was not unique to Fo and Rame, indeed it was a very common evolution among revolutionaries of the 1970s. Rather than minutely analysing the extent and nature of this evolution, which was far from uniform, what was odd about Fo's personal situation was his elevation to a national and international institution by the mid-1990s.

Conclusion

Dario Fo, Nobel Prizewinner – A *Mistero Buffo?*

The announcement of Fo being awarded the Nobel Prize for Literature in October 1997 brought many of the contradictions of his political evolution sharply into focus.

Most of the Italian literary establishment were furious, as they do not consider Fo to be a writer of drama. The poet Mario Luzi wrote in the national press: 'I greeted the news with great bitterness, nowadays nothing surprises me. I didn't know much about Dario Fo, I know that as an actor he is famous throughout the world, but I don't know him as an author'. The literary critic Geno Pampaloni commented in the same right-wing paper: 'A Nobel Prize? It's a joke.' Rita Levi Montalcini, who had won the Nobel Prize for Medicine in 1986, also revealed her ignorance: 'I don't know Dario Fo, I really don't know who he is. Is he Italian?'[1] Others, such as the philosopher Gianni Vattimo, had a more devious approach defining Fo as 'little more than a monument of an epoch which has totally passed'.

Politically, the neo-fascist National Alliance party predictably expressed its outrage, and the Vatican naturally took a dim view as well, while the Prime Minister Romano Prodi sent him a pompous but perfunctory telegram: 'Italy is proud. Your name is added to the glorious list of celebrated writers who have won this award.'[2]

Fo couldn't resist teasing his detractors. As regards his literary enemies he commented: 'It's not bad at all getting a Nobel, and making so many old fossils explode with rage.'[3] And during his acceptance speech in Stockholm he congratulated the Swedish Academy for what their decision meant metaphorically for those who had ignored or insulted Fo for decades: 'You've hit them and brought them down so that their noses and bellies have slammed into the mud of normality!' He was equally provocative towards the Vatican: 'God exists and he's a *giullare*, because with this prize he's made a load of people angry.'[4]

Fo's behaviour at the highest point of his career should be compared to the comments he made when it was first rumoured that he might win the Nobel Prize in 1975. Fo's immediate response was not to view it as a serious suggestion: 'I think the proposal of my candidature is a polemical and provocatory gesture aimed at a shrivelled up and fossilised institution which reflects the values and mentality of the most reactionary bourgeoisie.'[5] And although he didn't say he would refuse the prize, he would not accept it in a conventional fashion: 'I don't think I could ever wear a tailcoat: it doesn't suit me. As regards bowing, I have become famous for my aversion to reverence and genuflections of all types.' Yet in 1997 he carefully rehearsed his triple bow for the Swedish king and had a three piece suit made for the occasion. In many respects Fo's change of heart is not particularly surprising or unusual. Just as any other individual over a 20-year period he experienced the slow evolution of a different political situation compared to the 1970s. Fo has not had a mass movement to work with for roughly 20 years, so it is not surprising that he, as is the case with any artist, has been conditioned by the circumstances in which he lives and works.

While on the one hand Fo is perfectly at home with bourgeois etiquette, a far more important matter was the subject matter of his speech, delivered literally on a world stage, and at a moment which was undoubtedly the high point of his career.

The Latin title of his acceptance speech, *Contra Jogulatores Obloquentes*, was a 1221 decree from the Holy Roman Empire, which allowed the Emperor to kill *giullari*. It was a humorous speech, with some contemporary political asides – the Sofri case, the Vatican, genetic engineering, the Italian literary establishment – but nothing too controversial.

Apart from these specific political comments, Fo also recounted some of his major theatrical influences. However, in the following passage he outlines how for him art and society are inextricably linked together:

> Our duty as intellectuals, of people who go and talk above all to young people in universities or on stage, is not only that of teaching them how to move their arms, how you must breathe to act, how you use your stomach, your voice, falsetto, reverse field. It's not enough to just teach a style: you've got to tell them about what's happening around them. They've got to tell their own stories. Any theatre, literature or artistic expression which doesn't speak about its own time is non-existent.

The Italian establishment are still wary of him. His acceptance speech was shown in full in many countries, such as South Korea, yet in Italy just a four-minute section was inserted into news bulletins. At one point Rame even intended to produce a video cassette of his speech with the subtitle: 'This is what Italian television censored'.[6]

There are many criticisms to be made of the political mistakes made by Fo and many others, but at the same time the old lion can still roar. The following three paragraphs are a far from exhaustive selection of recent political campaigns that he has supported.

In December 1997 Fo held a show in favour of the left-wing daily *Il Manifesto*, which was then risking closure.[7] In March 1998 he put his name to a demonstration in support of a 35-hour week.[8] Later the same month he was the first signatory of an appeal intended to help the peace process in the north of Ireland, stating: 'The Sinn Fein comrades need maximum support internationally,' and calling for 'a campaign of mobilisation for the defence of the rights of the Irish people, who for decades have been demanding the implementation of the most elementary democratic and social norms'.[9] In May he was invited to speak at Italy's major book festival in Turin and used the occasion to attack the Pope over abortion: 'The Pope is wrong when he attacks the abortion law. He forgets about all the millions of children killed by private abortionists – victims of the terrible abortions which are performed throughout the world. The real battle to be fought is the one against disinformation, and for prevention.'[10] In June he sent a letter to President Clinton demanding the release of Leonard Peltier, an Oglala Sioux Indian sentenced to life imprisonment for a murder in 1975. Fo stated that his release 'would not only be an act of necessary justice towards the man and the individual, but also a real affirmation of a President who has the "courage" to state clearly to the world that the oppression, discrimination, domination and repression of native Americans have come to an end'.[11] In December he lent his support to homeless people squatting in unrented apartment blocks in Bologna.[12] And in January 1999 he was one of eleven Nobel Prize winners who signed an appeal to EU and US governments designed to 'force Turkey to give justice to the legitimate aspirations of its 15 million Kurdish citizens, agreeing with them a statute of autonomy and the guarantee of cultural and linguistic rights'.[13] In March Fo and Rame were co-signatories against a government bill proposing greater police powers and longer custodial sentences.[14] And in the same month, a few days before his 73rd birthday, Fo joined a protest march in Genoa which demanded that the Italian government ban all arms sales to Turkey.[15]

In January 1999 Fo and Rame became closely associated with a campaign in support of migrant workers in Italy. In a growing climate of racism a demonstration had been held in Milan against 'illegal immigrants', which was quickly followed by police raids on migrants' living quarters, often abandoned factories. Fo and Rame brought some camp beds to migrants living rough at the *Leoncavallo* social centre, where Rame indignantly commented: 'Those who were demonstrating should be forced to emigrate and sleep on the ground, or on park benches in the middle of January.' A counter demonstration of 20,000, led by Fo and Rame, was held within a week and was built for by launching a public appeal entitled 'We're all illegal immigrants' and demanding the closure of the so-called 'temporary residence centres' for migrants. After visiting a 'centre' in which migrants were held, Fo told the crowd: 'It is like being in a horror film. This structure has been devised by people who have lost their head, they're clutching at straws.'[16]

When the 1999 Balkan war broke out Fo and Rame signed a joint appeal which argued: 'Let's stop the NATO bombings! Let's stop the deportations and genocidal intentions of the Milosevic regime!' It called for 'immediate and unconditional asylum for all Balkan refugees' and condemned Western Europe's immigration policies, denouncing 'closed borders, concentration camps for immigrants, xenophobia and racism, exploitation and unemployment'. Perhaps the most important point made was the call for 'authentic solidarity from below towards all Balkan peoples'. Subsequent to their own signatures, they did their stint at stalls in a major Milan street, asking passers-by to sign a petition against the war.[17]

The same disapproval that Fo encountered as a Nobel Prize winner from the intelligentsia and the political world has also been reproduced in his theatrical activities.

The première of *Free Marino! Marino is Innocent!* in his home town of Milan in March 1998 was bizarre. Fo was performing his first play since winning the Nobel Prize for literature less than six months earlier, and apart from that he had been a national institution for years, indeed the country's most popular actor and playwright for most of the last 40 years. Yet according to Milan's main newspaper when the show premièred there were

Loads of people. But not politicians, magistrates, the arts world: Fo was snubbed by them.

Despite this, or perhaps because of this, the atmosphere was affectionate, a little nostalgic, and almost smelt of street barricades. Young people looked around amazed, radical bookstalls, leaflets, Che Guevara T-shirts, albums of struggle and even some old coats brought out for the occasion. It was like the golden years of the *Palazzina Liberty*, with the audience crammed all over the place ...

Beside them were ordinary people, the generation who was around at that time and who hasn't forgotten, as well as the generation who wasn't there but who wants to know. 'We've been from Sicily to Milan,' Fo recalls, 'and the expression on young people's faces has been vacant. Nobody teaches them anything about that period, only the Red Brigades get mentioned. The period of the massacres has been cancelled out, just like the state wants.'

And it is really for them that at the start of the show Fo provides a kind of revision of the 1970s and the strategy of tension. He uses bits of his famous *Accidental Death of an Anarchist*, which still cause outbursts of laughter.[18]

By the end of the show, the journalist continues:

> Indicating the audience he added: 'There are two women sat there who are still waiting for justice after so many years: Lidia Franceschi, the mother of Roberto, a student of Bocconi University killed by the police. And Licia Pinelli, the widow of the anarchist railway worker thrown out of a window.' Everyone is on their feet, with the applause both for these two women and Fo, Rame, Sofri and the others. An outburst of social and political passion which has been forgotten for a long while.[19]

Fo's life and plays are a celebration of the oppressed, of those fighting against an unjust world. And although his career is coming to an end it is clear that the political realities which drove much of his work remain as contemporary as ever. An International Labour Organisation report issued in September 1998 stated that 1 billion workers – one third of the world's labour force – are either unemployed or underemployed. And of that 1 billion, 150 million are entirely unemployed.[20] At almost the same time the United Nations issued its Human Development Report which revealed more details of worldwide misery. In the industrialised world alone 200 million people will not live until the age of 60 and 100 million are homeless. In Africa 7 million children – five per second – are dying every year due to the need to repay foreign banks. Alongside this misery the report also listed obscene wealth: the richest 225 individuals in the world have more wealth than the annual income of 47 per cent of the world's population, 2.5 billion people. The three richest men in the world (the richest is Bill Gates of Microsoft) have more money than the total wealth of the 48 poorest countries. The UN estimated that if Bill Gates paid the cost of basic education, health care and safe water supplies for the 4.4 billion people in the developing countries, he would still be a *billionaire* ten times over.[21]

When informed of such individual wealth Fo responded: 'They're greedy and they do nothing.' The growth of such obscene wealth has coincided with the recent election of centre-left governments in many European countries, and according to Fo, 'One thought that there would have been some action, some creative momentum ... Big projects are announced but they don't interfere with the interests of the powerful.' In such a situation Fo commented that young people have no role models to follow, but then added: 'We've got our own role models. We've got to provide them.'[22]

In a system riven with such injustices, defended by national governments, security forces and the media throughout the world, Fo's work remains extremely relevant. His plays and life are full of observations which can inspire people to change the world, and perhaps the world needs fundamental change even more so now than when Fo started out 50 years ago.

Appendix A: Fo's Theatrical Coup[1]

The first sign was a voice with a southern accent which suddenly emerged from the battery microphone that Dario Fo was wearing on his chest: 'Hello, hello, Dragon here. Dragon orders the patrol to move to the north.' The interruption occurred right in the middle of a monologue on Augusto Pinochet (the show, *People's War in Chile*, deals with the Chilean military coup). The actor rolled his eyes and attempted to explain it with a joke: 'They're always so close to us, these policemen. They even manage to get inside our microphones with their radios' and carries on acting as if nothing had happened.

But the interference quickly returned. You could hear urgent orders and code words. 'The telephones aren't working,' a youth with a megaphone suddenly shouts. 'The radio's gone dead,' says a voice from the stalls. 'Come on comrades, it's nothing,' urges Fo from the stage, now speaking his lines in a more and more laboured voice.

A member of the audience who appears to have lost control of himself starts a long monologue: 'But this is Italy, we're not in Greece or Chile. Here there's the Communist Party, the trade unions, a coup is impossible.'

Nervousness starts to spread among the audience. The rumbling of passing lorries is heard from outside, as are a few gunshots. A Chief Constable suddenly comes in and jumps on the stage, saying, 'The show is suspended, the people I am about to name will follow me to headquarters,' and he starts to read out the names of the best known far-left activists who are in the theatre.

The tension is at fever pitch, many people start to murmur, 'It's a coup, it's a coup.' Somebody strikes up the *Internationale* and everyone is on their feet with their fists clenched, singing at the tops of their voices in what they believe will be their last expression of freedom. As Fo explains immediately afterwards to a shocked and almost disappointed audience, it was a deliberate theatrical device to remind people how even in Italy certain scenarios are not completely improbable.

Performed with total success at the *Palalido* in Milan in front of 5,000 people ('It was almost like being in America when Orson Welles announced the arrival of the Martians on the radio: slowly the unreal became real, and we ended up with hysterics,' said Gino D'Ario, the 25-year-old actor who plays the Chief Constable), as well as in Turin, Mestre and Nuoro and another ten cities – Dario Fo's sci-fi political escapade fell to earth with a crash at Sassari.

Of the two shows that the company was planning to perform, one was transformed into a kind of public debate due to the presence in the theatre of real policemen, and the other did not even take place as Dario Fo and five other actors were arrested before the show, even though they were released soon afterwards. The reason given was 'obstructing an officer through verbal violence': the actor had opposed officers entering the theatre during rehearsals.

'When I felt the handcuffs click around my wrists at the end of my questioning by the Sassari police chief, Renato Vurria, I felt immobilised by the absurdity of what was happening. "A coup d'état is really happening" ran through my mind,' Fo told *Panorama* when he left Sassari jail ...

Success

Almost ignored by the press, Fo's theatre has become famous among the left, particularly the extra-parliamentary left. The result has been some mind-boggling box office statistics: audiences of 250,000 in the first year, 700,000 last year, almost all of them young people, workers, peasants – at least half of whom had never set foot in a theatre before. Recently many performances have been held in university buildings, in public squares, in occupied factories, and on one occasion even inside a church, at Vispa just outside Savona.

The impact he creates has always been enormous. One example is the audience's reaction to the fake coup: in Turin one young man ate ten pages of his diary, which were full of addresses he thought were compromising. At Merano a student tried to jump out of a window but just broke the glass. At Nuoro, where two coachloads of shepherds had arrived from Orgosolo, there were some who flashed the shiny blades of the knives they use to cut cheese as soon as they saw the fake Chief Constable ...

Other episodes: in Bologna, when the fake Chief Constable declared that 'nobody can leave, apart from those who are members of parties of the parliamentary left' a full-time official of a left-wing party, with his wife and son, went up and showed his party card and asked to leave. In

Salerno the fake Chief Constable narrowly avoided a knifing. At Rimini the mother of a comrade called on to the stage by the Chief Constable to follow him to headquarters ran down to the stage and attacked him: Franca Rame barely managed to restrain her, telling her in vain that 'it's part of the show'.

Appendix B: An 'Intervention Show' in Brescia[1]

Brescia, in the afternoon of 21 June 1974. We're at the local branch of *The Commune*. It is a whitewashed room with 100 chairs, a table at the end, and a bookshop. On the shelves are texts of *The Commune* theatre collective, books by Lenin and Mao Zedung, cultural and political magazines, and the newspapers of political organisations. There are posters on the walls which detail local initiatives (theatrical performances, film shows, debates) organised by the branch within the city and in nearby towns. The poster announcing the show which will take place in a few hours, at 9 p.m., has just been stuck up. The show will be staged in the main square: *No to fascist murderers and their backers*.

Fifteen days before a fascist bomb had exploded at an anti-fascist demonstration organised by the unions, which saw the participation of all progressive and revolutionary organisations: nine comrades were massacred, dozens were wounded.

A horrendous massacre. An unambiguous direct attack against the working-class movement. An act of war carried out by fascist bandits but wanted, created and organised by those who, at the level of economic and state power, mobilise and finance the fascist gangs.

The bomb exploded under a portico full of workers and students (it was raining), while a trade unionist was listing the crimes and provocations carried out by fascists from the massacre at the Milan Agriculture Bank on 12 December 1969 until today. He had just finished talking about the violent actions launched against workers' and students' struggles in Milan, and was starting to speak of the fascists' actions in the Brescia area, when the bomb went off ...

The meeting has started. It is attended by Dario Fo, Franca Rame, other members of the theatre collective and some comrades of the local branch, who lead off the discussion. Dario Fo has asked them to describe what happened both when the bomb went off and during the funerals, but above all – at the level of anti-fascist response – what has happened in schools, working-class areas and factories.

This is an indispensable moment of investigation to avoid a generic intervention, or one which will not ring true to the thousands of people who in a few hours will take part in the show in the main square. This is always the main problem which an 'intervention show' faces, that is, a show without an overall script, which is built (generally in a few hours) on the basis of the information gathered about a specific situation.

This is similar to what happens on the eve of political trials, when *The Commune* intervenes with the practical aim of contributing to a political mobilisation against the 'show' offered by the bourgeois courts. Above all, eyewitness statements are collected, as are personal histories, statistics and court documents; and the intervention is then built on the basis of this material. Already existing texts are always inserted within the parameters of debate which will be built into the show, texts which have already been used in other 'intervention shows', or those taken from the scripts of 'national' texts (*Mistero Buffo*, etc.). But all of them are contained within a narrative plan which is intended to be closely linked to the concrete situation in which the intervention is made.

This is also the case of tonight's show in Brescia: texts written on other occasions will be used, but within a framework which emerges from research done on the massacre and other events which have taken place in Brescia.

A woman from the local branch gives Fo a piece of paper: 'Here you are. This is a list of the factories which expelled fascists immediately after the massacre ... There were two fascists in this factory, one has moved to another city and the other is in hospital ... he fell over and hurt himself. The shop stewards' committee in this other factory passed a motion demanding the confiscation of property belonging to the bosses who finance them.'

Fo is writing on pieces of paper while this woman, and others from the branch, carry on talking, adding information and trying to be as accurate as possible.

'And the PCI?' asks Fo.

A comrade answers: 'The same old attitude ... the worry about losing control of the rank and file ... appeals for vigilance in defence of the Republic's institutions ... joint posters with the Christian Democrats, and appeals for vigilance against "adventurist" initiatives, etc. Many ordinary members, however, have been deeply shocked by the massacre, above all the ex-partisan members ... we're having lots of discussions with them ...'

Another member: 'One important thing is that a motion against fascism has come out of the prison signed by almost all the inmates ... I don't know whether you know, but three months ago there was a revolt inside, supported from the outside by hundreds of comrades ... we held a photographic exhibition and produced a pamphlet.'

'Can you give us some copies ... it's important for the work we do with *Soccorso Rosso* [Red Help]. But tell us something else: is it true that during the religious service the Gregorian chants were drowned out by *Bandiera Rossa* and *Fischia il vento?*'[2]

'Yes, there were hundreds of clenched fists in the church as well. The camera crews didn't know where to point their lenses ... I was close to one of them, and at one point they really didn't know what to do so they focused in on a fresco on the ceiling and just stayed fixed on that ... So I asked him: "Why don't you film the congregation?" He was embarrassed, he smiled, looked at me, and shrugged his shoulders as if to say, "It's the control room that decides," and he pointed to a group of generals who were sat to the right of the comrades' coffins.'

'Great,' Fo has stopped writing. 'Now let's see how to build the show, what pieces we're going to use, after an introduction that creates the tone for the whole show.'

'Also bearing in mind that there will be many ordinary members of the Communist and Socialist Parties in the audience' adds Franca Rame.

'As an introduction we could repeat what we did as the People's Court in Milan, together with the details given to us by the members of the branch ... As regards scripts we've already performed, we could use *Mamma Togni*,[3] do you agree Franca?'

'All right.'

'Cicciu's[4] piece on *Ciucciu Corno* is important because it deals with the failure of any collaboration with the bourgeoisie. Given that we're in Brescia, and all the discussion about linking back up with the past struggles of people in this city, we could also do that monologue of Arnaldo da Brescia on the violence of the boss ... and on revolutionary violence ...'

A branch member speaks up: 'We could also use the song about the GAP[5] ... and some Chilean songs ... there should be some discussion about Chile.'

'Definitely, right, so let's start to rehearse the songs. Then we'll decide the running order of the show, and we'll assemble the texts and the songs according to the rhythms and the tempo that we need.'

A member of the branch interrupts: 'There's going to be a number of speeches from several factories, an ex-partisan ... is it better to have them before the show or during it?'

'No, it's better to do it at the end otherwise there's a danger of creating a situation in which people lose their concentration, things can get bogged down. This is something that we've always experienced in our shows: that it is better to have speeches at the end. They're an introduction to a debate, comrades must be urged to make concrete speeches and avoid analyses of the general situation in Italy and around the world, or even on the moon ... instead they should bring us their experience of struggle, this is what is useful. After all, this is the practical benefit of our work, isn't it?'

As the research meeting is ending at the branch, and the members of the collective start to rehearse the songs for the show, in the square other members are assembling the stage and the amplification, and putting out hundreds of chairs. The branch has organised stewarding around the square (which is close to the one where the bomb exploded, which in turn was denied 'for reasons of public order'), and there are dozens of comrades with red armbands who are controlling the entrance of people into the square, who already start arriving at 8 p.m.

There is a bookstall on the left of the stage, with the publications of *The Commune*, which from 1968 onwards has always chosen to produce its own publications in order to keep prices low as well as to generate its own income.

It is after 9 p.m., the square has been filled by more than 5,000 people. Dario Fo tests the microphones on the makeshift stage and invites people to go back to their seats or to sit on the ground. He jokes with one or two comrades. None of this is accidental, it is part of a deliberate technique to make contact with the spectators, to break down the traditional division between 'actor' and 'audience', to break the ritual of a performance mediated by the 'fourth wall', as we shall soon see.

The show starts with a long monologue by Dario Fo, a 'presentation' contained in every show, whether it is one of 'intervention' or not.

In the 'presentation' he talks about the rebellion of Brescian workers against the hypocritical attempt by the state to 'worship' at one of its own funerals. The heckling of the President of the Republic is recounted in a grotesque fashion, and heavy irony is used against the system's various puppets.

And opposed to these ridiculous puppets, masters in crime, there is the strength of a movement of struggle which can't stand them any more. There are the expulsions of fascists from factories and schools.

The presentation takes life from the research done on the current situation. The narrative is clear, the audience recognise themselves in it and underline this through their laughter and applause when various references and allusions are made. The climate which is created is one of collective and active participation, people have a clear awareness of their own strength and intelligence, and the real possibilities of liberation.

Once contact has been made with the concrete situation of the audience, the main show begins.

Appendix C: A Telegram to *The Commune*[1]

The following telegram was received by *The Commune* from the small Lombard town of Sovere in March 1975, and is a good example of how Fo was perceived by many workers.

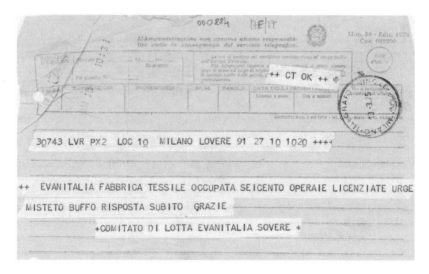

Evanitalia textile factory occupied 600 women workers sacked *Misteto Buffo* needed urgently immediate reply thanks *Evanitalia* committee of struggle Sovere

Notes

CTFR = Dario Fo and Franca Rame's personal archives.

Introduction

1. *Il Manifesto*, 20 March 1998.
2. *Guardian*, 10 October 1997.
3. *La Repubblica*, 19 September 1980. Cited in T. Mitchell, *Dario Fo: People's Court Jester* (Methuen: London, 1976), p. 75.

Chapter 1 The Bourgeois Period

1. D. Fo, in P. Agosti and G. Borghese, *C'era una volta un bambino* (Milan: Baldini & Castoldi, 1996), p. 66.
2. *Corriere della Sera*, 2 July 1993.
3. Ibid.
4. C. Valentini, *La storia di Dario Fo*, 2nd edition (Milan: Feltrinelli, 1997) p. 26.
5. *Corriere della Sera*, 2 July 1993.
6. Valentini, *La storia di Dario Fo*, p. 28.
7. See M. Zancan, *Il Progetto 'Politecnico'* (Venice: Marsilio, 1984), pp. 202–10.
8. See S. Gundle, *I comunisti italiani tra Hollywood e Mosca* (Florence: Giunti, 1995), pp. 56–60.
9. Interview in *Moda*, September 1985. Cited in D. Fo, *Fabulazzo* (Milan: Kaos, 1992), p. 60.
10. See T. Mitchell, *Dario Fo: People's Court Jester*, 2nd edition (London: Methuen, 1986), pp. 38–9.
11. See ibid., p. 40.
12. Valentini, *La storia di Dario Fo*, pp. 39–40.
13. R. Franzosi, *The Puzzle of Strikes. Class and State strategies in Postwar Italy* (Cambridge: Cambridge University Press, 1995), p. 214.
14. F. Rame, 'Introduction', in D. Fo, *Plays: 2* (London: Methuen, 1994).
15. Ibid.

16. R. Nepoti and M. Cappa, *Dario Fo*, new edition (Rome: Gremese, 1997), p. 37.
17. CTFR, busta 2a, 'I sani da legare', p. 59.
18. Ibid., p. 61.
19. Ibid.
20. Valentini, *La storia di Dario Fo*, p. 48.
21. Ibid., p. 58.
22. Ibid., p. 59.
23. Ibid., p. 64.
24. Ibid.
25. Nepoti and Cappa, *Dario Fo*, p. 45.
26. P. Ginsborg, *A History of Contemporary Italy* (Harmondsworth: Penguin, 1990), pp. 256–7.
27. Valentini, *La storia di Dario Fo*, p. 70.
28. G. Petrillo, *La Capitale del Miracolo. Sviluppo lavoro potere a Milano 1953–1962* (Milan: Franco Angeli, 1992), pp. 322–3. The traditional ideological divisions took the following form: the largest federation, the CGIL, was dominated by communists, the UIL by socialists and the CISL by Christian Democrats.
29. Cited in ibid., p. 330.
30. Valentini, *La storia di Dario Fo*, p. 72.
31. Ibid., p. 74.
32. *Le Ore*, 28 March 1960. Unless otherwise stated, pre-1999 amounts in *lire* have been converted into contemporary amounts in sterling. This has been done by using a table of historical coefficients published monthly by the financial newspaper *Il Sole 24 Ore*, called *Indici Mensili*. The January 1999 edition was used to convert pre-1999 *lire* amounts into contemporary prices; these figures were then converted into sterling using an exchange rate of 2,700 *lire* to the pound.
33. Valentini, *La storia di Dario Fo*, p. 74.
34. All of the details concerning censorship thus far have been taken from one single source from Italian state archives: ACS: M.I. Gab. 1957–60, busta 329, f. 17083. The quote by Flaminio Piccoli was originally published in *L'Adige*, 17 June 1960.
35. ACS: M.I. Gab 1961–3, busta 324, f. 17083.
36. *L'Unità*, 27 October 1963.
37. Nepoti and Cappa, *Dario Fo*, p. 38.
38. However A. Grasso, in his *Storia della televisione italiana* (Milan: Garzanti, 1992), p. 155, cites a senator complaining about a payment of £20,000 per show.
39. Valentini, *La storia di Dario Fo*, p. 77.
40. Cited in Fo, *Fabulazzo*, p. 239.
41. Valentini, *La storia di Dario Fo*, p. 78.
42. Mitchell, *Dario Fo: People's Court Jester*, p. 46.
43. Valentini, *La storia di Dario Fo*, p. 79.
44. Ibid., p. 80.
45. Cited by F. Rame, 'Introduction', in Fo, *Plays: 2*, p. xxi.
46. Valentini, *La storia di Dario Fo*, p. 80.
47. Ibid., p. 81.
48. Fo, *Fabulazzo*, p. 139.

49. Cited in M. Cesari, *La censura in Italia oggi (1944–80)* (Naples: Liguori, 1982), p. 187.
50. *Il Giorno*, 30 November 1962. Cited in Petrillo, *La Capitale del Miracolo*, p. 437.
51. Valentini, *La storia di Dario Fo*, p. 83.
52. Petrillo, *La Capitale del Miracolo*, p. 437.
53. Valentini, *La storia di Dario Fo*, p. 84.
54. Cited in Grasso, *Storia della televisione italiana*, p. 156.
55. *La Stampa*, 16 April 1966.
56. E. Santarelli, *Storia critica della Repubblica* (Milan: Feltrinelli, 1996), p. 128.
57. Interview with Nanni Ricordi. Born in 1932, Ricordi was Milan ARCI secretary and a PCI member during the 1960s, and a founder member of *New Scene* in 1968.
58. Valentini, *La storia di Dario Fo*, p. 88.
59. Mitchell, *Dario Fo: People's Court Jester*, p. 47.
60. D. Fo, *Le commedie di Dario Fo*, Vol. 2 (Turin: Einaudi, 1966), pp. 84–5.
61. Valentini, *La storia di Dario Fo*, p. 88. Fo accepted the challenge but only if it was fought under Thai boxing rules, as Fo claimed he was a regional champion. The officer was never heard from again.
62. Nepoti and Cappa, *Dario Fo*, p. 55.
63. ACS: M.I. Gab. 1961 3, busta 324, f. 17082/48.
64. Nepoti and Cappa, *Dario Fo*, p. 55.
65. Ibid., pp. 45 and 62.
66. Nanni Ricordi, interview.
67. F. Quadri, 'Introduzione', in D. Fo, *Le commedie di Dario Fo*, Vol. 1 (Turin: Einaudi, 1966), p. xii.
68. Valentini, *La storia di Dario Fo*, p. 104.
69. Rame, 'Introduction', p. xxii.
70. Ibid., p. xxi.
71. Interview with Nanni Ricordi.
72. F. Rame, 'Una testimonianza di Franca Rame', in D. Fo, *Le commedie di Dario Fo*, Vol. 3, (Turin: Einaudi, 1975) pp. vi–vii.
73. Cited in Valentini, *La storia di Dario Fo*, p. 8. Giullari were medieval travelling players, discussed in Chapter 5.
74. Ibid.

Chapter 2 The Revolutionary Period

1. F. Rame, 'Introduction', in D. Fo, *We Can't Pay? We Won't Pay!* (London: Pluto Press, 1978), pp. viii–ix.
2. C. Harman, *The Fire Last Time: 1968 and After* (London: Bookmarks, 1988), p. 194.
3. Cited in R. Franzosi, *The Puzzle of Strikes. Class and State Strategies in Postwar Italy* (Cambridge: Cambridge University Press, 1995), p. 272.
4. Ibid., p. 161.
5. Cited in ibid., p. 278.
6. Ibid., p. 270.
7. Cited in ibid., p. 281.
8. T. D'Amico, *Gli anni ribelli* (Rome: Editori Riuniti, 1998), p. 68.

9. G. Bedani, *Politics and Ideology in the Italian Workers' Movement* (Oxford: Berg, 1995), p. 168.
10. P. Ginsborg, *A History of Contemporary Italy* (Harmondsworth: Penguin 1990), p. 320.
11. S. Tarrow, *Democracy and Disorder. Protest and Politics in Italy 1965–75* (Oxford: Clarendon Press, 1989), p. 71.
12. Franzosi, *The Puzzle of Strikes*, p. 274.
13. Bedani, *Politics and Ideology*, p. 172.
14. Interview with Piero Sciotto. Born in 1943, he worked with Fo from 1973 to 1980, and again from 1984 to 1992.
15. C. Valentini, *La storia di Dario Fo*, 2nd edition (Milan: Feltrinelli, 1997), p. 12.
16. R. Nepoti and M. Cappa, *Dario Fo*, new edition (Rome: Gremese, 1997), p. 76.
17. D. Fo, *Le commedie di Dario Fo*, Vol. 3, (Turin: Einaudi, 1975), p. 77.
18. Interview with Nanni Ricordi. Born in 1932, Ricordi was Milan ARCI secretary and a PCI member during the 1960s, and a founder member of *New Scene* in 1968.
19. R.M., 'A colloquio con Dario Fo. Un esperimento totale', *Il Ponte* (July 1969), p. 892.
20. Ibid., p. 889.
21. *L'Unità*, 21 November 1968; *Sorrisi e Canzoni TV*, 26 January 1969.
22. R.M., 'A colloquio con Dario Fo', p. 892.
23. Interview with Arturo Peregalli. Born in 1948, Peregalli has seen virtually all of Fo's plays since the mid-1960s.
24. Born in 1932, this person was a member of *The Commune* from 1970 to 1973.
25. CTFR, busta 12A, July 1970, 'Fine Stagione', p. 5.
26. R.M., 'A colloquio con Dario Fo', p. 891. Emphasis in the original.
27. Nanni Ricordi, interview.
28. Interview with a member of *The Commune*.
29. Piero Sciotto, interview.
30. *L'Unità*, 21 November 1968. Emphasis in the original.
31. Valentini, *La storia di Dario Fo*, pp. 108–9.
32. Ibid., pp. 14–5.
33. Nanni Ricordi, interview.
34. CTFR, busta 12A, 9 September 1970, p. 5.
35. Valentini, *La storia di Dario Fo*, p. 15, no date given.
36. Ibid., p. 111.
37. F. Rame, 'Una testimonianza di Franca Rame', in Fo, *Le commedie di Dario Fo*, Vol. 3, p. viii.
38. *L'Unità*, 7 December 1972.
39. C. Harman, *Bureaucracy and Revolution in Eastern Europe* (London: Pluto Press, 1974), pp. 188–9.
40. Fo, *Le commedie di Dario Fo*, Vol. 3, p. 103.
41. Ibid., p. 104–6.
42. Ibid., p. 107.
43. S. Cowan, 'Theatre, Politics and Social Change in Italy since the Second World War', *Theatre Quarterly*, No. 27, (Autumn 1977), p. 36.
44. *L'Unità*, 19 December 1969.
45. D. Fo, *Compagni senza censura*, Vol. 1 (Milan: Mazzotta, 1973), p. 209.

46. *L'Unità*, 6 November 1969.
47. Valentini, *La storia di Dario Fo*, p. 113. The organisational structure with which Fo and Rame were increasingly coming into conflict had access to a mass working-class audience: at the end of 1970 ARCI officially had 3,299 local branches and a total of 533,112 members. (*Rinascita*, 18 June 1971).
48. *L'Unità*, 11 November 1969.
49. *L'Unità*, 15 November 1969.
50. *L'Unità*, 11 November 1969.
51. Valentini, *La storia di Dario Fo*, p. 114.
52. *Cineforum Pistolese*, March 1970.
53. Nanni Ricordi, interview.
54. Valentini, *La storia di Dario Fo*, p. 116.
55. *La Nazione*, 8 February 1972.
56. See Fo, *Compagni senza censura*, Vol. 1, p. 70, for details of the origin of this play.
57. Fo, *Le commedie di Dario Fo*, Vol. 3, pp. 137–8.
58. Ibid., p. 139.
59. Ibid., p. 140.
60. Ibid., p. 161.
61. Cited in Fo, *Compagni senza censura*, Vol 1, p. 203.
62. D. Fo, *Compagni senza censura*, Vol. 2, 3rd edition (Milan: Mazzotta, 1977), p. 230.
63. Valentini, *La storia di Dario Fo*, p. 131.
64. Interview with Emilio Orsino. Born in 1944, Orsino has attended most of Fo's plays since the late 1960s.
65. Nanni Ricordi, interview.
66. CTFR, busta 12A, 'L'attività svolta nella stagione 1970/71', p. 1.
67. Mario Soldati, writing in *Il Mondo*, 28 January 1972.
68. Cited in L. Binni, *attento te...!*, (Verona: Bertani, 1975), p. 227; translation of an interview in *Libération*, 9 January 1974.
69. Valentini, *La storia di Dario Fo*, p. 132.
70. Unsigned review of *United we stand!...*, in *Sipario*, May 1971, p. 42.
71. J. Lorch, 'Introduction', in D. Fo, *Morte accidentale di un anarchico* (Manchester: Manchester University Press, 1997), p. 22.
72. *Il Giorno*, 21 February 1973.
73. Nepoti and Cappa, *Dario Fo*, p. 27.
74. *Alto Adige*, 20 January 1972.
75. *Potere Operaio*, 26 November 1972, dealing with the activities of the Quarticciolo branch. Speakers included Giorgio Bocca, Carla Capponi, Joyce Lussu, Aldo Natoli and Giovanni Pesce.
76. *Brescia Oggi*, 19 July 1974.
77. Valentini, *La storia di Dario Fo*, p. 133.
78. Ibid.
79. Ibid., p. 134, note. See Chapter 6 for a discussion of Maoism.
80. Unsigned review of *United We Stand!...*, in *Sipario*, May 1971, p. 42.
81. This account is taken largely but not exclusively from Ginsborg, *History of Contemporary Italy*, pp. 312–6; and Harman, *The Fire Last Time*, pp. 200–19.
82. D. Fo, 'Teatro di situazione uguale teatro popolare', *Sipario*, May 1971, p. 43.

83. Unsigned review of *United We Stand!...*, in ibid., p. 43.
84. D. Fo, *Le commedie di Dario Fo*, Vol. 4 (Turin: Einaudi, 1977), p. 117.
85. Ibid., p. 165.
86. *Il Secolo XIX*, 8 June 1971. The 'One, Two, Three, a Thousand' slogan was an elaboration of a chant often used by Maoists, which called for the creation of more and more national liberation struggles along the lines of Vietnam.
87. Ibid.
88. Cited in Valentini, *La storia di Dario Fo*, p. 140.
89. *L'Unità*, 1 April 1971.
90. *Il Secolo XIX*, 8 June 1971.
91. Cited in Fo, *Compagni senza censura*, Vol. 2, pp. 221–2.
92. Fo, 'Teatro di situazione uguale teatro popolare', p. 43.
93. CTFR, busta 14A, ARCI leaflet dated 14 April 1972.
94. Nepoti and Cappa, *Dario Fo*, p. 27.
95. *Il Manifesto*, 14 October 1972.
96. Valentini, *La storia di Dario Fo*, p. 144.
97. *Il Giorno*, 21 February 1973.
98. Ginsborg, *History of Contemporary Italy*, pp. 323 and 361.
99. *Il Manifesto*, 31 July 1973.
100. Valentini, *La storia di Dario Fo*, p. 146.
101. Nepoti and Cappa, *Dario Fo*, p. 100.
102. *Brescia Oggi*, 14 June 1974.
103. *Quotidiano dei lavoratori*, 22 December 1974.
104. *Corriere di Napoli*, 19 February 1972.
105. Interview with a member of *The Commune*.
106. *Il Giornale*, 30 October 1974.
107. *L'Espresso*, 18 March 1973.
108. *Paese Sera*, 23 March 1973.
109. *Gazzetta del Popolo*, 10 May 1973.
110. *Il Manifesto*, 11 February 1998.
111. *La Repubblica*, 10 February 1998.
112. *La Repubblica*, 11 February 1998.
113. D. Fo, *Guerra di popolo in Cile* (Milan: Bertani, 1973), p. 7.
114. M. Gonzalez, 'Chile and the struggle for workers' power', *International Socialism*, No. 60 (Autumn 1993), p. 141.
115. Cited in Fo, *Compagni senza censura*, Vol. 2, p. 193. Debate held at Forlimpopoli, 6 May 1971.
116. *Guardian*, 2 February 1999.
117. *L'Unità*, 7 December 1998.
118. *Observer*, 28 February 1999.
119. *Socialist Worker*, 27 March 1999.
120. Fo, *Guerra di popolo in Cile*, pp. 60–1.
121. Cited in Ginsborg, *History of Contemporary Italy*, p. 355.
122. *Servire il popolo*, 20 October 1973.
123. *La Stampa*, 28 October 1973. Interestingly enough this journalist, along with most others at the time, didn't reveal the fake coup engineered by Fo and the rest of the cast.
124. Piero Sciotto, interview.
125. Valentini, *La storia di Dario Fo*, p. 152.

126. *Aria di golpe*, a video cassette produced by the *Il Manifesto* newspaper in 1994, containing an interview with Fo and Rame, and footage from their performance in Turin in 1973.
127. Ibid.
128. *Servire il popolo*, 20 October 1973.
129. *L'Unione Sarda*, 8 November 1973, report filed from Nuoro on 7 November.
130. *Avanti*, 6 November 1973.
131. *Paese Sera* and *Il Secolo*, 10 November 1973.
132. Binni, *attento te...!*, p. 372.
133. *L'Unione Sarda*, 10 November 1973, report filed from Sassari on 9 November.
134. *L'Unione Sarda*, 11 November 1973, and Valentini, *La storia di Dario Fo*, p. 153.
135. *Il Manifesto* and *Il Tempo*, 11 November 1973.
136. *Paese Sera*, 11 November 1973.
137. CTFR, busta 14A.
138. *L'Unità*, 11 November 1973.
139. *Corriere del Ticino*, 12 November 1973.
140. *L'Unione Sarda*, 11 November 1973, and Valentini, *La storia di Dario Fo*, p. 153.
141. Ibid.
142. *Gazzetta del Popolo*, 11 November 1973.
143. *L'Unione Sarda*, 11 November 1973, and Valentini, *La storia di Dario Fo*, p. 153.
144. CTFR, busta 14A, Ansa press agency comuniqué. (Palermo, 13 November 1973).
145. Interview with Emilio Orsino.
146. *Lotta Continua* and *Il Manifesto*, 17 March 1974.
147. Binni, *attento te...!*, p. 186.
148. Valentini, *La storia di Dario Fo*, p. 157.
149. Fo, writing in F. Quadri, *Il Teatro del Regime* (Milan: Mazzotta, 1976), pp. 148–9. The article was written in January 1975.
150. Interview originally published in December 1974. Reproduced in D. Fo, *Fabulazzo* (Milan: Kaos, 1992), p. 46.
151. Nepoti and Cappa, *Dario Fo*, p. 112. The birth of a puppet in fascist uniform is a reference to Fanfani's adherence to fascism as a young man.
152. Valentini, *La storia di Dario Fo*, p. 167.
153. A. Stille, *Excellent Cadavers* (London: Vintage, 1996), p. 65.
154. D. Fo, *Le commedie di Dario Fo*, Vol. 12 (Turin: Einaudi, 1998), p. 148.
155. Reproduced in Fo, *Fabulazzo*, p. 207.
156. See Fo, *Le commedie di Dario Fo*, Vol. 12, p. 151.
157. Ibid., p. 153.
158. Reproduced in Fo, *Fabulazzo*, p. 246.
159. Fo, *Le commedie di Dario Fo*, Vol. 12, p. 106.
160. Ibid., p. 112.
161. See *La classe operaia è forte*, (Edizioni Lotta Continua, n.d. [1974], no author), pp. 33–9, for an eyewitness account of the immediate response to the bombing in Brescia.
162. *Brescia Oggi*, 22 June 1974.
163. *Il Resto del Carlino*, 31 December 1977.
164. *La Stampa*, 28 October 1977.
165. D. Fo, 'Dario Fo explains', in *The Drama Review*, Vol. 22, N. 1, (March 1978), p. 48.

Chapter 3 *Accidental Death of an Anarchist*

1. D. Fo, *Marino Libero! Marino è innocente!* (Turin: Einaudi, 1998), p. 14.
2. C. Cairns, 'Introduction', in D. Fo, *Accidental Death of an Anarchist* (London: Methuen, 1991), p. xx.
3. In most translations of *Accidental Death...* into English, many specific political details concerning Italy have rightly been omitted by translators. The exception to this tendency is a translation by Ed Emery, published in D. Fo, *Plays: 1* (London: Methuen, 1992), which is the version used most extensively in this chapter.
4. D. Fo, *Pum, Pum! Chi è? La polizia!*, 3rd edition (Verona: Bertani, 1974), p. 20.
5. *Paese Sera*, 18 November 1969.
6. P. Ginsborg, *A History of Contemporary Italy* (Harmondsworth: Penguin, 1990), p. 318.
7. *Corriere della Sera*, 16 December 1970.
8. Ibid.
9. See Ginsborg, *History of Contemporary Italy*, p. 334.
10. Fo, *Plays: 1*, p. 194.
11. Fo, *Pum, Pum!*, p. 10.
12. *Lotta Continua*, 20 December 1969, cited in A. Sofri (ed.), *Il malore attivo dell'anarchico Pinelli* (Palermo: Sellerio, 1996), p. 96. Interestingly enough, under fascism Marcello Guida had been in charge of the jail on the island of Ventotene, which housed many of Italy's most important anti-fascist prisoners. Another policeman present in the room from which Pinelli exited via the window is currently police chief of Rome.
13. Cited in C. Cederna, *Una finestra sulla strage* (Milan: Feltrinelli, 1972), p. 25.
14. Cited in ibid., p. 41.
15. Ibid., pp. 38–9.
16. *La strage di stato*, (Rome: Samonà e Savelli, 1971), p. 91. See also J. Lorch's Introduction to D. Fo, *Morte accidentale di un anarchico* (Manchester: Manchester University Press, 1997), p. 14.
17. Even before his death Calabresi's behaviour gave rise to strong suspicion: six months before Pinelli's death Calabresi shouted at another anarchist suspect beside an open window: 'Maybe you aren't even capable of throwing yourself out.' For this reason he was known as 'Inspector Window' in anarchist circles. He also denied food and sleep to two suspects for 72 hours. Three hours after the bomb he too had defined it as 'clearly of anarchist origin'. Camilla Cederna, writing in *L'Espresso*, 30 May 1971.
18. Fo, *Plays: 1*, p. 207.
19. Ibid., p. 208.
20. Fo, *Marino Libero!*, pp. 16–7.
21. Cited in Cederna, *Una finestra sulla strage*, p. 78.
22. Ibid., p. 62.
23. J. Lorch, 'Introduction', in Fo, *Morte accidentale di un anarchico*, p. 29.
24. Cederna, *Una finestra sulla strage*, p. 63.
25. *L'Ora*, 17 December 1970.
26. CTFR busta 12A, NS, September 1970, 'Pinelli: Un caso che non è di coscienza', p. 1.
27. Fo, *Morte accidentale di un anarchico*, p. 111.

28. Ibid., p. 143. These points are developed in greater detail in the Introduction to the 1973 version published within *Compagni senza censura*, Vol. 2, in which there are several quotations from Lenin's *State and Revolution* and Engels' *The Origin of the Family, Private Property and the State*.

29. Fo, *Compagni senza censura*, Vol. 2, pp. 139–40.

30. Fo, *Plays: 1*, p. 195. This was not a new concept for Fo, he had already formulated it five years earlier in *Seventh Commandment: Thou Shalt Steal a Bit Less* in 1964. Here the subtle political exploitation of one particular scandal by the ruling class is outlined: 'It wouldn't be a bad thing if it was limited to the government's resignation and getting rid of a few Ministers. On the contrary this would be a healthy development, as Machiavelli rightly says: "Once in a while a few well-measured scandals reinforce government, and instil confidence into unhappy citizens."' In D. Fo, *Le commedie di Dario Fo*, Vol. 2 (Turin: Einaudi, 1966), p. 200.

31. Fo, *Plays: 1*, p. 195.

32. Ibid., p. 196.

33. Ibid., p. 201.

34. Ibid., pp. 201–2.

35. Ibid., p. 202.

36. Fo, *Morte accidentale di un anarchico*, p. 144.

37. Fo, *Plays: 1*, p. 191.

38. *L'Unità*, 12 December 1970.

39. *Corriere della Sera*, 16 December 1970.

40. *L'Ora*, 17 December 1970.

41. *Corriere della Sera*, 16 December 1970.

42. C. Valentini, *La storia di Dario Fo*, 2nd edition (Milan: Feltrinelli, 1997), p. 137.

43. Fo, *Plays: 1*, pp. 209–10.

44. Cited in Fo, *Compagni senza censura*, Vol 2, pp. 230–1.

45. Cederna, *Una finestra sulla strage*, pp. 110–15.

46. *La Voce*, 13 December 1994. Cited in an unpublished essay kindly given to me by John Foot: 'The Disaster and the City: Milan and *Piazza Fontana, 1969–99*'.

47. *La Repubblica*, 4 December 1987.

48. *Il Manifesto*, 6 December 1987. Fo is clearly referring to Pinelli's death, caused when he 'threw' himself out of the window.

49. *L'Avanti!*, 10 December 1987. When the play was first performed in 1970 the same newspaper, the organ of a then left-wing Socialist Party, called the play 'an example of political theatre in which art isn't suffocated either by dogmatic constructs or by propaganda'. *L'Avanti!*, 12 December 1970.

50. *Corriere della Sera*, 17 September 1992.

51. Cederna, *Una finestra sulla strage*, p. 31. Exactly a year after Calabresi's murder, in May 1973, a bomb was thrown into a crowd commemorating Calabresi's death outside the Milan Police headquarters, killing four and wounding 45. The initial explanation for the act, following in the tradition of the 'strategy of tension', was that the bomber was an anarchist. In reality the bombing was again a conspiracy of secret service officers, outraged by the government's investigations into neo-fascist groups. See *Il Manifesto*, 22 July 1998.

52. Cited in Fo, *Pum, Pum!*, pp. 94–5.

53. Ibid., p. 213.
54. Ibid., p. 217.
55. Fo, *Marino Libero!*, p. 13.
56. Ibid., pp. 65–6.
57. Ibid., p. 66.
58. Ibid., p. 39.
59. Ibid., p. 40.
60. Ibid., p. 43.
61. Ibid., p. 44.
62. Ibid., p. 45.
63. Ibid.
64. Ibid., pp. 21–2.
65. Ibid., p. 24.
66. Ibid., p. 28.
67. *Il caso Sofri Bompressi Pietrostefani*. Eight-page supplement distributed through the magazine *Una città* (Forli: n.d. [1997]).
68. Fo, *Marino Libero!*, p. 26.
69. Ibid., p. 28.
70. Ibid., p. 21.
71. Ibid., p. 59.
72. Ibid., p. 35.
73. Ibid., p. 77.
74. Ibid., p. 79.
75. *La Repubblica*, 6 April 1998.
76. Fo, *Marino Libero!*, p. 79.
77. Ibid.
78. Ibid., p. 9.
79. Ibid., p. 81.
80. Ibid., p. 9.
81. Ibid., p. 81.
82. Revealed in an article written by Adriano Sofri in *La Repubblica*, 26 March 1998.
83. *Il Manifesto*, 7 October 1998.
84. Fo, *Marino Libero!*, p. 80.
85. Broadcast on the RAI Due channel, 18 March 1998.

Chapter 4 *Can't Pay? Won't Pay!*

1. This literally translates as 'We won't pay! We won't pay!'
2. S. Tarrow, *Democracy and Disorder. Protest and Politics in Italy 1965–75* (Oxford: Clarendon Press, 1989), p. 315.
3. R. Lumley, *States of Emergency. Cultures of Revolt in Italy from 1968 to 1978* (London: Verso, 1990), p. 185.
4. *Rinascita*, 20 December 1968. Cited in ibid., p. 189.
5. *Il Manifesto*, October–November 1969. Cited in ibid., p. 189.
6. Ibid., p. 249.
7. C. Harman, *The Fire Last Time: 1968 and After* (London: Bookmarks, 1988), p. 197.
8. P. Ginsborg, *A History of Contemporary Italy* (Harmondsworth: Penguin, 1990), p. 353.

9. Under this system workers were laid off for a fixed period and received close to their normal wage. Generally they received 80 per cent of their wages; 72 per cent paid by the government and 8 per cent by the employers. When compared to an outright sacking, it was far more difficult to convince workers to oppose the introduction of such a measure. See G. Bedani, *Politics and Ideology in the Italian Workers' Movement* (Oxford: Berg, 1995), p. 204.

10. *Nord Est*, 26 December 1974.

11. Ginsborg, *History of Contemporary Italy*, p. 359

12. *Libera Stampa*, 12 November 1974.

13. *Il Manifesto*, 31 October 1974.

14. *Paese Sera*, 2 November 1974.

15. Interview with Piero Sciotto. Born in 1943, he worked closely with Fo from 1973 to 1980, and again from 1984 to 1992.

16. *L'Unità*, 31 January 1977.

17. See D. Hirst, *Dario Fo and Franca Rame* (London: Macmillan, 1989), pp. 94–106, for a detailed critique of the existing English translation by Lino Pertile.

18. D. Fo, *Le commedie di Dario Fo*, Vol. 12 (Turin: Einaudi, 1998), pp. 78–9.

19. Ibid., p. 79.

20. D. Fo, *Non si paga! Non si paga!* (Milan: La Comune, 1974), p. 98.

21. C. Valentini, *La storia di Dario Fo* (Milan: Feltrinelli, 1997), p. 159.

22. D. Fo, *Non si paga! Non si paga!* (Milan: CTFR, n.d. [1980]), p. 5. Shorter version in Fo, *Le commedie di Dario Fo*, Vol. 12, p. 7.

23. These details are taken from *Corriere di Napoli*, 19 October 1974 and *Il Mattino*, 20 October 1974; however, the coverage is very similar in all national newspapers. There is also one report of 500 shoppers paying 'old' prices the following day at the first of the two supermarkets raided.

24. Fo, *Non si paga! Non si paga!* [1980] p. 5

25. See note 9.

26. L. Binni, *'attento te...!'* (Verona: Bertani, 1975), pp. 385–6.

27. Interviewed in C. Meldolesi, *Su un comico in rivolta. Dario Fo, il bufalo, il bambino* (Rome: Bulzoni, 1978), pp. 201–2.

28. *Corriere d'Informazione*, 11 October 1974.

29. R. Nepoti and M. Cappa, *Dario Fo*, new edition (Rome: Gremese, 1997), p. 110.

30. Valentini, *La storia di Dario Fo*, p. 185.

31. *Corriere della Sera* and the *Corriere d'Informazione*, 7 October 1980.

32. *Gazzetta del popolo*, 26 September 1980.

33. *La Stampa*, 20 October 1980.

34. Fo, *Le commedie di Dario Fo*, Vol. 12, p. 81.

35. Ibid., p. 81 and Fo, *Non si paga! Non si paga!* [1980], p. 37. The latter version is slightly different, particularly as regards the reference to Gdansk.

36. Bedani, *Politics and Ideology in the Italian Workers' Movement*, p. 253.

Chapter 5 *Mistero Buffo*

1. Translating the title, '*Mistero Buffo*', presents many problems, and for this reason many translators have kept the Italian title. Ed Emery's translation in D. Fo, *Plays: 1* (London: Methuen, 1992) uses the expression 'The

Comic Mysteries', but some other alternatives which could be used include 'Strange Mystery', 'Funny Mystery'.

2. However, he has not sufficiently acknowledged his debt to the Russian playwright, Vladimir Mayakovsky. In 1918 Mayakovsky wrote a play with an almost identical title – *Mystery-Bouffe* – the subject matter of which has strong parallels with Fo's *Mistero Buffo*. This is not to suggest plagiarism, as Fo's play is much more varied and sophisticated. But the fact that Mayakovsky's work is not even mentioned in the five-page bibliography contained within *The Commune*'s editions of *Mistero Buffo* is highly surprising. See *The Complete Plays of Vladimir Mayakovsky* (New York: Simon & Schuster, 1968).

3. See D. Fo, *Tricks of the Trade* (London: Methuen, 1991), pp. 84–8, for a brief historical account by Fo.

4. See L. Binni, 'Dario Fo', *Il Castoro*, n.123 (1977) p. 52, for a good, brief definition of the activities of a *giullare*.

5. Fo, *Plays: 1*, p. 1.

6. The full English translation of the article can be found in A. Gramsci, *Selections from Political Writings, 1910–20* (London: Lawrence & Wishart, 1977), pp. 10–13.

7. Fo, *Plays: 1*, p. 3.

8. D. Fo, *Compagni senza censura*, Vol 1, 2nd edition (Milan: Mazzotta, 1977), pp. 59–60.

9. *Nord Est*, 26 December 1974.

10. Fo, *Compagni senza censura*, p. 59.

11. D. Fo, 'Dario Fo explains', *The Drama Review*, Vol. 22, No. 1, (March 1978), p. 42.

12. An interview with Fo originally published in the Italian edition of *Playboy*, December 1974. Reproduced in D. Fo, *Fabulazzo* (Milan: Kaos, 1992), p. 48.

13. *Nord Est*, 26 December 1974.

14. *Sabato Sera*, January 1984. Reproduced in Fo, *Fabulazzo*, p. 55.

15. *La Notte*, 30 May 1969.

16. *Italia Oggi*, 2 October 1989.

17. *Paese Sera* and *l'Unità*, 20 November 1969.

18. D. Fo, 'Dialogue with an audience' *Theatre Quarterly*, Vol 9, No. 35 (Autumn 1979), p. 10.

19. *La Stampa*, 14 January 1970.

20. Interview with Piero Sciotto. Born in 1943, he worked with Fo from 1973 to 1980, and again during 1984 to 1992.

21. Interview printed as part of a video package of *Mistero Buffo*, published by *l'Unità*, November 1997.

22. R. Jenkins, 'Dario Fo: The roar of the clown', in P.B. Zarrilli (ed.), *Acting (Re) Considered* (London: Routledge, 1995), p. 249. This article contains a very good general description of Fo's performing style in *MB*.

23. Piero Sciotto, interview.

24. *Stampa Sera*, 25 June 1973 and *Panorama*, 5 July 1973. Fo also performed *MB* at St Paul's Church in London in 1983.

25. *Panorama*, 26 April 1977.

26. Ibid.

27. *L'Osservatore Romano*, 24 April 1977.

28. *La Repubblica*, 25 April 1977. Cited in D. Fo, *Mistero Buffo* , new edition (Verona: Bertani, 1977), p. xix.

29. *Panorama*, 26 April 1977. See also C. Ginsburg's *The Cheese and the Worms. The Cosmos of a Sixteenth Century Miller* (London: Routledge, 1980) for a fascinating historical account one individual's interpretation of religion.

30. D. Fo, *Le commedie di Dario Fo*, Vol. 3 (Turin: Einaudi, 1975), p. 128.

31. *L'Osservatore Romano*, 24 April 1977.

32. *Panorama*, March 1977. Reproduced in Fo, *Fabulazzo*, p. 251.

33. *Il Messaggero*, 2 February 1982.

34. Account originally published in *Il Manifesto*, June 1984. Reproduced in Fo, *Fabulazzo*, p. 313.

35. Ibid., p. 310.

36. J.L. Wing, 'The Iconicity of Absence', *Theatre Journal*, Vol. 45, No. 3 (October 1993), p. 308.

37. J. Farrell, 'Introduction', in Fo, *Tricks of the Trade*, p. 3.

38. Fo, 'Dario Fo explains', p. 43.

39. *La Stampa*, 16 April 1966.

40. *La Stampa*, 24 May 1998.

41. C. Valentini, *La storia di Dario Fo*, 2nd edition (Milan: Feltrinelli, 1997), p. 184.

42. A. Gurr, *Playgoing in Shakespeare's London*, 2nd edition (Cambridge: Cambridge University Press, 1996), p. 46.

43. D. Fo, *Le commedie di Dario Fo*, Vol. 13, (Turin: Einaudi, 1998), p. v.

44. J. Lorch, 'Introduction', in D. Fo, *Morte accidentale di un anarchico* (Manchester: Manchester University Press, 1997), p. 17.

45. *La Stampa*, 24 May 1998.

46. Fo, *Tricks of the Trade*, p. 73.

47. A speech made at a meeting on culture held in June 1974, reproduced in Fo, *Fabulazzo*, p. 80.

48. Originally published in *Sabato Sera*, January 1984, reproduced in ibid., p. 53.

49. Cited in M. Pizza, *Il gesto, la parola, l'azione. Poetica, drammaturgia e storia dei monologhi di Dario Fo* (Rome: Bulzoni, 1996), p. 176.

50. S. Cowan, 'The Throw-Away Theatre of Dario Fo' in *The Drama Review*, Vol. 19, No. 2 (June 1975), p. 106.

51. Valentini, *La storia di Dario Fo*, p. 185.

52. Cited by Lorch, in Fo, *Morte accidentale di un anarchico*, p. 34, note 41.

53. Fo, 'Dialogue with an Audience', p. 16.

54. Ibid., p. 15. It is worth recalling that under Lenin and Trotsky's leadership of the Bolshevik Party, Mayakovsky was allowed full artistic freedom regardless of the fact he was not a party member; indeed Mayakovsky was one of the Soviet government's staunchest supporters. The censoring and banning of his work occurred later, during a completely different political period represented by Stalin's domination of the party.

55. *Europeo*, 19 January 1981.

56. *Nord Est*, 26 December 1974.

57. D. Fo, *Dialogo provocatorio sul comico, il tragico, la follia e la ragione*, 2nd edition (Rome-Bari: Laterza, 1997), pp. 116–7.

Chapter 6 The Downturn Period

1. C. Valentini, *La storia di Dario Fo*, 2nd edition (Milan: Feltrinelli, 1997), p. 187.
2. Ibid.
3. D. Fo and F. Rame, *Coppia aperta, quasi spalancata* (Turin: Einaudi, 1991), p. 8.
4. Interview with Emilio Orsino. Born in 1944, Orsino has attended most of Fo's plays since the late 1960s.
5. Cited in P. Ginsborg, *A History of Contemporary Italy* (Harmondsworth: Penguin, 1990), p. 412.
6. *Il Giorno*, 26 April 1982.
7. *Lotta Continua*, 16 September 1980.
8. *Giornale di Mantova*, 4 June 1980.
9. *Il Manifesto*, 16 January 1981.
10. Interview with Emilio Orsino.
11. *Corriere d'Informazione*, 10 September 1981.
12. *La Stampa*, 2 October 1981.
13. D. Fo, 'Per una nuova gestione degli spazi e degli spettacoli', in F. Quadri, *Il Teatro del Regime* (Milan: Mazzotta, 1976), pp. 141–2.
14. *Il Resto del Carlino*, 7 January 1982.
15. *Il Gazzettino di Venezia*, 28 November 1982.
16. *Il Giornale Nuovo*, 24 September 1981.
17. D. Fo, *Fabulazzo* (Milan: Kaos, 1992), p. 111.
18. Interview with Emilio Orsino.
19. Red Notes, *Dario Fo and Franca Rame: Theatre Workshops, Riverside Studios, London* (London: Red Notes, 1983), p. 64.
20. Ibid., p. 63.
21. Fo, *Fabulazzo*, p. 373.
22. *Paese Sera*, 2 June 1981.
23. *L'Unità*, 11 December 1987; and *La Repubblica*, 12 December 1987.
24. *Corriere d'Informazione*, 7 October 1980.
25. *La Classe Operaia è forte* (Edizioni Lotta Continua/Savelli, n. d. [1974]), p. 101. No place of publication.
26. C. Harman, *The Lost Revolution. Germany 1918 to 1923*, 2nd edition (London: Bookmarks, 1997), p. 209.
27. D. Moss, *The Politics of Left-Wing Violence in Italy, 1969–85* (London: Macmillan, 1989), p. 66.
28. Ibid., p. 185.
29. *Gazzetta del Popolo*, 12 October 1974.
30. G. Galli, *Il Partito Armato. Gli 'anni di piombo' in Italia 1968–86* (Milan: Kaos, 1993), pp. 97–8.
31. See the accounts in *La Stampa*, 6 and 7 July 1975.
32. D. Fo, 'The Sandstorm Method', *semiotext(e)*, Vol. 3, No. 3, (1980), p. 214.
33. *Lotta Continua*, 23 September 1977.
34. Fo, 'The Sandstorm Method', p.215. The present author would substitute the word 'power' with 'the system'.
35. *Corriere d'Informazione*, 18 September 1980. This was done at the première of the new version of *Can't Pay? Won't Pay!*, and the activist's name was Oreste Scalzone, who since his release from jail in 1981 has lived in exile

in Paris, along with several hundred other Italians wanted on charges of terrorism.

36. *Panorama*, 12 January 1981.
37. D. Fo, *Il Papa e la Strega* (Turin: Einaudi, 1994), p. 70.
38. *Europeo*, 19 January 1981.
39. D. Fo, *Plays: 1* (London: Methuen, 1992), p. 309.
40. *Il Secolo XIX*, 14 March 1982.
41. *L'Unità*, 17 January 1981. As a concept, the 'party of death' was comprised of all those parties who refused any negotiations with terrorists, not just the PCI.
42. Galli, *Il Partito Armato*, pp. 278–82.
43. *L'Unità*, 17 January 1981.
44. R. Nepoti and M. Cappa, *Dario Fo*, new edition (Rome: Gremese, 1997), p. 130.
45. *Gazzetta del Popolo*, 18 January 1981.
46. *L'Unità*, 24 January 1981.
47. *L'Unità*, 27 January 1981.
48. *La Provincia Pavese*, 11 March 1981.
49. *Il Secolo XIX*, 14 March 1982.
50. *La Nazione*, 24 November 1981.
51. See D. Fo, *Manuale minimo dell'attore* (Turin: Einaudi, 1997), pp. 192–222, for details on the genesis, structure and performance technique of *Tale of a Tiger*. Unfortunately this section is only included in this new Italian edition, and was unavailable for the 1991 English translation: D. Fo, *Tricks of the Trade* (London: Methuen, 1991).
52. D. Fo, *The Tale of A Tiger* (London: Theatretexts, 1984), p. 1.
53. *La Repubblica*, 30 March 1980.
54. *Il Manifesto*, 9 April 1980.
55. D. Fo, *Storia della Tigre e altre storie* (Milan: La Comune, 1980), p. 8.
56. Fo, *The Tale of A Tiger*, p. 4.
57. *Il Manifesto*, 9 April 1980.
58. Fo, *The Tale of A Tiger*, p. 25.
59. Ibid., p. 26.
60. Ibid.
61. Ibid., pp. 26–7.
62. *Il Corriere Mercantile*, 2 September 1989.
63. Ginsborg, *History of Contemporary Italy*, p. 302.
64. L. Bobbio, *Storia di Lotta Continua*, new edition (Milan: Feltrinelli, 1988), pp. 161–2. The difficulty for LC was that of attempting a dialogue with a mass movement which did not correspond to their expectation of a linear and rising mass working-class movement.
65. N. Harris, *The Mandate of Heaven. Marx and Mao in Modern China* (London: Quartet, 1978), p. 76.
66. C. Harman, *The Fire Last Time: 1968 and After* (London: Bookmarks, 1988), p. 348.
67. See C. Hore, *The Road to Tiananmen Square* (London: Bookmarks, 1991), Chapter 4.
68. J. Rees, 'Revolutionary Marxism and Academic Marxism' in J. Rees (ed.), *Essays on Historical Materialism* (London: Bookmarks, 1998), p. 172. The sense of this quote derives from an awareness that Maoism has all but disappeared internationally, and that the Marxist current which has

maintained itself has been that of Trotskyism, particularly those variants of Trotskyism which never believed that the USSR or Mao's China were examples of socialism.

69. *Panorama*, 25 September 1975.
70. *L'Unità*, 15 November 1989.
71. *L'Unità*, 8 December 1989.
72. *Corriere della Sera*, 11 October 1998.
73. Nepoti and Cappa, *Dario Fo*, p. 127.
74. Ibid., p. 122.
75. T. Mitchell, *File on Fo* (London: Methuen, 1989), p. 11.
76. Nepoti and Cappa, *Dario Fo*, p. 30.
77. Mitchell, *File on Fo*, p. 11.
78. SIAE, *Teatro in Italia '97* (Rome: SIAE, 1998), p. 5.
79. CTFR, Soccorso Rosso, busta: ricevute.
80. *Il Resto del Carlino*, 7 January 1982.
81. Fo, *Il Papa e la Strega*, pp. 158–9. In the original, reference is made to the House of Savoy and not the House of Windsor. The Italian royal family was removed from power following a popular referendum in 1946 which voted to create a Republic. Many commentators have explained such a vote as condemnation of the king's collusion with fascism. The royal family were then forced to go into exile in 1948, although their descendants were recently given permission to reside in Italy once more.
82. *Guardian*, 29 May 1992.
83. Nepoti and Cappa, *Dario Fo*, p. 147.
84. *Il Mattino*, 20 January 1993.
85. The same text can be found in either *L'Espresso*, 28 February 1993, or in *Settimo: Ruba un po' meno* (Milan: CTFR, 23 February 1993), p. 12. 1991 figures converted to 1999 prices.
86. *Il Venerdì di Repubblica*, 24 December 1993.
87. *L'Espresso*, 28 February 1993.

Conclusion

1. *La Stampa*, 9 October 1997.
2. C. Valentini, *La storia di Dario Fo*, 2nd edition (Milan: Feltrinelli, 1997), p. 183.
3. Ibid., p. 192.
4. Ibid., p. 191.
5. *Corriere d'Informazione*, February 1975. Cited in D. Fo, *Fabulazzo* (Milan: Kaos, 1992), p. 274.
6. *Il Manifesto*, 20 December 1997.
7. Ibid.
8. *Il Manifesto*, 6 March 1998.
9. *Il Manifesto*, 21 March 1998.
10. *Il Manifesto*, 25 May 1998.
11. *Il Manifesto*, 26 June 1998.
12. *Il Manifesto*, 17 December 1998.
13. *Il Manifesto*, 5 January 1999.
14. *Il Manifesto*, 18 March 1999.
15. *Il Manifesto*, 6 March 1999.

16.   *Il Manifesto*, 17, 21, 22 and 24 January 1999.
17.   *Il Manifesto*, 20 April, and 8 May 1999.
18.   *Corriere della Sera*, 17 March 1998.
19.   Ibid. Roberto Franceschi was a student shot dead by the police during a demonstration in March 1973.
20.   *Il Manifesto* 24 September 1998, and *Socialist Worker*, 3 October 1998.
21.   *Socialist Worker*, 19 September 1998.
22.   Interview with Dario Fo, 23 September 1998.

Appendix A: Fo's Theatrical Coup

1.   Source: C. Valentini, *Panorama*, 22 November 1973. Also reproduced in D. Fo, *Guerra di Popolo in Cile* (Verona: Bertani, 1973), pp. 106–10. The last paragraph is taken from L.Binni, *'attento te'...!'* (Verona: Bertani, 1975), p. 370. See D. Fo, *Tricks of the Trade*, (London: Methuen, 1991), pp. 192–6, for further details on the construction of the hoax.

Appendix B: An 'Intervention Show' in Brescia

1.   Source: L. Binni, *'attento te'...!'* (Verona: Bertani, 1975) pp. 99–106.
2.   *Bandiera Rossa* (Red Flag) was effectively the anthem of the Communist Party, while *Fischia il vento* (The Wind Whistles) was the most popular song from the anti-fascist Resistance of 1943–45.
3.   *Mamma Togni* was the true story of a woman partisan.
4.   Fo is referring to the Sicilian story teller Cicciu Busacca, who joined *The Commune* in the spring of 1973.
5.   The GAP were urban anti-fascist terrorist groups which were active during 1943–45.

Appendix C: A Telegram to *The Commune*

1.   Source: CTFR archives, busta 17F.

Index